FAMILY, HOUSEHOLD AND GENDER RELATIONS IN LATIN AMERICA

FAMILY, HOUSEHOLD AND GENDER RELATIONS IN LATIN AMERICA

Edited by Elizabeth Jelin

KEGAN PAUL INTERNATIONAL
UNESCO

First published in 1991 by
Kegan Paul International Ltd
PO Box 256, London WC1B 3SW, England
and UNESCO, 7 Place de Fontenoy,
757 c/o Paris, France.

Distributed by
John Wiley & Sons Ltd
Southern Cross Trading Estate
1 Oldlands Way, Bognor Regis,
West Sussex, PO22 9SA, England

Routledge, Chapman & Hall Inc
29 West 35th Street
New York, NY 10001, USA

The Canterbury Press Pty Ltd
Unit 2, 71 Rushdale Street
Scoresby, Victoria 3179, Australia

© Unesco 1991

Set in Baskerville, 10 on 12pt
by Input Typesetting Ltd, London SW19 8DR

Printed in Great Britain by T.J. Press

Kegan Paul International ISBN: 0 7103 0399 8

Unesco ISBN: 92–3–102657–7

British Library Cataloguing in Publication Data
Family, household and gender relations in Latin America.
　1. Latin America. Women. Social conditions
　I. Jelin, Elizabeth
　305.42098

Library of Congress Cataloguing-in-Publication Data
Family, household and gender relations in Latin America/edited by
　Elizabeth Jelin.
　　　229 p. 21.6 cm.
　　Includes bibliographical references.
　　ISBN 0–7103–0399–8
　　1. Family–Latin America.　2. Households–Latin
　America.　3. Sex role–Latin America.　4. Women–Latin
　America–Social conditions.
I. Jelin, Elizabeth, 1941–　.　II. Unesco.
HQ560.5.F355　1990
306.85′098–dc20
　　　　　　　　　　　　　　　　　　　　　　　90–31956
　　　　　　　　　　　　　　　　　　　　　　　CIP

CONTENTS

CONTENTS

PREFACE

The present collection of studies of family, household and gender relations in Latin America not only illustrates how these issues have been approached by researchers from the region during the last decade but also reflects the advances made over the past fifteen years in studies that concern the work and place of women in society. The insights, methods and research findings provided by the authors make a solid contribution to our knowledge of Latin American society as a whole and to the development of substantive areas in the social and human sciences.

The volume, commissioned within the Unesco subprogramme 'Research, training and international co-operation concerning the status of women', is compiled and edited by Elizabeth Jelin, Director of the Centro de Estudias de Estado y Sociedad (CEDES), Buenos Aires, Argentina, and Executive Committee Member of the International Sociological Association (ISA). Dr Jelin has selected from her extensive reading in the Latin American academic literature two contributions for each of the four sections of the volume: Analytical perspectives on family and gender; Production and reproduction; Family and kinship networks; Social classes and life styles. Both the selected articles and the introduction to each section amply demonstrate the essential contribution that women make to Latin American society.

It is hoped that this collection of readings will serve as a useful teaching aid not only in Latin American universities but also for courses in family sociology and social studies in other regions of the world. The research paradigms underlying the contributions have led to new and valuable insights into the relationship between the family and the wider institutional context. Within this perspective, the links between the social processes of production and reproduction, and the mutual determinants of the private and public domains are revealed and clarified.

The authors are responsible for the choice and presentation of the facts contained in this book and for the opinions expressed therein which are not necessarily those of Unesco and do not commit the Organization.

INTRODUCTION

EVERYDAY PRACTICES, FAMILY STRUCTURES, SOCIAL PROCESSES

Elizabeth Jelin

For the last three decades, that is since the beginning of the tradition of systematic studies on the empirical reality of the region, the mainstream of the social sciences in Latin America has been strongly biased towards dealing with the 'grand' subjects: economic development, political stability, population growth, urbanization. Within this tradition, transformations of productive structures were regarded as the central process; the political will to carry them out as the problematic issue in the region. Social and cultural aspects were relatively absent from the analyses. The institutional level and micro-social relationships were subordinated to, submerged even, in the major trends of the economy and changes in politics. In any case, they could be seen either as obstacles or as consequences. Seldom were they regarded as 'producers' of significant effects or results for what was considered the core of intellectual and political concern.

The incorporation of the institution of the family – or, more widely, paying some attention to the micro-social level and to every-day life – in the analysis of the main social, economic and political processes of the region is the result of several transformations in Latin American social sciences during the last two decades. In the first place, from the 1960s onwards, there has been a major crisis in the developmentalist paradigm. Earlier optimism, based on the hope of a linear mechanism linking economic development to social transformations, started to give way to new interpretations of the region, ranging from recognition of external dependence and its effects on social structure to the reality of social marginality. From these, the need arises to search, question and study concrete social practices in the different sectors and social classes, and to explore their articulations. In order to study 'the information sector', it is

1

not enough to have data on the proportion of independent workers within the economically active population. It is necessary to understand how, within a given family unit, the processes of insertion in the productive system become articulated with the satisfaction of consumption and reproductive needs. The analytical logic that was previously used for peasant units – where the processes of production and reproduction are permanently interconnected – had to be extended to urban areas and to other sectors of the population. Household organization then became the focal point of many studies.

In the second place, and simultaneously with the previously mentioned trend, the region started feeling the impact of debates and discussions stemming from international feminism. For the subject of this volume, the recognition of the invisible labour of women in the domestic domain is fundamentally important, as is its explicit incorporation in models of analysis: on the one hand, in debates about the cost of reproduction of the labour force; and on the other, in the analysis of the determinants of the supply of female workers in the labour markets. The implicit reconceptualization of the notion of 'work' is part of this process. At the symbolic and cultural levels, the analysis of the notions of 'public' and 'private' developed by the feminist debates gained in relevance, in so far as this becomes a key axis for rethinking the gender division of labour and distribution of power domains.

In the third place, developments in the Latin American region are not detached from international academic trends. The limitations of modernization theory on the analysis of the family, progress in the field of family history, analyses centred on the notion of the 'life-course' and its social organization, have also had their impact.

Finally, the impact of new social phenomena, or at times the intensification of trends that were previously marginal, both in Latin America and the industrialized countries, brings to the fore the need to understand these trends and new phenomena. The increase in the number of households formed by a woman and her children without the permanent presence of a man; the increase in the percentage of marriages that end in divorce; the gradual increase in the elderly population, with the concomitant problem of who takes care of their maintenance; the increase in the percentage of women in the labour force and the characteristics of their insertion are all cases in point. These trends have implications for the transformation of household organization and imply the restructuring of co-residence bonds and of kinship-based obligations, rights and duties. In so far as such trends become manifest, and more so when they are magnified in periods of crisis, they encourage research and analysis of the underlying social processes, thus contributing to the renewal of studies on the family.

From an analytical point of view, three main issues arise from this review and renewal of perspectives. In the first place, there is the relationship between the social processes of production and reproduction. If the emphasis of economic analysis – which for a long time was also transferred to sociological and anthropological studies – used to be placed on the social processes of production, the systematic and explicit inclusion of reproduction helps to close the cycle of the economic process. After all, social production is complemented by the distribution and consumption of what is produced; and consumption is carried out primarily within the domain of families and households. Furthermore, unless the agents of production reproduce themselves – both in the sense of reproducing new generations of people to replace the previous ones, and of reproducing the working capacity through the daily maintenance of the people – the whole cycle is interrupted. Which tasks are required? Who will carry them out? How is the group that socializes its resources for these tasks to be formed? These questions are aimed at domestic organization in everyday social life.

In the second place, there is the classical anthropological theme of kinship and the family. The hypotheses of the modernization and convergence of historical developments towards a nuclear family have been contradicted by actual trends in certain societies. In Latin America, recent studies stress the importance and vitality of extended kinship, even if this does not imply co-residence. At the same time, the basic dimensions of the family, the legitimate channelling of sexuality and procreation and the establishment of filiation bonds are in the process of transformation, caused in part by the increase in divorce and the liberalization of sexual practices that in turn indicates a significant change in the formation and stability of the family as an institution. Consequently kinship, family, residence patterns and domesticity have to be considered in depth.

Thirdly, since the industrial revolution, during which the separation between 'home' and 'work' and between life environment and production space took place, a gradual differentiation between 'private' and 'public' has emerged – a differentiation geared to separating the domains of action of women and men, of power and affection. The 'exit' of women to the public world and the 'entry' of social controls in the private domain are phenomena that have only recently been acknowledged, even though in practice they have been with us for a long time. The recognition of their importance fosters the revision of social practices and the ideological matrices that justify them.

Cutting across our subject-matter, a theoretical and methodological concern is recognizable: the relationship between individual and society, between the level of micro-social interaction and that of social structure. The study of the family must be placed at an intermediate level, at which it is possible to discern some of the mechanisms of mediation and transformation of that relationship. The issue will not be tackled explicitly in this book. However, in so far as the studies included are at this intermediate level, they can provide an impetus for the analysis of the ways of transference and passage from the individual level to the social, collective or structural one.

The volume intends to present a wide and varied panorama of recent work on the subject. The basic criterion utilized for selecting the studies, beyond the quality of the research work and its contribution to the substantive knowledge of a subject, has been to provide the greatest possible heterogeneity – in terms of countries and social classes, of time or historical coverage, of urban and rural areas, and of analytical themes: intra-domestic dynamics, kinship networks, the community, public life. The result is not a complete panorama, either in terms of the countries included or in terms of issues. Furthermore, there is a predominance of qualitative studies, undoubtedly resulting from the nature of the subject-matter.

The book is organized into four sections. The first presents theoretical perspectives relating that which is new to classical anthropological traditions and to the perspectives of current social sciences. Durham's chapter, which discusses the issue of the family, takes into account the biological bases and the cultural trends towards the 'naturalization' of the family; it lays out the constant or universal features of its subject, focusing attention on themes that are classical in anthropology, such as the incest taboo and the organization of kinship. Jelin's study includes a review of recent literature on production and reproduction, on the social conformation of the private domain, and on intra-domestic dynamics.

The second part of the book deals with the relationship between production and reproduction, anchored in the relationship between the family and productive organization. The two studies included are of a different nature: Stolcke's study provides a historical perspective of the transformations in the structure of workers' families in relation to the changes in the structure of coffee production in a region in Brazil. Oliveira's study analyses the presence of women in the labour market in relation to migratory processes and family organization in several areas in Mexico. Family organization is presented within its socio-economic context, both in the migrants' places of origin and in their places of destination, thus allowing an understanding of its role as mediator in the migratory processes and in the supply of labour.

The third part of the book focuses on the relationship between households and kinship networks. The studies included aim to show the household as part of such networks; they show the prevalence of family units that have relatively little autonomy, immersed in a larger space of mutual aid and obligations, often based on kinship bonds. Lomnitz and Perez-Lizaur's chapter concentrates on the 'grand-family' present both in poor neighbourhoods as well as in the Mexican bourgeoisie, whilst Fonseca, in her study of a marginal district in Porto Alegre (Brazil), questions the hypotheses of the absence of men in the daily life of the Latin American working-class sectors. The study proves that women permanently resort to men's help, but that these men are usually consanguineal relatives (fathers, brothers, sons) rather than sexual partners.

The fourth and last part of the book, made up of two studies, is more heterogeneous. Jelin's study is centred on the internal dynamics of the household, dealing especially with the relationships between parents and children and men and women as regards the organization of daily consumption and reproduction. Rapp's study is more theoretical, focusing on the links between material and ideological dimensions in the process of family formation within a social class context. Even though it refers not to Latin America but to the United States, it was selected for two reasons: to enrich the comparative dimension of the analysis of the working classes, and to take advantage of the author's in-depth perspective regarding the relationship between family and social class.

Section 1

ANALYTICAL PERSPECTIVES ON FAMILY AND GENDER

INTRODUCTION

Elizabeth Jelin

All of us live in families. Family identity and belonging, as well as everyday interactions, are so much part of our lives that we seldom think about them. In most situations it is taken for granted that family, that 'basic cell of society', refers to a couple and their children, i.e. the nuclear family. In this, many levels and dimensions intermingle: everyday life together, socially legitimate sexuality, descent and reproductions, shared intimacy, the warmest feelings.

A closer look at everyday life and changes in intimate relationships during the life cycle and, even more dramatically, a comparative look at other societies and cultures, all lead to a fundamental conceptual reformulation: the family form to which we refer in everyday life and language is no more than *one* of the modes of manifestation of the family institution – neither unique, nor the most advanced, nor the best. If we consider it as 'natural' without questioning it, this is because we have undergone a complex process of cultural formation that has led us to assume our family form is a natural fact, based on the biology of sexuality and reproduction; to think of our kinship structure as a 'natural' extension of the family; to see our pattern of gender division of labour as a phenomenon that is *given* by our anatomical and biological make-up.

To review such cultural assumptions from a scientific perspective, one has to analyse the social dimensions that make up the phenomenon under study, to deconstruct the implicit social relationships and activities, to incorporate systematically a comparative and historical framework. Only then can the social tranformations and cultural patterns designed to answer issues of sexuality and reproduction be understood. In that sense, it is worthwhile referring to the conceptualization of the family arrived at by Eunice Durham (p. 51 in this volume):

> The family has to be defined as an *institution*, in Malinowski's sense. That is, in reference to a concrete social group, which exists as such in the representation of its members, and is organized to perform the tasks of (biological and social) reproduction, through the manipulation of the formal principles of alliance, descent and consanguinity on the one hand; and of the substantive practices of the sexual division of labour on the other. (*Malinowski, 1944; Durham, 1978*)

First, there is a reference to the representation of its members, that is, to the way in which a world view and a subjectivity are constructed within a given culture. A useful and illustrative exercise in this direction is to ask, when beginning a study or reflection about the family, for a written description of each participant's family. The richness and variety of implicit social definitions and the complexity of the social dimensions to which people refer is, without doubt, highly valuable empirical material for the learning process.

Second, the conceptualization refers to the reproductive function, with all its implicit social normativity. In fact, every society elaborates acceptable and unacceptable ways to handle sexuality, and some way in which sexuality is linked to reproduction. Who takes care of child-rearing, and who is recognized (both men and women) as responsible for descent, are among the basic principles of social organization.

Thirdly, references to patterns of alliance, consanguinity and descent, as well as to the sexual division of labour, point to the need to study, in each concrete historical condition, how a given society or social class prescribes ways in which everyday life and inter-generational relations are defined: patterns of co-residence, of household organization, of kinship and inheritance rules.

In summary, we are proposing a multidimensional approach to the family, which calls for explicit consideration of the material aspects of daily and generational reproduction, of the social system of interaction, of the symbolic and cultural dimension in the family and kinship, and of the political dimension involved in the relationship between the family and the wider institutional system.

The studies included in this section address the themes and dilemmas implicit in the analytical reflection that stems from questioning the naturalness of social processes. Eunice Durham takes up some of the classical themes of anthropology, from cultural universals such as the incest taboo to the enormous cultural variability in solving the demands of constructing a social order. Jelin's study deals with several basic themes for analysis: the relationship between social processes of production and reproduction; questioning the distinction between the private and public worlds stemming from the recognition of the presence of the 'social'; gender division of labour in the daily life of domestic organization. The studies selected are intended more to raise questions and discuss alternative perspectives than to present theoretically neat and closed systems.

1

FAMILY AND HOUSEHOLD: OUTSIDE WORLD AND PRIVATE LIFE*

Elizabeth Jelin

The social processes linked to a population's daily and generational reproduction constitute a complex set of mechanisms and organization that have not been thoroughly studied within the social sciences. The description and analysis of these processes were considered part of the ethnographic tradition of anthropology, but were not studied with the same precision in Western societies, whether central, peripheral or socialist. This omission has recently been repaired and the subject-matter seems to have been rediscovered.

The revival was linked to several thematic developments within the social sciences. On the one hand, there has been intense debate concerning the political economy of domestic labour, promoted by women's liberation movements and by the new analytical and critical trends within the Marxist tradition (Malos, 1980). On the other hand, the crisis of the welfare state in central Western societies has brought to the fore, as a significant social and political matter, the issue of the social mechanisms for the protection and maintenance of non-earning individuals and social groups.

In the last decade, the discovery and politicization of domestic labour appeared in the academic world to be a reaction to the functionalist sociology of the family. This theory claimed that, in so far as the process of modernization involves increasing institutional differentiation, it brings about a functional specialization of the family. The main social functions of the family in the modern world would be the emotional support of adults and the early socialization of children. Within this framework, domestic labour – including the daily activity of final transformation of goods for consumption and

---

* A preliminary version was published as *Familia y unidad doméstica: mundo público y vida privada*. Buenos Aires, CEDES, 1984.

several personal services – seems not to exist nor to require analysis or interpretation. In so far as it is performed in the privacy of the family and the home, the social relevance of domestic labour appears to be focused on its importance as an expression of the love and devotion of women rather than as a socially necessary, concrete activity. The recent crisis in the delivery of these 'invisible' services, partially due to women's questioning of the 'naturalness' of their responsibility for these tasks, has turned the issue of the daily maintenance of the population into a matter of social and political relevance. Within the social sciences, the subject has become an issue for reflection and analysis.

Within the Latin American social sciences, the origin of this concern may be traced to an attempt to understand the linkage between processes and styles of development on the one hand, and the structuring of new social groups on the other. During the 1960s, attention started to focus on the relationship between external dependence, with its imprint on style of development, and social marginality and its consequence from the point of view of changes in working-class sectors (Cardoso and Faletto, 1969; Nun, 1969; Kowarick, 1975). This analysis was centred on the formation of new social groups, especially in urban working-class sectors. The imbalance between rural–urban migration and the productive absorption of modern industry was regarded as a mechanism for transforming rural into urban marginality (Quijano, 1968; Singer, 1975). However, a more detailed analysis of its social and economic organization led to a reconsideration of the place of these social groups in the new urban structure. Their relatively autonomous role was recognized in the so-called 'informal sectors', and their creative characteristics were re-evaluated, whilst the connections between them and the more dynamic sectors of the economy became more evident (Roberts, 1978; Peattie, 1979).

The analysis of the organization of productive units in the informal sector necessarily implied an explicit consideration of the linkage between the processes of production, reproduction and maintenance, given their reciprocal determinations (Schmukler, 1981; Jelin, 1976). In turn, at the macro-social level, reconsideration of subordinate social groups in the process of development led to seeing the urban scene not only as the location of certain production styles (the modern factory or street vending) that give birth to differentiated actors (the working class, the marginals), but as several superimposed, related scenarios. Among them, increasing importance was attached to the organization of collective consumption in the urban milieu (utilization of land, transport, housing, health, etc.) as a determining factor in the level of living and lifestyle of the common people. Hence, the consideration of organizations and social movements related to collective services is a crucial dimension of social organization. Furthermore, during the last few years, there have been important developments in research on, and conceptualization of the family and its strategies for survival (Torrado, 1981).

The approach followed here centres on a consideration of maintenance and reproductive activities within the framework of family analysis. Its objective is to contribute towards a conceptualization of the internal dynamics of domestic organization on the basis of concrete 'utilitarian' tasks. The intention is not to leave aside the emotional bonds and ideological and cultural images that set the background for, and justify the existence of the family and the household, but rather to anchor these feelings and images in the material aspects of daily life.

Domestic domain, public world and private life

The anthropological literature has specialized in analysing and discussing the social organization of the family and reproduction (Yanagisako, 1979). The first important point to be understood from this literature is the analytical distinction between residential group, reproductive unit, productive unit and consumption unit. On the basis of already traditional studies on the subject, and after reviewing the various approaches and conceptualizations, Jack Goody proposes:

> We used the phrase 'domestic group' in order to circumvent some of the definitional problems and introduce an element of flexibility. This phrase is an overall term for three main kinds of unit, namely, the dwelling unit, the reproductive unit, the economic unit. The economic unit is again a generic term which covers the persons jointly engaged in the process of production and consumption. In agricultural societies (as well as in craft production) these units tend to be closely linked together; in industrial societies they are usually quite distinct. (Goody, 1972: 106)

The analytical differentiation between kinship, residence, productive and reproductive units has shown its usefulness in comparative analysis, given the enormous intercultural variability in forms of social organization. Its acceptance poses two basic problems, one empirical, the other analytical. If social units differ in their specific activity, only through empirical investigation will it be possible to determine the degree and type of overlap, superposition and disjunction in membership and boundaries of co-residential social groups, families and production and consumption units. Their interrelationship is also open for discussion.[1]

From an analytical point of view, the problem is how to establish explanatory relationships between the various dimensions, that is to say, to formulate hypotheses about the basic principles of social organization, thus allowing the interpretation of inter- and intra-social regularities and variations, as well as an explantion of processes of change. In this sense, a strong current within anthropology has emphasized the structure of kinship, deriving therefrom arrangements regarding residence and conformation of productive and consumption units (Bender, 1967; Fortes, 1969). Other studies, however, have placed emphasis on the mechanisms of property transmission, i.e. on marital and inheritance norms (Goody, 1976; Goody, Thrisk and Thompson, 1978). Here an explicit reference to the connection between these mechanisms and the productive organization of the society under discussion is required (Meillassoux, 1977; Bourdieu, 1976).

As Yanagisako states, this approach may be useful when property is the central defining element of domestic units:

> Where this is not the case, as among landless peasants, hunter-gatherers, or wage-laborers, we may usefully identify other significant components of family organization, including the commensal group, the production group, and the budget group in which reciprocal exchange occurs without accounting. However, the aggregate of people engaged in any of these activities may change throughout the production cycle, the exchange cycle, or the individual's life cycle. Consequently, it seems more analytically strategic to begin with an investigation of the activities that are central to the domestic relationships in each particular society, rather than with its domestic groups. (Yanagisako, 1979: 186)

The acceptance of the author's proposal, centred on domestic activities implies an initial delimitation of the core of the analysis.

In our case, as already mentioned, the focus is placed on activities related to the maintenance and reproduction of the population, in the context of a given productive organization.

From an analytical point of view, the term 'reproduction' refers to three dimensions or levels: biological reproduction, which at the family level means bearing children and at the social level refers to socio-demographic aspects of fertility; daily reproduction, that is, the maintenance of the existent population through domestic tasks for subsistence; and social reproduction, that is, all the extra-productive tasks aimed at maintaining the social system (Edholm, Harris and Young, 1977). The *domestic domain* includes activities of daily production and consumption of food and other goods and services for subsistence, as well as those related to generational replacement, that is to say, bearing children, taking care of them and socializing them.

√The emphasis on the household does not imply conceiving it as a unit isolated from the social world, nor identifying domesticity with privacy as opposed to the public domain of power and social production. Both are common errors in the literature on the subject. In effect, beginning with the analytical differentiation of the contexts in which activities are carried out and of the norms ruling each domain, the distinction between the domestic and the public worlds has been taken as an actual split in the real world, with meanings way beyond the implications of Fortes' original conceptualization (Fortes, 1969).

The difficulty is not so much in the theoretical and empirical reference to the public world, but rather in distinguishing between the domestic and the private worlds, invisible and impenetrable from the outside and, consequently, considered to be of lesser social importance.[2] Furthermore, the distinction between these domains has been identified with gender differentiation – men in charge of public tasks, women confined to the private and domestic world – as if this were a universal and constant feature of social organization. Recent comparative anthropological research shows that the model based on the opposition between the domestic/private/female/powerless domain and the public/male/powerful one is fundamentally cultural and ideological (Rapp, 1979).[3]

The approach proposed here stems from criticism of these dualistic conceptions and is nurtured by ideas developed in the last few years from several converging perspectives. From that of the history of mentalities, Donzelot has set forth a convincing argument on the formative presence of the 'social' in the family world:

> The method we have employed tries to avoid this danger by positing the family, not as a point of departure, as a manifest reality, but as a moving resultant, an uncertain form whose intelligibility can only come from studying the system of relations it maintains with the socio-political level. This requires us to detect all the political mediations that exist between the two registers, to identify the lines of transformation that are situated in the space of intersections. (Donzelot, 1979: XXV)

According to Donzelot, the historian's task consists in:

> identifying lines of tranformation fine enough to account for the singularities assigned to family roles . . . perceiving those roles as the strategic resultant of these diverse forces. . . . This first object, the family, will thus be seen to fade into the background, overshadowed by another, the social, in relation to which the family is both queen and prisoner. (Donzelot, 1979: 7)

The key concept for this historical search is 'policing':

> not understood in the limiting, repressive sense we give the term today, but according to a much broader meaning that encompassed all the methods for developing the quality of the population and the strength of the nation. (Donzelot, 1979: 6–7)

The family and the household are formed in relation to the public world: the services, various sorts of legislation, mechanisms of social control, the changing definition of the applicability of medicine, the mechanisms regulating the prevailing social images of the family and of 'normality', educational ideologies and institutions, social definitions of the place of philanthropy and public charity (Donzelot, 1979; Aries, 1962). Throughout history, the family domain has been shaped by transformations in institutions and ideas. From this point of view, household and family are obviously not to be regarded as part of the private world but as part of the social world, that over which 'policing' and control are exercised.

In reviewing the various sociological and psychological theories of the family, and in trying to probe the issue of the future of the family, Lasch also uncovers the degree of politicization and de-privatization to which this institution is subject (Lasch, 1977). According to this author, traditional patriarchy has been eroded by the invasion of social, professional and expert agencies, thus reducing the jurisdiction of family members themselves. However, as stated by Donzelot, the penetration of the 'social' into the family is not a recent phenomenon related to the increasing professionaliz-ation of services in the Western world – though no doubt it has intensified during this century – but a long-standing social force revealed in the power and influence of different social institutions (philanthropy and charity, legislation on minors and the family, medical and psychological practices, and so on). Undoubtedly, this force has been transformed over several centuries of history.

The contribution of the study of women to the discussion of this subject-matter is centred on the analysis of female identity, gender division of labour and power relationships. Within this perspective, a first intellectual current anchors woman's subordination in the public–private duality identified with the differentiation man––woman. The subordinate position of women is explained by their specialization in domestic tasks:

> Generally speaking, the domestic obligations and demands seem to help explain the reasons why women everywhere are limited in their access to prestigious masculine activities. (Rosaldo, 1980: 399)

The system of social relationships that defines feminine identity appears to members of society and culture as a direct consequence of the biological facts of reproduction.

The critical analysis of this dualistic approach emphasizes the public and social character, be it real or potential, of domestic activities carried out by women. For example, Yanagisako concludes her critical review of the literature on household organization by saying that 'the domestic relationships are an essential part of a society's political structure' (Yanagisako, 1979: 181). In a different vein, Elshtain criticizes the archetypical stands of feminisim and anti-feminism: the type of feminism that calls for a public identity for women on an equal basis to men, while at the same time rejecting their roles and identities rooted in the domestic domain; and the traditional position that accepts gender differentiation linked to public–private distinction. To explain her position, the author traces an analogy with the legend of Antigone:

The standpoint of Antigone is of a woman who dares to challenge public power by giving voice to familial and social imperatives and duties. . . . To recapture that voice and to reclaim that standpoint, and not just for women alone, it is necessary to locate the daughters of Antigone where, shakily and problematically, they continue to locate themselves: in the arena of the social world where human life is nurtured and protected from day to day. This is a world women have not altogether abandoned, though it is one both male-dominant society and some feminist protest have devalued as the sphere of 'shit-work', 'diaper talk', and 'terminal social decay'. This is a world that women, aware that they have traditions and values, can bring forward to put pressure on contemporary public policies and identities. . . . To define this world simply as the 'private sphere' in contrast to 'the public sphere' is to mislead. For contemporary Americans, 'private' conjures up images of narrow exclusivity. The world of Antigone, however, is a social location that speaks of, and to, identities that are unique to a particular family, on the one hand; but, on another and perhaps even more basic level, it taps a deeply buried human identity, for we are first and foremost not political or economic man but family men and women. (Elshtain, 1982: 55–6)

This chapter, in line with Donzelot's argument, calls attention to the political and social aspects inherent in the domestic sphere of reproduction and consumption (Jelin, 1984). In summary, the domestic domain to be studied is bound by the set of shared activities related to the daily maintenance of a social group, as it is shaped and changed in relation to other institutions and spheres of society. In this relationship, the household does not only play an adaptive or 'functionally necessary' role in social reproduction, but itself has innovative politicized potential.

Family and household throughout the life cycle

The selection of the household as a focal point for analysis is justified in so far as it is the social organization with the specific objective of carrying out the activities related to daily maintenance and generational reproduction of the population. What is a household? What are the structural parameters of its composition and membership criteria? How does the unit vary and rearrange itself throughout the lifetime of its members?

The first point that requires attention is the analytical distinction between household and family. On the one hand, the family has a biological substratum related to sexuality and procreation, constituting the social institution that rules, channels and confers social and cultural meanings to these two needs. On the other hand, the family is part of a larger network of kinship relations – rights and obligations – governed by established social rules and principles. However, the social importance of the family goes beyond the norms of sexuality and filiation. It also constitutes an interacting social group, inasmuch as it is co-resident and co-operates economically in the daily tasks related to the maintenance of its members (Murdock, 1949).

The shared activities related to daily maintenance define households, in which members' skills, capacities and resources are combined for productive and distributive tasks.

> Household activities are continuously part of the 'larger' processes of production, reproduction, and consumption; as such, they vary by class. Household activities cannot be analysed as separate from the socio-economic relations of the societies in which they are embedded. (Rapp et al., 1979: 176).

The family is the basis for recruitment of members for households, thus revealing a significant aspect of social norms:

> ✓It is through their commitment to the concept of family that people are recruited to the material relations of households. Because people accept the meaningfulness of family, they enter into relations of production, reproduction, and consumption with one another – they marry, beget children, work to support dependents, transmit and inherit cultural and material resources. In all of these activities, the concept of family both reflects and masks the realities of household formation and sustenance. It also glosses over the variety of experiences that social categories of persons have within households. These experiences alter radically depending on gender, generation, and class. (Rapp et al., 1979: 177)

Empirically, most households are made up of members who are related by kinship ties, but the degree of coincidence between the household and the family and, even more so, the social definition of the scope of the co-resident group (in terms of kinship bonds) greatly varies among societies and through the life cycle of members. This subject has been tackled from several disciplinary and analytical angles. From a comparative perspective, the differentiation of households has been related to changes in the world economy (Wallerstein and Martin, 1979). From the perspective of historical demography and family history, the discussion has focused on the changes in size and composition of households (Laslett, 1972; Berkner, 1972 and 1975). Analytical models based on the life cycle and the domestic cycle have also been applied to historical data, resulting in contributions that stress, for example, the circumstances and importance of the presence of boarders and guests in certain social strata (Hareven, 1977), the changes in marriage criteria and patterns (Modell *et al*, 1978) and the transformation of patterns of transition throughout the life cycle (Hareven, 1978).

In another line of research, recent studies of urban anthropology have stressed the importance of large kinship networks in the daily maintenance of household members (Lomnitz, 1975; Stack, 1974b; Ramos, 1981). Stack has thus shown that among poor black people in urban areas of the United States, the relevant unit for daily activities is the 'domestic network', more than the household. The domestic network is a vast kinship network where reciprocal relationships are set up through children, marriage and friendship, joining together to satisfy domestic functions. This network is dispersed over several homes. The interesting feature is that fluctuations in the composition of individual households does not alter wider co-operative arrangements (Stack, 1974a).

In the contemporary urban world, the composition of the household, always guided by family and kinship norms, is the result of several processes during the life cycle of its members. On the one hand, there are the events related to the history of family formation, including marriages, separations, births and deaths, as well as residential moves, migration and other accidents or decisions at certain specific moments, that leave traces in the composition of the domestic group in future moments. On the other hand, changes in the economic and political situation – especially regarding social policies – in which the various transitions in the life cycle take place, constantly influence domestic organization and affect its subsequent dynamics. In summary, domestic organization tends to endure, following an established pattern of activities and task-assignments, responsibilities and authority. Changes come about as a result of transitions in the members' life cycle or as a response to special economic situations – internal or external – that require an adjustment in customary strategies.

Nowadays couples attempt to establish independent households upon marriage. Their success depends in part on their resources and in part on conditions beyond their control. A relevant external condition is related to governmental housing policies determining the real estate market at the time of marriage and the possibilities of access to housing. In terms of more immediate decisions, the couple will be able to set up as an autonomous unit depending on the commitments of each of the partners to their respective families: sick or widowed mothers, family businesses or properties, will condition the options open to them.

The subsequent history is complex and multidimensional: the birth of children, changes in commitments and responsibilities towards families of origin, possible assistance from informal networks, changes in governmental policy or in the real estate market, etc., condition the possible options or choices that changes in the couple's monetary resources may permit. These options are not continuously rationally assessed but are updated at the time of significant transitions in the life cycle of the family group – such as the birth of children, death of parents, marriage of siblings, separations – or at times of crisis directly or indirectly related to housing conditions – evictions, changes in rent legislation, access to special loans, etc.

In this way, even though most of the domestic groups are composed of people with immediate family bonds, the inclusion or exclusion of certain members is not solely established by closeness in the kinship bond, nor can it be explained only by the current situation of members of the household. Parents whose children do not live with them, who in turn are responsible for children of close or not so close relatives, patterns of double residence (for example, children whose parents have separated, grandmothers that live alternatively in the homes of several of their children) constitute common phenomena that must be taken into account in any research project.[4]

The lack of coincidence between the kinship unit and the household in turn gives rise to another important issue: by definition, kinship bonds outside the unit are different for each one of its members. Each household member has his or her kinship network, with its system of mutual relationships, reciprocities, rights and obligations, relatively independent from the networks of the other members. This obviously varies according to the phase of the person's life cycle. More systematically, the various members of a household contribute differently to daily maintenance tasks. In terms of both monetary resources and personal time devoted to these tasks, each member's contribution to the common activity varies according to the type of duties and obligations towards his or her own kinship network.

At the same time, the household does not necessarily concentrate all the activities related to the maintenance of its members. The household seems to be the basic social unit for some activities and areas of consumption, especially those related to daily maintenance – food, hygiene, cleaning. But other activities, including those related to health, housing and domestic equipment, may be carried out in larger units (neighbourhood, community or kinship networks) or smaller units (isolated individuals) than the household itself. With respect to the generational reproduction of the population, family relationships, whether or not they coincide with the household, constitute the fundamental social relationship.

The limits of the household and of the family are extremely permeable. The degree of participation in household activities and the commitment towards these activities do not vary at random. There are strong social norms that goven the differential commitment expected from the various members according to their position in terms of age, sex, and kinship ties with other members. That which is expected of a child daughter is different from that which is expected of an adolescent girl, and of course, of an adolescent boy. And different behaviour patterns are expected of mother and father, siblings, uncles, aunts and grandparents. That is to say, even though it is the same social institution, charged with emotions and feelings, 'the family' has different meanings and is experienced in a diverse fashion by different individuals, according to their sex, age and social class.

The household in the processes of production and reproduction

Household activities conceal material linkages connecting them to the wider social processes of production and reproduction. A comparative analysis of a wide range of societies and cultures indicates a great variety of household forms, and their relationship to the organization of prouction. Even within a given society and within a given social class or sector, households vary in terms of the insertion of their members in the productive process. Thus, households depending on wage-work differ from family-based productive units (be they in farming, crafts, commerce or services) and the latter from those based on occasional or unstable work.

A significant part of the reproductive activities of the household are concrete consumption tasks. Consumption of goods and services produced by the eoconomic system requires time and work. As Galbraith notes, in the modern Western world these tasks are carried out fundamentally by the family and especially by women. The work performed by the latter has no monetary compensation, but is rather justified in terms of 'social virtue' (Galbraith, 1973).[5]

Household activities of consumption and reproduction are not limited to the tasks of transforming market-produced and commercialized goods. The provision of goods and services of a collective nature is a very important input to the household. The provision of services by the State – which services, for whom, when, and at what cost – has historically constituted a battlefront for the incorporation of social sectors into the benefits and rights defining social citizenship. Responsibility for providing services is so important that it has become a defining dimension of the various models of the State: on the one hand, the liberal model that theoretically provides minimum collective services and gives priority to the competitive market; on the other hand, the different variants of the welfare state, where the scope of services defined as governmental obligations is considerably wider; finally, the socialist states, in which these services are the keystone of their public action. In the historical transformation of the State's social role, class conflict shows up in the struggle for the extension of citizenship rights and for the application of redistributive policies (Marshall, 1964; Bendix, 1969; van Gunsteren, 1978). Differential access (and the differential need to accede) to these services has become a defining feature of social classes. At each specific moment, the social context in which the daily reproductive tasks of each social class take place is determined by the result of these struggles in the past.

There are clearly differentiated types of collective goods and services. On the one hand, these are collective or public services geared to the maintenance of the population as a whole (transport, drainage, electricity and gas, sanitation, etc.). Even though these may be organized as profit-making enterprises, they require co-ordination and centralized regulation of social space. The historical experience shows that the extension of these services is related to direct State action, since they often render insufficient profit to attract private investment. Consequently, these services are subject to fluctuations in the State's social policy (Castells, 1976). On the other hand, there are social welfare services that establish a minimum level of welfare for the population (in terms of health, education, and so on) to be ensured by the State. The justification of these services is based on the enlargement of specific rights and benefits as an extension of social citizenship.

Another side of social welfare policies is aimed at answering the issue of who is responsible for the maintenance of the people who are not self-sufficient, that is to say, those whose income is either non-existent or insufficient to cover their basic survival needs. This side of social policies deals with determining the social mechanisms for the legitimate transfer of income and consumer goods. Thus, in the welfare state model, the costs of these tasks and activities are borne collectively; on the other hand, the liberal competitive market model implies that these maintenance costs must be covered individually or, more specifically, by the households of which the beneficiaries (children, elderly or sick persons, housewives, students, the unemployed) are members.

Moving on from inter-societal variations in productive and reproductive organization, we can now concentrate specifically on the situation of the subordinate classes in urban capitalist societies, with special attention to Latin America. Here, the way in which households are inserted into the processes of production, reproduction and consumption defines their class positions and their access to, accumulation of and transfer of resources. In principle, it is possible to distinguish three types of urban common people's households, defined according to the prevailing insertion of their members into the productive system: the worker's household, the small family enterprise, and the social organization of the poor.

The economic base of the worker's family, allowing its continuing existence and reproduction, is the wage-work of its members. There is a clear separation between the workplace and the home. Of course, the amount of labour the unit offers to the market varies:

How much labor-power a working-class household needs to send out is determined by many things: the cost of reproducing (or maintaining) the household, the work careers and earning trajectories of individual members, and the domestic cycle (that is, the relations between the gender and the generations, which specify when and if wives and adolescent children are available to work outside the home). (Rapp, 1978: 283)

Workers' households inherently contain some elements of tension and contradiction: the basic production relationship is established on the labour market among individuals who offer their labour in exchange for wages and social benefits, whilst the household bases its existence on the collectivization and solidarity of its members. Due to the individuality of the wage-worker's participation in the labour force and of his or her income, the bonds within the domestic unit must be very strong in order to oppose the centrifugal and individualizing trends of the market. Family ideology based on love and the ideal of the nuclear family constitute elements of these bonds.

The gap between ideals and reality constitutes a second source of contradictions. Ideally, the worker's household would be a nuclear family, autonomous and self-sufficient with regard to the resources necessary for its maintenance and reproduction. However, this ideal of autonomy is constantly contradicted by the reality of unsatified needs, by the need to share and loan. 'It is women who bridge the gap between what a household's resources really are, and what a family's position is supposed to be.' (Rapp, 1978: 288) The stable insertion of women in kinship and neighbourhood networks functions as an adjustment mechanism helping to maintain some stability in the worker's household (Ramos, 1981; Lomnitz, 1975).

In opposition to the relative stability of the worker's family, a second type of urban domestic organization – into which the worker's family may fall temporarily or permanently – is unstable insertion in the labour market. In this case, the monetary income related to the sale of labour power does not exist or is insufficient for the maintenance and reproduction of the unit. The household then loses its autonomy and self-sufficiency. This often implies high instability in household composition and family bonds, as well as a constant appeal to networks of informal relationships and/or mechanisms of social welfare, should these exist. This instability may be temporary and transient, related to migratory processes or periods of transition. The most typical case is that of peasants who migrate seasonally, keeping ties in their place of origin (Arizpe, 1982; Balan, 1981). But chronic instability is one of the constant

26

features of urban reality, varying in magnitude and social significance according to the economic situation of the country (especially the unemployment rate) and to welfare policies.

A third type of household among the common people are family enterprise, based on the work of its members, being at the same time a productive and reproductive unit. Within it, domestic and market-oriented tasks cannot clearly be distinguished; there is no separation between workplace and domestic domain; nor is there a clear division of labour between the sexes and generations, although there is a differentiation in power and authority. The woman/mother carries responsibility for domestic work; however, she – as well as the children – may actively participate in the family enterprize. In this case, intra-family bonds are reinforced by the unification of productive and reproductive tasks, always within a framework of internal differentiation in power and authority. In so far as the reproductive logic of the unit is based on the participation of members in family work with no pay, the process of individualization and autonomy of the subordinate members – wife and children – may consequently be more difficult and conflictual. Informal sector households are often a fluctuating (or intermediate) category between the second and third types.

Of course, these three types of urban common people's household are not found in pure and totally clear forms. Transitions between one and another are fluent and there are many possible combinations. At the same time, whilst the living conditions of the common people depend on shared macro-social factors – such as level of economic activity and labour market situation, social services and the existence of channels for expressing interests – the relative homogeneity in the position of the subordinate classes regarding consumption and reproduction creates the potential for unification of the common people, above and beyond differences in their insertion in the productive structure.

Internal dynamics: the household as a formal organization

In a well-known sociology textbook, the chapter devoted to formal organizations begins:

> There is a fundamental difference between activities that are systematically planned to achieve some purpose and those that are spontaneous. Generally we call systematically planned,

purposeful activities 'work', and spontaneous activities 'leisure' or 'play'. . . . But the most important distinction is whether a man plans his own activities, or whether his activities are planned *for him*. . . . Any social arrangement in which the activities of some people are systematically planned by other people (who, therefore, have authority over them) in order to achieve some special purpose is called a *formal organization*. (Stinchcombe, 1967: 154–5)

From this point of view, a household devoted to daily maintenance activities, based on a division of labour and responsibilities among its members, with established activities and routines for each one of them, is a formal organization. This does not deny the existence of other important and significant aspects of households, especially the affective components and kinship organization. However, the application of the formal organization model to the household is justified when the objective – as is the case here – is to emphasize its instrumental dimensions, and therefore to reveal actual social activities and relationships that have been been relatively invisible to society.

As in all organizations, there is a specific objective towards which the planned activities of a group of persons are aimed. The specific purpose of households may be characterized in a very global manner: to ensured maintenance and reproduction of its members according to criteria and parameters that refer to an 'adequate standard of living'. This objective is difficult to grasp. Theoretically, it should be possible to define a minimum threshold of satisfaction of certain biological needs for survival (such as eating or sleeping). The very process of meeting these minimum biological needs, however, sets the foundations of cultural and social organization, since the required activities are carried out as social relationships with meanings. Thus, even biological needs have a social component inherent in the process of their satisfaction. Needs are historically and culturally determined, and vary for different groups or classes of the population.[6]

At the micro-social level of the household, the definition of needs changes throughout the domestic cycle, whilst the standard of living (as a consumption pattern related to satisfying a set of 'standard' needs for a given social group in a certain historical period) is defined and redefined throughout the biographical cycle of the unit and of each of its members.[7] Several household factors intervene in this definition of needs and living standards: a) the combination of the needs of each of the household members, according to his or her social insertion (age, sex, occupation); b) the changing adaptation of domestic needs to socio-economic conditions along the domestic cycle; c) the domestic group's own history, in so far as it includes the temporal process of accumulation (or loss) of the necessary resources for the activities related to the maintenance of its members.

The theme of need satsifaction presents an additional difficulty: the distance between the definition of needs as part of an analytical model (following parameters that are external to the actors) and the definition of needs expressed by the actor themselves. In everyday life, needs are defined as that which one lacks. For example, from a theoretical point of view, housing is a constant need of domestic groups; people only perceive it as a need when they feel a lack of satisfaction with their housing level. Social groups identify needs with 'shortages', that is to say with those needs that cannot be met by habitually available resources.

In summary, the objective of the household is to carry out activities related to the maintenance of its members, following culturally-defined 'normal standards of living'. And this 'normality' must, in turn, be broken down into the statistical normality of the most common behaviour among members of the group, normality in terms of beliefs and values (Skolnick, 1975).

Performing activities to meet needs requires access to the necessary resources. As in any organization, obtaining resources is problematic, and the household must elaborate social mechanisms for procuring or creating them, defending them, continuously reproducing them and managing them. In urban sectors of the common people, household resources may derive from different sources – the direct effort and work of its members, formal transfers from institutions authorized to this effect (particularly the State) and informal transfers based on exchange and mutual aid networks. Resources may be in cash, in kind, or in services for direct use.

The study over time of the process of creation, defense, reproduction and management of resources can start at marriage, the moment of formation of the family/household. Spouses bring some material resources to the new enterprise (from the bride's trousseau to wedding presents, basic household goods, including at times their own dwelling) and their time-as-work capacity to be offered on the labour market or utilized in domestic activities. They also bring a

Table 1.1

Source	Type of Resource	
	Monetary	**Non-monetary**
Work of the members of the household	Participation in the labour force	Domestic production
Formal transfers	Pensions	Access to public services, social security, indirect subsidies
Informal transfers from relatives or neighbours	Mutual aid based on reciprocity/exchange	

'social capital' consisting of a network of kinship and friendship relations, to which they can resort, providing certain services in exchange for others. And they bring 'information capital' regarding the obtention of goods and services required to carry out activities related to meeting needs (knowledge on means of transport, social security, medical services, etc.).

As time goes by, the structure of the household may be modified by the addition of new members and the separation of others. In turn, the composition of resources also changes. There is a social expectation that the 'economic capital', the basic domestic infrastructure, will go on increasing and improving, adapting itself to the changing needs of the group (improvements in the house or in domestic equipment, for instance). Likewise, what could be called 'social capital' (following Bourdieu's terminology, although not strictly the author's conceptualization, 1977) must also be constantly increased and re-created. In order to maintain the network of reciprocity, it must be constantly activated through exchanges, the function of which is always two-faced: to obtain or render the specific good or service, while at the same time 'oiling' the system of reciprocity relations to keep it going (Ramos, 1981). And it is also necessary to maintain and update what could analogically be called the 'cultural capital' of domestic activities, that is to say information on resources and sources of procuring them (changes in a hospital's timetable, new rights acquired by a worker regarding family allowances, handling of bureaucratic structures and paperwork, and so on).

The working capacity of members changes throughout their life cycle, determining changes in domestic organization. There are two types of important decision: in the first place, when and how much each member can and must work, that is to say, who will contribute to what activities related to the maintenance of the group and at what moment. Changes in domestic roles are related to transitions in the life cycle: at what moment must a boy (or more often a girl) assist in domestic tasks or get a paid job outside the home? When does an elderly man or woman give up working on extra-domestic or domestic tasks? In the second place, decisions must be made regarding the assignment of working capacity to obtain a monetary income or to domestic production, that is to say, the divison of labour and responsibilities. These two subjects constitute the main axis of domestic organization.

With respect to the management of resources and their allotment to different activities, someone must assume responsibility for activities and ensure that resources are not utilized for objectives other than those prescribed. There is a need for internal organization, control and discipline. These tasks are traditionally assigned to women/housewives. Although a woman's responsibility for domestic organization does not always grant her power, she may have varying degrees of discretion and authority in the implementation of the intra-domestic division of labour. In part, these are not matters related to resource management but to the system of authority and control within the organization.

In summary, to carry out the prescribed activities, the household requires diverse resources. As expressed by Stinchcombe with respect to formal organizations, the defense of resources and their re-creation are the main problems that lead an organization to establish relations with the outside world. The financial control and management of these resources are the main parts of the organization's system of internal discipline (Stinchcombe, 1967: 167).

A fundamental element of the characterization of organizations is the *system of authority* by which the people are organized and guided when carrying out their activities. This includes assigning responsibilities, supervising tasks and a disciplinary system. The household may differ from other formal organizations in the incentives utilized to encourage the members to carry out the tasks assigned to them. It is not simply a matter of assigning tasks from a position of authority but a much more complex operation in which feelings and solidarity are at stake. Members must be prevailed upon to contribute to the common task, incorporating the money obtained into the family budget and/or participating in domestic labour. Individual utilitarian calculation of the monetary costs and benefits of co-residence does not seem here to be the basic criterion for a person's permanence in a given domestic group.[8] Even though the economic reality of shortages and the economies of scale of multipersonal units are present in the process of household formation, either implicitly or explicitly, they do not suffice to explain the matter. Predominantly moral appeals become necessary, with relatively little use of purely monetary or coercive incentives. The moral appeal addressed to various members differs according to their place within the structure of the household: a mother's abnegation, a father's responsibility, a child's obedience, are traditional social principles on which the system of incentives is based.

In fact, the typification of sexual roles (the man as 'head of household' and supplier of resources, the woman looking after her home and children) and the system of duties and obligations between parents and children constitute the ideological pillars on which proof of morality rests. Beyond this, the use of moral rewards and punishments according to social definitions and traditions, based on an ideological process of normalization of the division of labour between sexes and generations, makes the whole authority system less explicit and clear – especially in the 'modern' family where democratic and egalitarian values have already left their traces. In the family, values and ideologies are part of a highly personalized system of social relationships, charged with feelings and desires. The complexity of these bonds and the various levels and meanings into which these may be broken down and analysed, indicate the need to investigate in an empirical manner, the variety of domestic practices regarding the assignment of responsibilities, task-control and discipline. In this way, it will be possible to differentiate and to relate them to verbal expressions of norms and ideologies on this subject.

Finally, all formal organizations have their theory or conceptualization on how to organize activities. The planning of activities lies in the capacity to theorize or reflect on the best way to attain an objective. In this regard, the truth-value of the theory, that is to say whether it is true or false according to scientific criteria, is not of primary concern; it is the degree of acceptance of the theory – and of its consequences – by planners and actors which is important. This theorizing constitutes the system of basic beliefs that governs domestic organization. More than a rational theory, it is a system of changing representations, sometimes internally contradictory: a cultural system of values, norms and behavioural principles, grounded in Latin American and Western societies on the basic distinction between public and private spheres of life, in the 'naturalness' of the family and of the gender-based division of labour. At the same time, this system of beliefs is in contradiction with the ideological principles of individualization and personal autonomy. Thus, family organization and ideology is subject to contradictory forces that bring about change. Only an empirical analysis of the internal dynamics of households in concrete historical and class conditions can discover the bases of solidarity and unity among members, while at the same time exposing sources of conflict and rupture.[9]

The social bases of intra-domestic solidarity and conflict

The household is a mutifaceted social organization. Although activities and tasks carried out within it have more or less immediate concrete material results as far as the survival of its members is concerned (food is going to satisfy hunger, clothes are going to protect from the cold), they also contain an affective dimension, linked to reinforcement or re-creation, or to the breach or search for autonomy of bonds and social relations, and a symbolic dimension related to values and ideologies of specific social sectors or classes. In turn, it is a unit with shared interests, but in which the division of labour and the distributive processes that accompany it create conditions for divergent interests among its members, including struggles for exercising control:

> It is income pooling that enables the household to be perceived as a unit with unitary interests, despite the very different relationships to production of its separate members. Because of the division of labor among family members, disunity is thus inherent in the 'unity' of the family. (Hartman, 1981: 374)

Thus, the household is not an undifferentiated set of individuals who share activities related to their maintenance. It is a social organization, a microcosm of productive, reproductive and distributive relationships, with a structure of authority and strong ideological components that cement the organization and foster its continuation and reproduction. At the same time, there are structural bases for conflict and struggle within the household. Although collective and shared tasks and interests exist and bring the members together, each has his or her own distinct and at times incompatible interests, based on individual positions within intra- and extra-domestic production and reproduction processes.

In so far as households are mainly formed according to families, the basic principles of internal organization follow lines of internal differentiation linked to age, sex and kinship. Activities and tasks can be divided into two major types: production tasks that require the organization of the division of labour, and consumption tasks, that is to say the organization of the distribution of goods and services to meet specific needs. Decisions on the division of labour are centred on deciding who does what, who works outside the home and who does the domestic work and how, and according to which standards, etc. Regarding consumption, the question is how to organize expenditure or the family budget. How much is spent? Which are the priorities? Who exercises control and makes decisions? There is a third intermediate area that covers the amount of the work and/or income of each member that is socialized and alloted to shared activities, and how much to the individual's own use. Undoubtedly, these are the main issues causing intra-domestic conflicts and struggles as well as alliances and solidarities.

Within the socio-political and ideological context of patriarchal capitalist societies, children are subordinated to their parents, whom they must respect and obey. This is evident in their obligation to collaborate and participate in tasks for the common welfare, as defined and enforced by paternal authority.[10] During the last few centuries, the Western world has undergone a very deep process of individualization of children and of breaching (or gaining early autonomy from) paternal authority. Anderson (1971) compares the situation in rural areas of origin of migrants to Lancashire during the early English industrial revolution, with their condition in the textile cities. Based on historical reconstruction, he shows that in the city, youngsters had the option of becoming independent and autonomous in relation to their parents. If they stayed in the parental household, it was due to material convenience.[11] Anderson's analysis concentrates on the situation of children at the time the financial autonomy through incorporation into the labour force, a time at which it is clearly possible to identify differentiated interests.

Given the present stage of increasing autonomy of children and the loss of patriarchal authority, the confrontation between generations may nowadays show up earlier in the life cycle. The reason for conflicts may be the contribution of children to domestic labour, parents' requirement that the children find employment to help in the family maintenance, or the decision as to whether the resources thus obtained are for the individuals themselves or for the family. Confrontation between generations also appears in the area of consumption, especially due to adolescents' demands for a series of goods – ranging from fashionable clothes to electronic sound-systems – imposed by the consumer society of youth. Within the domestic domain, such pressures turn into conflict when it comes to establishing priorities in consumption and the distribution of benefits (Jelin, 1984).

Historically, the process of increased autonomy and the assertion of individual interests took place earlier between the generations – the young *vis-à-vis* their parents – than between the sexes. In this regard, the patriarchal system started to break down when the material bases of subsistence were transferred from the ownership of land inherited by children from their parents to the supply of labour on the market, for which the relevant unit is the individual and not the family. The process of individualization and recognition of women's interests and rights *vis-à-vis* the man head of family is more recent. Hence, the issue of the dynamics of the division of labour and the struggle for power between the sexes has only become important in the literature on domestic work, on women's subordination and on the social organization of reproduction in the last few years.

In domestic dynamics between the sexes, lines of confrontation appear in connection with the distribution of domestic responsibilities when the participation of women in the labour force increases. Time budget studies clearly indicate that women bear the heaviest burden as regards work and this is becoming an issue of women's demands, both in the privacy of the home as well as in social movements. However, in the realm of the intra-household pattern of consumption and distribution, the woman/mother seems to maintain her position as 'gate-keeper of the common good' in the domestic domain, resisting attacks of other members of the unit. This situation may change in various ways. On the one hand, it may lead to an increasing individualization of women, through an increasing attempt to defend their personal interests. Alternatively, it may bring about an increasing extension and socialization of the basic defense of humanitarian interests implicit in women's domestic role.[12]

Conclusions

The aim of this chapter has been to discuss the contributions of several disciplines which propose new ways of thinking of and presenting the family and domestic organization. In the first place, emphasis is placed on the complexity and multidimensional nature of daily life. Rather than separating and selecting a level or dimension of household organization, it seems important to make the effort to reveal how various dimensions – the economic and material, the cultural and symbolic, the political – are present and converge in each of the social relations and events of everyday life. In effect, all socially related practices contain messages that may (and must) be interpreted according to several codes. It is not a question of classifying patterns of behaviour as economic, political, or symbolic, but of interpreting the meaning of the same pattern of behaviour in these different analtyical levels:[13] in one and the same social practice, there is at the same time an exchange of material objects, affections and feelings, cultural symbols, identities and power.[14]

Secondly, it is necessary to consider explicitly intra-domestic dynamics, both in respect of the patterns of the division of labour and of interaction and decision-making related to the assignment of rewards, consumption and budgeting. In daily life, decisions on expenditure (what is going to be bought and for whom) are part of a complex system in which at the same time discussions and decisions take place regarding the division of labour (who does what and is responsible for what) and the criteria of authority and control (who has the right to judge and evaluate the others' actions). All this takes place in a setting in which love and feelings, mutual duties and obligations are also at stake. Within this complex ensemble of relations, two basic lines of intra-domestic conflict and alliance may be analytically identified, based on the distinction between gender and generation. The first sets the norms for the division of labour – women in charge of domestic tasks, men primarily responsible for extra-domestic work. The second line, the generational one, is especially important for understanding the dynamics of consumption (Jelin, 1984).

In the third place comes the interpenetration between intra-domestic dynamics and the wider social and political world. The distinction between the public and private domains constitutes a starting point for the investigation of the presence of the 'social' in family life. At an ideological and symbolic level, it refers to a way of conceptualizing and elaborating the specificity of family life. But it does not adequately describe the reality of social and political relations. The family is constituted and its functions are set in its interrelation with other social institutions; it never was, nor will be, detached or isolated from wider social determinations. In this sense, the family and daily domestic relationships do not constitute a 'private' world, but rather, the private world of each social agent is built on the social relations and controls within which everyday life unfolds.

Notes

1. These issues become crucially important when domestic organizations of divergent cultural traditions are compared, such as the Chinese family (Greenhalgh, 1981) or the social organization of different African and Asian cultures (Oppong, 1982; Goody, 1976). The overlap and the differences between domestic units, families, residential groups and households have been the subject of intense discussion when deciding on criteria for operationalization, especially whilst trying to standardize census enumerations to ensure intersocietal comparability (Burch *et al.*, 1976). This point is also of great importance when dealing with analyses of income distribution that take into consideration family composition (Kuznets, 1976).

2. Yanagisako (1979) refers to the shallowness of the descriptions of households found in ethnographical reports, even those written by first-class anthropologists, that can be traced to these confusions.

3. Larguia and Dumoulin have extended the implications of this distinction by showing how the separation between socially visible and invisible work has served to mask the subordination of women (Larguia and Dumoulin, 1975).

4. Generally, socio-economic studies consider the composition of the household as an explanatory variable or as a control variable for other phenomena, without posing the opposite question: that of the determinants of the composition of residential units. An exception to this rule is the increasing interest in the study of households headed by women (Buvinic and Youssef, 1978).

5. 'The convenient social virtue ascribes merits to any pattern of behaviour, however uncomfortable or unnatural for the individual involved, that serves the comfort or well-being of, or is otherwise advantageous for, the more powerful members of the community.' (Galbraith, 1973: 30) Galbraith identifies the role of women in consumption as that of a 'crypto-servant role of administrator.' (p. 37)

6. The concept of 'needs' presents many analytical difficulties. There are several definitions, varying from the administrative-bureaucratic or normative ones based on discussions of 'basic needs', to those that make reference to the actors' point of view or to shared social definitions

of welfare or of an 'adequate' or 'normal' standard of living (Heller, 1976; Leiss, 1976).

7. At the macro-social level, the definition of welfare and inequality in the social distribution of public services is analysed in a vast literature, ranging from the classics in welfare economics up to specific analyses on urban services and rights.

8. Anderson has applied this utilitarian model to explain the reasons why working children remained in their parental home in England, during the industrial revolution at the beginning of the nineteenth century, contrasting them with the 'traditional' bonds of their rural places of origin. His text concentrates on monetary benefits, making totally explicit the presence of this dimension in domestic organization, but does not suffice to express the complexity of the bonds therein (Anderson, 1971).

9. The approach followed here implicitly criticizes micro-economic analyses of domestic activities proposed by 'new home economics'. In effect, the existence of a conceptualization of tasks does not necessarily imply that actors move according to a rational theory of cost and benefit of domestic activities, a hypothesis on which the neoclassic micro-economic analysis is based. It is highly likely that rational-choice assumptions on marginal utility and opportunity costs are adequate for certain specific activites in which parameters are clear. Discovering this should be the result of empirical research rather than an assumption. Neither are the logical principles which guide the action of household members clear. To assume, as does this school, that action is ruled by a marginalist logic of the household constitutes in fact an inversion of the research process: the starting premise is what should – if reality so indicates – constitute the result of the research work. Moreover, the assumption that the household is a decision-making unit requires in-depth reviewing, in so far as it conceals the social condition of women, intra-domestic mechanisms for generating and solving conflicts and the intra-family authority system (Galbraith, 1973).

10. Recent literature on transfers between generations stems from two paradigms, modernization and demographic transition theories, and the micro-economics of the value of children. Both set forth the dichotomy between selfishness and altruism as an incentive for bearing children: children are borne because the material benefits that parents will eventually receive exceed costs; or children are borne for the altruistic 'satisfaction' of giving without expecting anything more than moral rewards and satisfactions in return (Caldwell, 1976; Willis, 1981).

11. Anderson's study completely omits the analysis of affective bonds, as if they did not exist or had nothing to do with binding parents and children. Rather, the analysis seems to assume that, even though parents might have expected some recognition from their children, the latter had the option of not fulfilling these expectations.

12. With respect to this issue, Elshtain formulated a hypothesis on broadening the scope of 'maternal thinking': 'Maternal thinking reminds us that public policy has an impact on real human beings.

As public policy becomes increasingly impersonal, calculating, and technocratic, maternal thinking insists that the reality of a single human child be kept before the mind's eye. Maternal thinking, like Antigone's protest, is a rejection of amoral statecraft and an affirmation of the dignity of the human person.' (Elshtain, 1982: 56)

13. The approach followed here is inspired by the type of ethnographic research that Geertz refers to, within the framework of his interpretative theory of culture, as 'dense description' (Geertz, 1973).

14. There is a more established tradition in the social sciences regarding the analysis of some of these dimensions than of others. Hence, there are more tools available for analysing the economic or political aspects of action than for the analysis of the affective or symbolic aspects, with the exception of tools for individual psychology, clearly insufficient.

2

FAMILY AND HUMAN REPRODUCTION

Eunice R. Durham

INTRODUCTION

Common sense usually conceives the relatively stable institutions of society as 'natural' forms of the organization of collective life, rather than as changeable products of social action. In the case of the family, however, the tendency towards its 'naturalization' is greatly reinforced by the fact that it refers to the institution in charge of the social regulation of activities with definite biological bases: sex and reproduction.

Although this naturalization of the family takes place in all cultures, it becomes particularly insidious in Latin American society, given its special type of family and the manipulation of scientific conceptions in its legitimation. Thus, besides its incidence in everyday life, this view of the family tends to intrude and contaminate scientific thought itself, in obvious or subtle ways. This is exemplified by the readiness to take the conjugal group as the basic or elementary form of the family, and to claim its universality. Furthermore, since we recognize in Latin American society an essentially bilateral kinship structure (though with a certain predominance of patrilinearity), kinship itself is taken as equally 'natural' and is conceived as an *extension* of family ties.

The process of naturalization of the family does not end with its formal structure; it also includes its internal organization, grounded in the sexual division of labour. The relationship between this sexual division of labour and the role of women in the reproductive process leads to a view in which all female roles are seen as derived from biological functions.

The study of the family has to start by dissolving this apparent naturality in order to perceive it as a changeable human creation.

Starting with the conjugal group, and given the universality of the institution of marriage, it is possible to identify husbands, wives and children in all societies. The problem is to determine to what extent this cluster is recognized as a specific social group or sub-group; whether it constitutes a household or residential unit; and whether it forms a kinship unit. Through comparative studies, anthropology has shown that this is not always the case, and that different societies conceive and combine marriage, kinship, residence and domestic life in varying forms, producing arrangements that may be quite different from those in Latin American society. The essential point in order to 'de-naturalize' the family is, therefore, to understand that the relationships we expect to find among the conjugal group, the family, kinship, and the division of labour, can be separated, giving birth to very different institutions.

Anthropology has a crucial role to play in this task. Among the social sciences, it is the only one that is aimed specifically at analysing differences and alternative forms of social organization. It can therefore allow us simultaneously to look at what is general and to perceive the infinite variety of concrete social formations.

The sexual division of labour

All known human societies have some form of sexual division of labour, a differentiation between female and male roles. This differentiation finds its foremost manifestation within the family. The structure of the sexual division, and the extension and degree of rigidity of the separation between prescribed male and female tasks vary greatly. This diversity is analysed below, but it should be stressed that there are certain constraints within this diversity.

First of all, it is necessary to recognize that there are no proved cases of proper matriarchal societies, that is, societies in which decisions regarding the entire society are concentrated in the hands of women. Everywhere, war and politics are essentially masculine activities; when women do participate, it is in a secondary or complementary manner. On the other hand, childcare and the initial stages of socialization are always the tasks of women – men only intervene in a complementary or auxiliary way. It seems necessary to recognize that the variability in the concrete forms of the sexual divison of labour is built around an almost universal tendency to split social life into a public sphere, distinctively male, linked to politics and war, and a feminine, domestic, private sphere, linked

41

to reproduction and childcare (Lamphere, 1979). This does not imply that women are absent from public life; even less so, that men are excluded from the domestic domain. It is only in a limited sense, therefore, that it can be said that all known human societies have so far been characterized by varying degrees and forms of male dominance, which is not the same as saying that in all cultures women are equally oppressed or dominated by men (Rosaldo, 1979).

In order to understand the universality of these aspects (as well as the possibility of their future transformation in Latin American society), it must be admitted that the cultural construction of the sexual division of labour is built upon biological differences. This is not to say that there is a 'natural' explanation for the distinction between male and female roles; rather, that in this particular issue, cultures organize, orientate, modify, stress or exclude traits that have a biological basis.

It is always difficult to speak of biological determinations in reference to human societies, because the very physical evolution of the species has been subject to the development of culture, originating much earlier than the emergence of the *Homo* gender itself. Nevertheless, man is undoubtedly an animal, a mammal and a primate, with clearly defined physical traits, and it is perfectly possible and valid to analyse the similarities and differences between *Homo sapiens* and other species, particularly those that are biogenetically closer to it. This comparison seems to be especially relevant regarding reproduction.

Among mammals, there is an innate tendency on the part of the females to feed and protect their babies. The period in which this takes place, however, is highly variable, although it tends not to overlap with the birth of the next baby. Among anthropoid apes the period of offspring dependence on their mothers is quite long; females are not in heat again, and therefore do not have new babies, while they are taking care of an immature offspring.

In the human species, the period of total dependence of the offspring is equally or even more extended; it also tends to overlap with the birth of the next child. Breast-feeding usually lasts for more than one year, and the child still needs to be fed by an adult long after that. Until they turn three years of age, children can barely control biped walking techniques and must be carried around most of the time. Only at five or six can they start helping with work, and very seldom do they become completely productive before the beginning of sexual maturity, that is, at eleven or twelve years of age for girls and at fourteen or fifteen for boys. Moreover, this long period of physical dependence is aggravated by the absolute need for systematic cultural training to transform a baby into a human being. This means that, although women seldom have multiple deliveries, they spend a large part of their adult life taking care of more than one child, of different ages. These biological and cultural peculiarities of the reproductive process of human beings, and the burden they represent to women, set the conditions for the development of the sexual division of labour. The fact that these tasks tend to be attributed to mothers cannot be seen simply as a masculine imposition; they also constitute a cultural product built upon tendencies and traits shared by the human species and other mammals, prominent among the anthropoids, our closest relatives: the protracted dependence of the offspring on their mothers.

On the other hand, it is possible culturally to modify this pattern by providing surrogate mothers, although this is much more complicated in the first year before weaning (adequate forms of artificial feeding of babies represent a very recent invention in the history of humanity). Furthermore, these conditioning factors of a biological nature impose themselves more forcefully and broadly in 'primitive' societies, that is, in those characterized by the limited complexity of their social division of labour. In such societies, all fecund women are necessarily mothers and are equally bound by childcare, which is essential for group survival. In stratified societies, on the other hand, especially among the dominant classes, women are frequently liberated from at least part of this task by the emergence of wet-nurses, maids, governesses, and so on. For this very reason, and taking for granted that the general aspects of the sexual division of labour are likely to be cultural elaborations of traits found in the development of the species prior to the development of culture itself, it becomes necessary to analyse further the scope of the cultural developments and transformations built on these bases.

Firstly, the sexual division of labour is never limited to these general aspects, but tends to encompass a great number of other activities. Its extension and rigidity, in fact, vary from one culture to another. Moreover, specific activities such as braiding, weaving, making ceramics, planting vegetables, may be defined in one society as feminine tasks, in another as male ones, and in a third as gender-neutral, carried out by either sex. Also, the very conception of the feminine character varies: the same universal aspects of the sexual division of labour may be associated with conceptions which attribute to women in general a strong sexual drive, or the opposite, a tendency to frigidity; women may be seen as fragile and irresponsible beings, or as reliable beast of burden; they may be defined as unable to carry out commercial activities, or a natural ability for business may be ascribed to them; finally, the degree of autonomy, independence and initiative granted to women in different societies and in different activities varies enormously.

Thus, the recognition of the existence of general aspects of the sexual division of labour and of the prevalence of male dominance does not imply accepting that women's submission is a natural or universal phenomenon. The actual extension of the sexual division of labour determines a high degree of mutual dependence between women and men, not restricted to sexual satisfaction, that is essential to the well-being and even to the economic survival of both. The sexual segregation of activities creates an area of autonomy and independence for both men and women. The more rigid the separation, the wider this area becomes. Secondly, in so far as this division of labour is largely 'arbitrary', it can produce entirely diverse conceptions of the role and the position of women in society. In the same way, the acceptance of male dominance in certain sectors of public life does not necessarily imply the submission to male will in others or in private life. It seems that men tyrannized by women exist in all societies, even in the most chauvinistic ones.

The analysis of cultural diversities demonstrates the need to break up the confinement of the relationship between men and women to the domination–submission dichotomy, and to start thinking about a complex combination of areas of influence or autonomy, of different degrees of imposition and acceptance of real or formal authority.

Marriage, kinship and the family

If the study of the biological factors related to reproduction and sexual differences can help us understand certain universal aspects of the sexual division of labour, it proves much less enlightening when we try to understanding the family, the hub of our analysis.

Consider again the primates, which are closest to the human species in terms of evolution. Permanent mating is very rare among primates. Among the anthropoids, only the gibbon lives in small groups formed by a male, a female and their immature offspring;

as a corollary, while having a 'family', the gibbon does not properly have a 'society'. The orangutans, however, are lonely animals who live together only briefly during the mating period, the progeny remaining entirely under the care of the mother. Chimpanzees and gorillas, on the other hand, live in bands and do not have anything similar to a family. The bands are hierarchical units in which the male adults dominate the females, and one male dominates the others. The stronger males guarantee themselves a privileged access to the promiscuous females during their heat period. Outside this period, there is no stable mating and the offspring are cared for by their respective mothers. In a somewhat simplified way, we can say that among anthropoids and primates either 'families' or bands are usually found, never both simultaneously: it seems impossible to erect families as building blocks of a broader social life, or to think about the family as the natural foundation of society.

If a natural group existed in human society, it would not be the family, but one formed by a woman and her immature children (Fox, 1967). Indeed, it can be argued that pregnancy, lengthy breast-feeding, and the need to protect, feed and carry around human babies during a long period of time, must contribute to the creation of relatively lasting ties between mother and children. It can also be deduced that the long maturation period of children, which outlasts the interval between one pregnancy and the next, allows brothers and sisters to live together, facilitating sociability among them. Meanwhile, sexual relationships, although certainly necessary for reproduction, do not necessarily develop lasting ties (contrary to breast-feeding). It seems, in fact, that human societies exert large measures of coercion to stabilize these relations. Similarly, excluding the strictly genetic point of view, the relationship between a man and the children he generates is necessarily indirect, not presenting the 'naturalness' of the relationship between mother and children. After all, human families in all societies establish social ties between a woman's children and certain men, ties which are created through *representations* (ideas, systems and symbols) embodied in kinship beliefs and mediated by marriage. Therefore, in order adequately to understand the familial institution, it becomes necessary to understand the nature of marriage and of kinship systems, both of which are regulated by the incest taboo.

The incest taboo consists of the proscription of sexual intercourse and, by extension, matrimonial relationships between men and women linked by certain social ties, generally (but not exclusively) defined by kinship categories. It exists in all known human societies, constituting, as a prohibition, a universal cultural creation, although extremely variable in its range and in the nature of the relationships to which it applies. It has no counterpart in any other animal species. Though there are certain mechanisms that seem to inhibit the mating of individuals of the same brood, especially among birds, certainly nothing would restrain the interbreeding of 'brothers' from different broods or even of fathers and daughters, or of mothers and already independent adult sons, not to mention even more distant relationships, such as uncles, nephews, or first-, second- and third-degree cousins.

The key to understanding the incest taboo, as demonstrated by Levi-Strauss (1968), is not to confuse it with the cultural elaboration of a biological trend or requirement (a supposedly natural aversion between genetically close individuals or the species' need to avoid consanguineous mating). Contrary to this, the prohibition of incest consists of a norm imposed (and as such it is a social creation) on the indeterminate natural space which concerns the choice of sexual partners. When considering family and kinship, the central importance of the incest taboo lies in that; while *conceptually* distinguishing between forbidden and permitted partners, it destroys the possibility of the natural manifestation of sexuality, subjecting it to rules and turning it into an instrument for the creation of social ties.

Through the taboo of incest, societies regulate marriage, which is also a univeral institution, although it varies in intensity and permanence of the ties established, as well as in the degree of sexual exclusiveness it presupposes. What is most general in marriage is that in all societies it is conceived as a prerequisite for the legitimization of the children borne by a woman (Gough, 1962). In the same way that the taboo of incest destroys the naturalness of sexual relationships, the universality of marriage as a prerequisite for procreation destroys the naturalness of the relationships between a mother and her children, attributing to a specific man the responsibility for the progeny of each woman.

In order to avoid the reintroduction of an undue naturalization, it is important not to confuse the universal requirement of marriage with the need to determine biological paternity. Because, even if marriage as a contract establishes which man is responsible for the children of which woman, this responsibility is not necessarily assigned to the husband, much less to the sexual partner. In matrilineal societies, for example, a great part of this responsibility (and attendant rights) is invested in the mother's brother, not in the consort.

A comparative analysis helps us understand marriage, according to Levi-Strauss, as a relationship among three people. Marriage involves not one man and one woman, but one woman and two men: the one that takes her and the one to whom she is denied, due to the incest taboo. From this perspective, marriage is seen not only as an element for the creation of family and kinship groups, but also as a mechanism of communication between these groups, establishing an 'exchange of women'.

By the fact that our culture privileges matrimonial relations over sororal ties, and paternity in lieu of avuncular ties, this basic characteristic of marriage remains hidden to common sense, blurred by the issue of paternity, which is culturally conceived as the social recognition of a biological relation. Conversely, the comparative viewpoint allows the dissociation of paternity from family and kinship, showing at the same time that the social group where reproduction occurs does not necessarily constitute a kinship unit.

With this approach, we can define marriage as a mechanism regulated by the taboo of incest, that attributes the specific responsibilities and rights of a woman's children to certain men who maintain the basic and antagonistic ties of brother and husband in relation to her, either favouring one of these terms or establishing a complementary relation between them. For this same reason, kinship cannot be conceived of as an extension of family ties: on the contrary, it is a presumption that is manipulated in the process of the formation of groups that can be called families.

From the anthropological viewpoint, kinship systems should be conceived as formal structures involving arrangements and combinations of three basic relationships: of descent (between father and children and/or mother and children), of consanguinity (between brothers), and of affinity created by marriage). What characterizes a kinship system is not the content of the relationships established through it, but the way these relationships are combined. In this sense, kinship systems are actually a language; similar systems may be found in societies with vey different economic organization and even with diverse types of family.

An important source of a kinship system's variability stems from the fact that the ties between mothers and children may be seen as essentially different from the ones between fathers and children. Ultimately, both of them may be totally excluded from the social definition of kinship (though not simultaneously). In rigidly patrilineal societies, for example, people may believe that the baby is entirely formed by its father's semen, the mother being no more than a receptable where the baby is developed – kinship is then delineated exclusively in the paternal lineage, taking the mother's side as only an affinity relationship. Conversely, in matrilineal societies, there are examples in which the male's role in conception is denied. In such societies, the father's image does not exist, only that of the mother's husband.

A concrete example helps to highlight these problems: that of the Trobriand family, justly famous in the literature for the richness of its documentation and for its exotic organization. (Malinowski, 1922). To a casual observer, Trobriand families are units that look very similar to those in Latin American society. Great circular villages are formed by huts where a man, a woman and small children live. The chiefs, mainly those in the highest ranks of the hierarchy, have several women, each one in a separate dwelling. Common men have only one. However, this understandable and seemingly familiar appearance is radically altered when we realize that the Trobrianders are a matrilineal society. This means that filiation, inheritance and descent succession take place exclusively through the maternal lineage, that is, between maternal uncle and nephew.

The Trobriand islanders constitute one of the (relatively rare) societies that totally deny the participation of the progenitor in the reproductive process. They believe that children are conceived through spirits that wander about the water and penetrate the women's vaginas while they are bathing. Sexual intercourse has nothing to do with it, except in the mechanical sense that the loss of virginity is necessary to widen the vaginal opening in order to permit the penetration of the baby-spirit (which, according to the Trobrianders themselves, may be attained through means other than intercourse). The relationship with the mother is at the same time physical and spiritual, and all relatives from the maternal lineage are thought of in very similar terms to what we call 'blood community'. On the other hand, the father is strictly related by affinity and is not kin – he is the mother's husband, someone corresponding to the western notion of a stepfather.

The situation becomes even more confusing when we consider that the Trobrianders are patrilocal and practise exogamy of villages extensively. This implies that when married, wives move into their husbands' villages. Since citizenship in the village, as well as land-ownership, is transmitted through the female line, all children in the village are actually foreigners. Their village is the one where their uncle lives. As he grows, the young man gradually leaves his father's village and progressively joins his uncle's, which is in fact his own village and where he will settle when getting married. Girls, for their part, generally move from their father's to their husband's village; in other words, they never live in their own village.

This society provides an excellent example of the widest range of possibilities in the combination of principles of kinship, marriage and domestic group organization; it shows clearly to what extent a reality like Latin American society is not a natural solution, but rather a specific arrangement of various structural principles that cannot be generalized.

When comparing the Latin American type of family with the Trobrianders, it is easy to conclude that the differences derive from the fact that in the latter society, kinship is exclusively matrilineal, so that if the term 'family' is used to refer to the domestic group, in the Trobriand case it does not constitute a kinship unit, in spite of its being a reproductive unit. If, on the other hand, the term 'family' is used to refer to a kinship unit, the family will be the group formed by the brother, the sister and her children, which is neither a reproductive unit, nor a residential one, nor, for that matter, a domestic group.

There are still other very different cases, such as the Mundurucu Indians of Brazil, living by the Tapajós River (Murphy, 1960). These Indians are formally patrilineal, recognizing clans, phratries and moieties. They are also matrilocal (the husbands live in their wives' villages) and marriage tends to be exogamous in relation to the village. Moreover, they have developed thoroughly the insti-tution of the men's house. Thus, all men and boys spend most of their time in the men's house, a structure that is usually in the centre of the village. Unlike most societies where this institution exists, among the Mundurucu not only do the young and single males eat and sleep in the men's house, but so do the married males.

Collective houses among the Mundurucu, on the other hand, are permanently occupied by the women, their daughters and their small sons. There, wives are visited during the night by husbands who wish to have sexual intercourse. Generally, the women within a house are related among themselves through the maternal line, that is the houses are occupied by grandmothers, mothers, aunts, daughters, sisters, nieces and granddaughters. However, in so far as it is a patrilineal society, this relationship is not formally recognized in kinship terms for the construction of descent groups – quite the opposite, given their system of marriage and kinship, women of the same house belong necessarily to different clans and opposite moieties.

Within the houses, the group formed by a woman and her small children occupies a certain space; however, each house has a common pantry where the produce of the fields owned by the women's husbands is kept together. Also, there is only one fire for cooking the collective meal. In general, when a man comes back from hunting, which is the main male occupation, he delivers the slaughtered animals to his wife. The women will prepare a meal, using the game brought by the husbands, as well as the produce of the fields. Once the food is ready, part of it is sent to the men's house where, together with contributions from the other houses, the male collective meal is consumed. In their house, the women distribute the remaining food amongst themselves and their children.

The economic complementarity created by the sexual division of labour links each of the houses and the collectivity of men. The group formed by a man, his wife and their children is not a domestic unit nor a household, but constitutes a basic reference for the *organization* and mutual distribution of the products of male and female labour.

Within this system, what is the *family*? The group formed by the husband, the wife and their children is important; it forms the reproductive, inheritance and descent unit, as well as the instance of the organization of the redistribution of products of female and male labour. The father generally develops very intense affectionate ties with the children, which constitutes an important factor in the stability of the marriage. However, this group is neither a productive, a residential nor a household unit. On the other hand, the women of one house, together with their children, are a residential and a household unit, but not a reproductive one, nor a kinship unit, and only partially do they form an economic unit, since they depend on the game brought by the husbands, and they work in the fields, which also belong to them, although only in a formal sense. There is no special institution to join together the men married to the women of a given house. In fact, what we find are subgroups corresponding structurally to our nuclear family, subordinated at the domestic level to an extended family of women.

The examples could be multiplied indefinitely (Radcliffe-Brown and Forde, 1958; Fortune, 1963). The analysis of these family types reveals that the difficulty in harmonizing them with the Latin American view of the family rests in the fact that they dissociate organizational principles which are combined in Latin American culture. The variety of possible arrangements makes it necessary to redefine the concept of the family or to limit its applicability to Latin American society. The effect is the dissoluion of the apparent naturalness of the family conceived as a conjugal group, and of kinship understood as an extension of family ties.

Therefore, to preserve the applicability of the notion of the family to other societies, it is essential to take into account the possible dissociation between reproductive and kinship units, and to favour either one of these terms. To define the family as a kinship unit means giving the concept a formal reference, well fulfilled by Levi-Strauss's term *kinship atom*, (Levi-Strauss, 1958). I believe that it is more interesting to privilege its reference to the groups responsible for reproduction. In effect, in all human societies, children are born and incorporated into groups formed according to kinship and affinity criteria, that become immediately and directly responsible for taking care of them. The emphasis of the concept then reverts upon two basic notions: the *group*, as an empirically demarcated and socially recognized unit, and *reproduction*.

In this sense, the family has to be defined as an *institution*, in Malinowski's sense. That is, in reference to a concrete social group, which exists as such in the representation of its members, and is organized to perform the tasks of (biological and social) reproduction, through the manipulation of the formal principles of alliance, descent and consanguinity on the one hand, and of the substantive practices of the sexual division of labour, on the other (Malinowski, 1922; Durham, 1978).

Alliance and kinship may be combined in different ways, giving origin to structurally different groups. As groups, families are constituted by persons who maintain among themselves relations of alliance, descent and consanguinity, although they may not necessarily form the basic unit of kinship. On the other hand, as procreative groups, they are also consumption groups (although not necessarily productive units) and tend to be organized as domestic and residential units or subunits, at least during part of their existence.

In this respect, they are the privileged locus of the incidence of the principles of the sexual division of labour, which to a great extent accounts for the degree of autonomy or subordination of women.

This definition of the family leads us to consider the superposition and separation of this concept from those of domestic group and residential unit. As already mentioned, at least during a stage of their life cycle, families tend to coincide and/or to integrate with domestic groups and residential units. As residential units, however, domestic groups can either restrict themselves to the members of the family, or expand themselves to include persons not related by kinship or affinity (like slaves, servants, and boarders of various kinds). They can even be made up of exclusively non-kin (which is the case, for example, of student fraternities) and clearly do not form a family. Finally, residential groups may be neither families nor domestic groups, as is the case of tribal groups where the young people live in the men's house, although they might eat with their families and contribute to the domestic pantry (Bender, 1967; Levy and Fallers, 1959).

Without confusing the concepts, it becomes necessary in each case to analyse the overlap in the definition of concrete social units, since families are the units that articulate relations of consanguinity, affinity and descent in nuclei of social reproduction.

Sex and family

Up to this point, we have examined thoroughly the organization of reproduction, but we have said very little about sex – and this is not by chance. Although both issues are obviously related, they are relatively autonomous, and in order better to understand the family, the analysis of reproduction proves to be more useful than that of sexuality.

In fact, the recognition that the *biological function* of sexual attraction is the reproduction of the species should not be confused with the idea that reproduction is the social and individual motivation for sexual activity: from the individual's point of view, reproduction, which is frequently unwanted, is a by-product of sexual activity, which follows its own dynamics. In extreme cases, as with the Trobrianders, the society does not even recognize the relationship between these two phenomena, although in many others it is exactly this relationship that becomes the privileged object of social regulation.

We could even say that the cultural development of the sexual impulse takes into account its *pleasure function*, which is not easily or directly compatible with its reproductive function. In this case, the comparison made so many times between sex and nourishment is illustrative. We all know that the intake of food is vital for the life of the organism, but people (and also animals) do not eat in order to maintain themselves in good physical form (excluding fanatics and athletes). They eat because they wish to do so and because food is a pleasure; for this reason, people frequently eat dangerous or even harmful substances. Thus, all societies have (usually highly refined) cultural constructs that refer to the preparation of food and the social conditions of its consumption. Such constructs simultaneously contribute to enhance and prolong pleasure, they regulate and assign meaning to it, transforming it into a means of bringing into being social ties – the immense variety and broadness of food restrictions, ritual banquets, and the universal importance of food in celebrations of all kinds must be recalled. Something similar occurs with sex: culture creates ways of refining, enhancing and prolonging pleasure; at the same time, and through extremely complex symbolic constructs, culture establishes restrictions and directions that transform sex into the basis of social relations, at least partially independent of its reproductive function.

As Levi-Strauss observed with great insight, 'Among all instincts, the sexual one is the only one that needs the stimulation of the other to manifest itself.' (Levi-Strauss, 1947: 14). It therefore simultaneously represents an overflow of culture into nature and, in nature itself, a fragment of social life. For this reason, it emerges as a privileged path in the passage from the 'state of nature' to the 'state of culture'.

But Levi-Strauss also reminds us of the double 'exteriority' of sexual life in relation to society, since it expresses, more than anything else, 'the animal nature of man and testifies, in the very core of humanity, to the clearest survival of instincts' (Levi-Strauss, 1968: 14). Furthermore, it depends on *individual* desires, which are least respectful of social rules.

We can add to Levi-Strauss's observations by mentioning that precisely because it demands the presence (even if only symbolic) of *the other* for attaining satisfaction, the manifestation of sexuality implies the permanent possibility of attempting to turn the other into a mere *object* or *instrument* of individual pleasure. Perhaps it is

53

due to this that sexual relationships present the constant threat of falling to asocial individualism and interpersonal violence.

When considering these manifestations of sexuality and their constant disruptive potential of social relations, it should be remembered that the females of the human species are unique in not having a definite period of heat (oestrus). In the species where this occurs, females are simultaneously attractive and receptive to males during very limited periods. During the rest of the time they remain, one might say, asexual. Whereas in the human species sex represents a constant and permanent possibility of interpersonal relationships. This is the origin of its double character: as a powerful instrument for developing enduring social ties, and as a constant threat to pre-established rules.

Nevertheless, if family life always implies some form of control of sexuality, it is important to recognize that family life is never restricted to this aspect. On the contrary, issues of sexuality greatly exceed questions of the family and it is never possible completely to equate these two issues with each other.

This observation is especially important in the analysis of the changes wrought on the family in Latin American society, given that this institution is closely linked to very rigid forms of sexual regulation. This fact has hindered the recognition of the relative separation of these problems. For this reason, the discussion about sexuality affects, in a very direct and immediate manner, the Latin American conception of the family.

The model and empirical reality

In the analysis developed thus far, the category of the family, as it is culturally defined in Latin American society, has been identified with the model of the conjugal or nuclear family. The next step is, therefore, to analyse this identification.

In Latin American society, any population census will reveal that regarding household composition there are as many exceptions as there are positive cases of the nuclear family pattern. These exceptions may be of various types. First, there are those residential groups in which the domestic group is larger than the nuclear family, including either other relatives (in the majority of cases, members of the family of origin of one of the spouses), or other members of different types (godchildren, protegés, friends, boarders, or even servants). There are also cases in which the group is smaller than the nuclear family: couples without children, single brothers without parents. But the most common case of 'incomplete' families is that of matrifocal families, that is, households formed basically by mother and children, where the presence of a spouse-father tends to be temporary and unstable. We know that this kind of family is very common in the poorer sectors of the population. Finally, there are very complex cases, which have increased over time, resulting from the dissolution of marriages, where the relationships of the couple with their own children, with children from other marriages of one or both of the spouses, and the relationship between those various children themselves may lead to very different arrangements.

It is precisely the variety and broadness of these exceptions that have created many problems in the definition of the types of family that characterize Latin American society. Besides, they frequently raise the issues of the disintegration of the family and its progressive destruction. In this respect, it is essential to distinguish three types of problem. In the first place, that of the exceptions to, and the elasticity of, the family model; secondly, the emergence of alternative patterns; and, finally, the disappearance of the institution as such.

In order to understand the nature of this distinction, the statement that the family is a model or cultural pattern must be clearly explained. Such a statement is linked to the concept of institution as defined above. Starting from the idea that social life is organized through culturally elaborated *rules*, concrete social groups should be seen as specific social structures that use the cultural models to handle problems of collective life. In Geertz's words, cultural patterns are simultaneously *models of* and *models for* social behaviour, that is representations of ordering arrangements that exist in social life and ordering arrangements for collective life (Geertz, 1973). As models, in this double sense, they are in the first place changeable; in the second place, they are synthetic constructions, into which social reality never fits completely. That is exactly why the existence of innumerable exceptions does not necessarily imply the denial of the rule; it may represent only its flexible application, in order to allow the solution of different problems. Regarding models that regulate sexual life and procreation, the difficulty in following the model or the need to accommodate a very high number of exceptions may characterize not only Latin American society but the great majority of societies. It seems that in this field it is a type of behaviour that is particularly resistant to social impositions.

In the cases of the primitive societies analysed above, we mentioned only the model; its performance depends, among other things, on the compliance with specific prohibitions of relationships considered incestuous and on very rigid rules concerning residence. However, in all of these societies, the rules are constantly being broken and there is enough flexibility to incorporate a great number of exceptions. So, marriage generally presupposes conjugal faithfulness. In all societies unfaithfulness occurs. It is true that the degree of tolerance of unfaithfulness does not imply either rejection or total disregard for the rule, nor does it imply that unfaithfulness creates no serious problems. The same can be said, to greater or lesser degrees, of incestuous relationships, of residence rules, of forms of co-operation, of compliance with the pattern of sexual divison of labour, and so on. Cultural rules certainly mould behaviour, but they never determine it absolutely. The existence of the rule is separate from its application to specific cases that never fit the model perfectly.

Although the diversity and the degree of variation in the composition of concrete families represents a fundamental problem for research, empirical deviations from the cultural model cannot be taken as a sign of its ineffectiveness, failure or transformation. It is necessary, first, to analyse to what extent the variations correspond to adaptations or extensions of the model, and in what sense they imply a challenge to it. The *concept* of the family, although referring to concrete social groups, refers primarily to the cultural model and to its *representation*. The analysis, on the other hand, always takes into consideration the utilization of the model in the organization of social groups and in collective behaviour, within the context of a dynamism that usually involves the transformation of the existing models themselves.

Secondly, in the analysis of the model itself, it is possible to distinguish between the formal structure (which defines the composition of the group) and the organization of social relations, which functions according to the patterns of sexual (and age) division of labour, given that there is a certain degree of autonomy between these two levels. This is particularly important in analysing ongoing changes in the family, which refer to alterations in the sexual division of labour and which may affect, in varying ways, the structure of the institution.

The model seems to be very clear in Latin American society: the family is a unit composed of the husband, the wife and their children, which form a household. The basic structural characteristics of this model first of all imply a specific developmental cycle of the domestic group, which comes to a close through its successive fragmentation due to the marriage of sons and daughters. Secondly, in this kind of family, characterized by bilateral kinship, the sororal relationship (among siblings) is totally overshadowed by the conjugal relationship, strengthened even more as the father's role is identified with that of the progenitor (biological father). Furthermore, there are many sexual patterns associated with this type of family, especially the scope of the controls exerted traditionally over feminine sexuality, related to the need to identify physical paternity. Finally, since adults belong to two different families – one of origin and one of procreation – the system of affinity-kinship may be thought of as relationships between families. For this same reason, the term 'family' may signify, metonymically, the total affinity and kinship network.

Due to the nature of the family model, which is simultaneously the minimum unit and subject to progressive fragmentation, old couples or widowers whose offspring have already married, orphan children or young migrants, are in fact fragments of families, usually incapable of constituting autonomous residential units, especially when their income is limited. They then join families of kin or friends, where they can contribute as producers and gain benefits from the collective efforts. Alternatively, they can form heterogeneous domestic groups that do not follow the family pattern. In either one of these cases, the existence of such exceptions, even if frequent, does not affect in any way the predominance of the family model, which continues to be the ideal and the basic reference in the norms of behaviour, a pattern to which people return whenever possible.

The same holds true for many of the so-called matrifocal families, so common in low-income sectors of society. This type of family – without a stable male provider – is more a demonstration of the impossibility of organizing subsistence in acceptable minimal terms than an alternative model of the family (Durham, 1980).

All of this refers to the model's structure. Something similar occurs with respect to the sexual division of labour, through which the relationships between husband and wife take place. The traditional model of the sexual division of labour determines that wage

57

labour is the function of the husband who, as the head of the family, provides for its maintenance. The wife is assigned responsibility for domestic work and the children. We know that, despite this fact, women increasingly feel forced or motivated to look for profitable activities inside or outside their homes. However, since this contribution is defined as 'helping' that of the husband, and is therefore subordinate and merely complementary in its partial maintenance of the house, the total validity of the traditional model is preserved, thus keeping its complete strength in defining the woman's position in society.

Once again, exceptions to the model, although frequent, do not necessarily imply a denial of it, nor an emergence of alternative models. Nevertheless, it is obvious that no model can preserve its legitimacy if it is totally ineffective. That is precisely why we are not stating that challenges to the model do not exist, nor that alternative patterns for the sexual division of labour are not being proposed. Rather it is necessary to locate them correctly.

The transformation of the family model

Classical analyses of the family in Latin American society have pointed out the transformations that result from the loss of its old function as productive unit (Durham, 1980). However, with the emergence of the feminist movement, new problems have been given priority, especially those dealing with the transformation of the sexual division of labour associated with male domination (Franchetto *et al.*, 1981).

The emergence of an explicit questioning of the asymmetry of the sexual division of labour, perceived clearly as a form of male domination, is a phenomenon specific to Latin American society. It did not occur by chance but is related to the development of capitalism, as shown by those who have studied this problem.

Industrialization not only socially separated production from reproduction, but it also polarized these two spheres of social life into two very different and physically separate spaces, thus creating a special form of feminine isolation in domestic life. The literature on women emphasizes the fact that capitalism affects the division between the public and the private, excluding the woman from the public sphere and locking her up in the domestic domain, so promoting her subordination. But this process presents only one side of the coin. What actually took place was the inclusion of women in both spheres, the public and the private, but in a contradictory manner. As a result, women began to experience a fundamental ambiguity (or contradiction): the perception of equality as individuals in the sphere of the market and of inequality in the domestic sphere of reproduction.

It is necessary to remember in this respect that the distinction between the public and the private/domestic, assigned to men and women respectively, constitutes a cultural category that is very common in primitive societies, and that, within Latin American culture, antedates capitalism.[1] In non-capitalist societies, male—female opposition cuts across all the spheres of social life uniformly, and the distinction between the public and the domestic is not given by a radical separation (physical and social) between the production of material goods (or social labour) on the one hand, and human reproduction on the other. The domestic group is not the only important unit of production; there are also diverse forms of collective labour that, together with the differential participation of men and women, produce a complementarity between the feminine and masculine roles, informing public life as much as private life. There are also societies, as in some Mediterranean civilizations, especially those more influenced by Islam, where the seclusion of women within the home (at least among some social sectors) is virtually absolute. In this case, their position is clearly subordinate but not contradictory.

✓ In Latin American society, although the feminine character of the domestic space remains, the tendency towards the elimination of the sexual division of labour in the productive sphere dominated by capital shapes the entirety of public life. Within it, in an increasingly visible manner, men and women confront each other as apparently free and equal individuals.

Given the dissociation between the public and the domestic, equality at work creates the phenomenon of the double workday, and therefore produces a new inequality (or increases the previous inequality); this in turn promotes a challenge of the sexual division of labour maintained within the domestic sphere. Furthermore, the tendency towards a reformulation of the sexual division of labour in the domstic sphere, in so far as it is influenced by the model of equalitarian individualism generated in the public sphere, can appear as a threat to the family itself, and with it, to the only structured and permanent primary group that seems able to halt the dissolution of interpersonal relations in the anonymous individualism of mass society. Indeed, the family, as the last terrain to be reached by the individualizing tendency inherent in the development of Latin American society, was established as the basic group of cohabitation and solidarity; also, firmly structured within the sphere of private life, the family is conceived as a refuge against the anonymity of the market, the authoritarian character of the State, and – contradictorily – as a space of freedom (Durham, 1980).

The family, like any other institution, changes historically in often unpredictable ways. However, these alterations do not occur as a function of rational planning, but are conditioned by conceptions and values rooted in the historic tradition. In the case of the family, the legitimacy of the model is fundamentally subject to very profound childhood experiences that mobilize intense affections. The entire notion of the family in Latin American society is tied to the conjugal bond and to a certain conception of paternity, thus making it extremely difficult to conceive the possibility of their substitution by other notions, such as the bond between brother and sister. A solution such as this one would hardly solve the basic problem, namely that of the manifestation of individualism within the family group.

On the other hand, it must be recognized that the new technology of birth control dramatically modifies the parameters within which the problem was posed traditionally. The possibility of entirely separating reproduction from sexuality opens, for large segments of the population, the possibility of permanently avoiding maternity without an effect on sexual life. At the same time, there has been an increase in the market supply of products and services that previously could only be obtained within the domestic sphere, anchored in the sexual division of labour. Thus, it becomes viable for a growing number of men and women, through the use of contraceptive methods or the choice of homosexuality, to place themselves outside the arena of reproductive issues, feeling free to develop diverse forms of non-familial privacy and domesticity.

Meanwhile, although visualized as an option, reproduction implies a constant revision of the problem of the family. The persistence of the social recognition and valuation of paternity, be it explicit or implicit, implies also the persistence of the positive evaluation of the conjugal model, which implies the maintenance of the public–private dichotomy. From this perspective, the challenge lies in the trend towards the dissolution of the sexual monopoly of the husband over female sexuality, a tendency that is closely related to the development of contraceptive methods. It also involves the search for models of the sexual division of labour within the domestic sphere that would be simultaneously more egalitarian and would allow the entry of women into the labour market. In this attempt, the State is often sought to assume partial responsibility over children, through the provision of day-care facilities and other institutions that would curtail neither the rights nor the responsibilities of parents for their children. However, the basic conflict between the free expression of individuality in professional as well as emotional terms, which tends to weaken the conjugal relationship, and the shared responsibility over the children, which requires the strengthening of the conjugal bond, persists.

The fundamental problem with this proposal is that it simultaneously makes demands on and weakens the conjugal relationship. Individual competition of each spouse in the labour market generates for each of them a tension between the time dedicated to domestic work and the time dedicated to wage labour and leisure. This tension can be seen reflected in an internal struggle, each spouse trying to make the other assume a larger domestic load. Given the lack of new stable models, the establishment of patterns of division of labour within the family depend on interpersonal confrontation between spouses, creating a large realm of potential conflict. On the other hand, as mutual emotional support and reciprocal sexual pleasure are valued and expected, the conjugal relationship is increasingly stressed by the multiple demands laid upon it.

The impossibility of satisfying all the conditions posed as necessary to the maintenance of the egalitarian conjugal relationship finds its resolution in the increasing social acceptance of divorce, which carries with it the fragmentation of the original family and the construction of a new one through the possibility of remarriage. If both ex-spouses retain rights and responsibilities over the children as the only egalitarian solution, future marriages face new forms of tension: relations between the previous partners, and between new partners and children from previous marriages of one or both spouses, relations among children of different marriages, and so on. All these relations, potentially very conflictive, must be established without the help of defined cultural models, excepting the illegitimacy of any type of coercion, all of which demand very painful processes of individual accommodation.

In fact, society did not elaborate new consensual solutions for these problems. A space was opened for experimentation of new ways to attempt an equilibrium between public and private life, between participation in the marketplace and domestic reproduction of use values, between individual liberty and responsibility towards children, between equality and the differentiation of roles. It could be said, however, that the same intensity of the conflicts generated around and inside the family constitute, in a certain way, a confirmation of its importance and vitality.

In relation to the permanence and vitality of the family, much has been said about its reduction in Latin American society. There is, in fact, a clear tendency towards a declining number of children; and in this sense the family is becoming a smaller unit. At the same time, especially in Brazil, there has also been the emergence of a certain mythology around the disappearance of the supposedly patriarchal extended family and its replacement with a nuclear or conjugal family. In fact, the conjugal model is very ancient and is widely diffused, in Latin American society as well as in Europe, except in the peasantry; that is to say, the children tend to leave the paternal home once they marry and establish independent domestic groups. Instead of extended families, in the past strong ties of kinship between different conjugal groups were to be found, especially between families of origin and families of procreation. Without doubt, there has been a weakening of those kinship ties and the resultant isolation of the conjugal group. This phenomenon worsens the tensions within the conjugal nucleus, but cannot be interpreted directly as an indicator of the weakening of the family.

In conclusion, it seems correct to state that, despite all the criticism and questioning, despite the creation of new forms of private, institutionalized, non-familial life as legitimate options, reproduction always brings us back to the conjugal nucleus, in a new version of the old family model. This persistence of the conjugal model is supported by very powerful ideological forces. First of all, there is the valorization of sexuality itself: if on the one hand it appears as an expression of possessive individualism, it also shows up as a privileged instrument for the establishment of intimate and affectionate interpersonal relations. In this sense the conjugal link (despite its temporality) constitutes the recurrent basis for the construction of the private sphere of social life. Furthermore, one has to recognize the weight of scientism in the legitimation of social relations: the recognition by biology of the male role in reproduction, especially the equivalent contributions of mother and father to the genetic constitution of the children, ends to validate and confirm the social recognition of paternity. Finally, this recognition, scientifically validated, is postulated by the egalitarian ideals which demand the participation of men as well as women in the social process of human reproduction, a participation that is both legitimized and concretized by the conjugal tie.

Notes

1. This does not mean to negate the existence of a distinctive form of intimate domesticity, specific to the bourgeois family, as seen by Habermas (1981).

Section II

PRODUCTION AND REPRODUCTION

INTRODUCTION

Elizabeth Jelin

Traditionally, economic and social analyses have concentrated their attention on the social organization of production: factories, public bureaus, peasant units; the supply and demand of workers; the varieties of wage-work and the dynamics of the informal sector; technological transformations and labour productivity. The organization of production, however, cannot function without its complement, the organization of reproduction. The latter has two basic functions: permanently to renew the labour force required for production, that is, to maintain and reproduce the workers for the productive system; and to destroy the goods produced through consumption, thus allowing the renewal of the productive cycle. Both functions are simultaneous and coexist in the domestic realm. At a macro-social level, they imply movements of products and of producers, commerce and migration. At a micro-social level, they refer to the organization of everyday life. Family and household organization is not a world isolated from the productive system. On the contrary, it has an intimate relationship with it, in so far as it is in charge of the tasks of consumption and reproduction. In turn, it adjusts, influences and limits the action of the productive system.

The emphasis in this section is on the relationship between the organization of production and the family. This relationship can be analysed at various levels; at the material level of concrete social practices linked to survival and reproduction; at the level of the organization and symbolic meanings of these practices for the actors themselves; at the level of the forms of articulation of diverse social organizations.

Verena Stolcke's chapter on coffee in Sao Paulo analyses the historical process of transformation of the relationship between the family and the productive organization. At one time in the evolution of the coffee plantation, producers opted for a certain type of labour force and family, the resident *colono* family, thus creating a whole new economic-cultural complex: a type of immigrant family, with a given organization of both labour and intra-domestic division of labour, linked to the productive organization of coffee expansion. Subsequent evolution, especially during recent decades, has brought about a fundamental change in the organization of labour and of domesticity: the resident worker's family is replaced by a temporary and unstable labour force; workers move to urban areas and organize their everyday life in a form analogous to that of the urban working-class family. In all this process, the patterns of family morality and gender division of labour play a key role as mediating mechanisms in the relationship between productive and reproductive organization.

At the macro-social level, aggregate data on migration and labour force supply could, and should, be analysed in terms of the conditions and limits that families put on individual behaviour. This statement turns out to be more important for women than for men, since the position of women in the family and their domestic responsibilities seems to be much more crucial in determining their participation in the labour market and in migratory flows than those of men. Orlandina de Oliveira's study, based on Mexican data, shows explicitly how these family mediations operate in concrete social contexts. Epistemologically and methodologically, it should be borne in mind that individual behaviour is mediated by family and social class, in the sense that these constitute the field and structure the options open to particular individuals (Przeworski, 1982).

3

THE EXPLOITATION OF FAMILY MORALITY: LABOUR SYSTEMS AND FAMILY STRUCTURE ON SAO PAULO COFFEE PLANTATIONS, 1850–1979

Verena Stolcke

> Coffee growing demands not the contribution of casual labour but, indeed, that of 'well constituted' families, of at least three hoes.
>
> *Boletin do Departamento do Trabalho Agricola* (Sao Paulo), ano II, 72, 1932: II.

It is now generally recognized that neither the nuclear family nor gender hierarchy was created by the industrial revolution or capitalism for the sake of capital accumulation. Despite the warnings and fears of the political right and some scholars like Lasch (1979), it does not seem either that we are to witness the family's early demise. Instead, the relevant question continues to be: what is it in advanced industrial society that accounts for the extraordinary resilience of the family and gender hierarchy? Though their forms may change, they remain basic social facts. How do we explain the paradoxical coexistence in class society of an ethos of individualism, self-reliance and personal achievement along with the persistent mediation of the individual's place in society by family ties? As Barret and McIntosh have argued, there has been an 'under-emphasis of the extent of the cultural hegemony of familial ideology ... 'the family' ... is not only an economic unit, nor merely a kinship structure; it is also an ideological configuration with resonance far beyond these narrow definitions.' (Barret and McIntosh, 1982: 129–30)

69

Accumulating evidence on the persistence of gender hierarchy, despite rapid and often profound economic change, requires a rethinking of the structural link between the economy and the family. We need to examine the 'ideological configurations' referred to by Barret and McIntosh and to discover the way in which ideology and culture act upon, and interact with, processes of socio-economic change. The ideological constitution of personhood in class society (as free agent but at the same time the bearer of immutable essences) decisively shapes bourgeois family values and practice (Stolcke, 1981). However, no single model will suffice to explain the family in class society. Although bourgeois ideology typically seeks to universalize its own institutions and values, an explanation of working-class family structure and meaning must be sought in the particular relation between the working class and the bourgeoisie. There are at least two sides to the question of the persistence of the working-class family: namely, bourgeois class interests, both economic and ideological, in maintaining the nuclear family; and, equally significant, the forces and motives that account for working-class adherence to the family.

Extensive research into the evolution of the working-class family and gender hierarchy in capitalist society has shown the contribution made to the cheap reproduction of labour power by the family and women's domestication (Coulson, Magas and Wainwright, 1975; Seccombe, 1975; Gardiner, 1975; Himmelweit and Mohun, 1977; Hartmann, 1976). Still, research has shown little awareness of the contradictions generated within the working-class family, and for women in particular, by capitalist development. Nor has it paid attention to the cultural forces and ideological processes that might mediate the impact of economic change on the family and modify the intra-household conflicts generated by that change.

A recent exchange over the political meaning of the working-class family's persistence under capitalism has made explicit the contradiction embodied in an institution that both constitutes a source of subordination for women and is able to offer support and solidarity to family members in the face of economic hardship (Humphries, 1977; Hartmann and Markusen, 1980; Sen, 1980). This new perspective challenges the idea that the family is a collectivity of reciprocal interests, a pooling of efforts for the benefit of all members (Harris, 1981; Whitehead, 1981), and suggests that it is as important to detect the effect that economic change has on power relations within the household as it is to trace historical linkages between economic process and family structure.

Assessing the effect of socio-economic change on the condition of women is a central concern of the historical analysis of the family and gender hierarchy. However, research on the subordination of women during the expansion of capitalism in Latin America has displayed an underlying tension (Young, 1982; Deere and Leon, 1982; Roldan, 1982). At the core of this tension is a persistent uncertainty about the degree to which capitalist development, understood as the mercantilization of social relations, will undermine traditional links of personal dependence and subordination based on gender and enable women to enjoy the formal freedom that men are supposed to enjoy.

This chapter seeks both to trace the transformation of the social relations of production on Sao Paulo coffee plantations from the introduction of free labour in the 1850s to the present and to detect specific links and interactions among family ideology, gender hierarchy, the sexual division of labour, and the labour systems chosen by the planters. Central to this analysis is the idea that socio-economic change does not occur in an ideological vacuum. On the contrary, the objective processes of material change are shaped decisively by the pre-existing family ideology and gender hierarchy, from which the new conditions derive their meaning. Whereas much research into the subordination of women aims to measure women's relative access to once exclusively male privileges, the effect of capitalist development on the condition of women can only be understood if we realize that subordination is a social and political status, historically determined by the circumstances of men in relation to women in society. Rather than being just another attempt to rescue women from their historical invisibility, this chapter seeks to trace an anthropological history of which women are an active part.

Educating labour for intensive work

The introduction of free labour into agriculture in Sao Paulo is exceptional in that it was based from the beginning on the preference of the planters for contracting labour in family units. Immigrant labourers were recruited by agents in Europe under a sharecropping contract. According to this contract, the planter financed the immigrants' transportation from their country of origin to the

71

port of Santos, advanced the cost of transport from Santos to the plantation, and provided food and tools until the labourers could obtain them with their own labour. He assigned them enough coffee trees to tend and harvest and granted a piece of land to produce food crops. The labourers were obliged to refund these expenses with at least half of their yearly returns from coffee cultivation. There was no time limit in the contract, but the amount of the debt incurred for transportation and other advances was clearly stated. Until that debt had been redeemed the immigrants could not move off the plantation. (See Stolcke and Hall, 1983 for successive changes in the contracts.) Upon their arrival on the plantation the immigrant families were settled in often very poor individual houses, built, however, especially for them, separate from the slave quarters.

Why did Sao Paulo planters opt for the share-cropping system rather than recruiting individual wage labour? Why did they prefer whole families, and what effect did this labour system have on the immigrants' families? These are related questions.

Share-cropping in a situation of scarce labour is more efficient than wage-labour; it is similar to a carefully negotiated piece-work system. Both are forms of the incentive wage system, ways of securing extra effort from labour, of making labourers work harder and better for only a small increase in total remuneration over that of wage-labour. Also, share-croppers are typically recruited in family units, for one or more agricultural cycles. Sao Paulo planters usually explained their preference for family labour by arguing that immigrants accompanied by their families were less prone to abandon the plantations. This is at most a partial truth, for it hides the ideological notion of the family as an inherently solidary unit, a notion cherished by the planters themselves who considered it inconceivable that a person would run away and abandon his family.

This notion of the family had material consequences for the planters because, in fact, the immigrants' families constituted a cheap labour reserve. A share-cropper would usually accept a division of the product that would not fully cover the potential market price of family labour, for if he did not, family labour would remain under- or unemployed; planters at times even prohibited immigrants and their families from working outside the plantation (Davatz, 1941). The planter obtained this additional labour at a cost below that which he would have had to pay had he contracted it as wage-labour. Coffee is a labour-intensive crop, requiring varying amounts of labour throughout the agricultural year; harvest requires a fifth more labour than cultivation (Ramos, 1923: 358). The labourers' wives and children made up this increased demand during the harvest.

The food plot assigned to the immigrant families was a way of further reducing unit labour costs. Crops were produced, primarily by women and children, when labour demands for coffee were low. The share-cropping family was expected to produce its own subsistence, without, however, neglecting the coffee groves, which were the planters' main concern. Food crops were intercropped with coffee, planted in low-lying areas not suitable for coffee, or grown on virgin land that would later be planted to coffee.

The ideology of solidarity and co-operation within the family, as distinct from non-kin, was an important element favouring the planters' aim to exploit the whole immigrant family to the fullest. As one observer lucidly commented in 1877:

> The colonization that has really been useful for us has been that of Germans and Portuguese; the German *colono* [immigrant labourer] is always hardworking and honest, and when he has a numerous family he offers an incalculable advantage. The head of the family attempts to demonstrate in practice the English proverb – that time is money – and with his family they turn time into their property in such a way that even when they are working in the coffee grove for the planter, they make use of the weeds that grow there to feed their pig and chicken, and when they return home, the children start to work; all of them go to school and when they rest they remove the maize kernels from the cob, build fences, cultivate the food plot, raise chickens and pigs and calves which are the source of subsistence. The wife and the daughters prepare the famous maize bread which is the basis of their food. (Jaguaribe Filho, Domingos, 1877: 19; my translation)

This ideology was shared by the workers themselves. One example is their reaction to the clause in the contract requiring all members of a family to be collectively responsible for the family's debt. This clause was especially resented because communities of Swiss origin often forced families to take along non-kin – 'people with whom they had nothing to do' – in order to rid the communities of a burden on their finances (Karrer, 1886: 69; Natsch, 1966: 176; Heusser, 1857: 14).

Still, in the 1850s and 1860s, the majority of planters were dissatisfied with the immigrants' assiduity in work. The initial debt, by reducing the labourers' expected share in profits, discouraged effort in coffee cultivation. The immigrants systematically diverted labour to food production, where the product belonged to them directly. Productivity in coffee was low, and the planters lacked the means to impose the necessary labour discipline. Only after the 1880s, when the government assumed the full subsidization of the mass immigration that brought a million Italian immigrants into Sao Paulo agriculture over a twenty-year period, did labour productivity in coffee reach a satisfactory level. Subsidized immigration eliminated the initial debt, encouraged significant contract changes, and created the conditions for the constitution of a labour market. Initially one labourer tended no more than seven hundred trees throughout the year. In the 1880s the average number was between two thousand and two thousand five hundred trees.

The share-cropping system, the labour-leasing contract that succeeded it, and the *colonato* – a mixed task- and piece-rate arrangement that was to predominate in coffee cultivation in Sao Paulo until the 1950s – all presupposed the recruitment of labour in family units. Although the planters' choice was in part inspired by a specific family ideology, the labour system had an equal effect on the labourers' family structure, morality, intra-household relations and reproductive behaviour, and on the sexual division of labour.

The family presupposed in the contracts was the nuclear family as a separate residential unit. The contract defined explicitly the functions of this nuclear household: joint labour in coffee cultivation and the growing of the food strictly necessary for the family's consumption.

Retrospectively, it is difficult to assess the quality of intra-household relations. The *colonato* as a wage-incentive system put a premium on work commitment by, and co-operation among, family members and reinforced their interdependence. It strengthened the commonality of interests of the household. The allocation of family labour was decided by the husband or father, as household head, and following a division of labour by sex and age (see Table 1).

The contract was always signed by the head of the family, who also received the family earnings. Children of either sex were expected to contribute their share in looking after small animals and participating in the harvest. The wife was primarily responsible for domestic tasks and the cultivation of the food plot, with the aid

Table 1 Allocation of family labour under the *colonato* contract during the annual agricultural cycle

Crops/tasks	Family members	Period
Coffee: weeding	Men	Sept to April/May
Coffee: harvest	Men, women, children	May to August
Food crops: cultivation and harvest	Women and children*	Oct/Jan to April/May
Occasional wage	Men	Occasional days throughout the year
Childbearing, child-rearing and domestic tasks	Women	Throughout the year

* When corn or beans were intercropped with coffee, men weeded the crops simultaneously.

of the adult men when they had time left from their main task of tending coffee trees, which required several weedings. Men, women and children worked together in the harvest. Significantly, the number of coffee trees assigned to women was usually about half that assigned to men.

The husband's or father's pre-eminence and authority over family members derived in part from his relative autonomy to organize the labour process and allocate the family's labour. More difficult to assess are the material benefits he may have derived from this pre-eminence. There is no information on allocation of income and resources within the household or on decision-making beyond the organization of work. As regards work effort, though the tasks differed by sex, all household members worked from dawn to dusk in response to the incentives. The income the family received was family income and expressed not individual effort but that of all household members. At times food surpluses were sold, and men would work at odd jobs on the plantations for a day wage. There is no indication that these additional earnings were individually attributed.

At the level of meaning, however, there is a significant difference between tasks carried out predominantly by men and those carried out by women. Both the weeding of coffee and the cultivation of food crops were regarded as *servico da gente* (this is, 'our own job')

75

in contrast to day wage-labour, which was regarded explicitly as work for the plantation. The coffee harvest paid piece-rate was part of 'our own job', but the product was for 'the boss'.

In the category of 'our own job', a further distinction was made between coffee weeding and food growing. Coffee weeding was paid at a task-rate per thousand coffee trees per year, that is, a kind of incentive wage. The number of coffee trees tended by a family depended as much on its work capacity, as determined by household composition, as on its labour intensity. The allocation of family labour was left to the husband or father, but labour intensity depended largely on family members' own will to work. Coffee weeding, carried out mainly by men, was, in fact, regarded as *trabalhar por conta* (to work of one's own accord); one stopped when one wanted, and there were no set times. A significant characteristic of this task was the degree of autonomy it allowed the worker. The workers perceived the fact that this relative autonomy was the precondition for high labour intensity, but appreciated it as an opportunity to increase their income. Food growing, predominantly carried out by women, was seen by contrast as *trabalhar para a gente* or *plantar para a gente* (to work or grow food for ourselves).

Analysts have frequently regarded the food plot given the workers under combined cash-crop and self-provisioning systems as a form of payment in kind (Palacios, 1980; Kageyama *et al.*, 1982; but see also Sallum, 1982). This is a double mystification. It obscures the labour input required to produce foodstuffs and the fact that self-provisioning reduced not only the money wage; the labour invested by workers in growing their own food also diminished the cost of reproduction of labour in absolute terms. The workers themselves, in this case predominantly women, invested part of their labour power in producing food for the family, a practice that allowed the planters to pay work in coffee at a lower price. Self-provisioning was thus an additional source of exploitation, specifically of women. But the definition of good growing as 'work for ourselves' indicates that this mystification was shared by the workers themselves, both men and women. Only one woman among my informants pointed out that when she was weeding corn she was not earning anything.

Planters not only preferred families to single workers; they favoured large families. The greater the proportion of workers to consumers in a family, the greater its productive capacity. Under the share-cropping system, the labourers' income depended directly on the intensity of their work in coffee. Under the *colonato* system, however, coffee cultivation was paid at a fixed task-rate per thousand trees per year. Income thus depended not only on the number of trees taken by the family but also on the task-rate set by the planters, calculated on the basis of a family of at least three adult workers. Thus, under the *colonato*, small families were even worse off than under the preceding system (Maistrello, 1923). As one experienced planter rejoiced in 1877:

These families are truly patriarchal both because of their size and their morality, solidarity and love of work. . . . The families from the Tyrol are still the most advantageous ones for the planter because of their size. This advantage is considerable. (Visconde de Indaiatuba [ca. 1878], 1952: 245; my translation)

The planters' interest in the size and composition of immigrant families influenced demographic behaviour by placing a premium on high fertility. This emphasis in turn, affected the sexual division of labour. Having a large number of children, although it might initially have meant a considerable burden on the mother and father, implied that after the first years the family's productive capacity would increase year after year. By contrast, a family with few children was disadvantaged throughout the family life cycle (Heusser, 1857; Ozorio de Almeida, 1977). A mother with a large number of children would be fully occupied with childbearing and rearing during a considerable period of her life and would have less time left for extra-domestic activities. Domestic tasks were, however, recognized as essential and duly valued. As a French observer noted in 1879:

The conclusion to be drawn is that . . . the more numerous a family, the greater the help it can offer its head to redeem the initial debts. . . . The help and arms of his children constitute a natural aid, the more precious the more numerous they are, and the woman, while she minds her own business, is also productive in the home, without her presence being indispensable in the fields, a thing that will become necessary if the family is composed of few members. (Turenne, 1879: 451; my translation)

By allowing only those families with good productive capacity to redeem their debts and accumulate, the *colonato* had consequences for the wider social structure as well. The degree of exploitation to which the immigrants were subjected and the opportunities for upward mobility offered by the *colonato* are much-debated issues (Holloway, 1980; Dean, 1976; Stolcke and Hall, 1983; Sallum, 1982). With the beginning of mass immigration in the 1880s, living and working conditions became particularly harsh. Restriction of output in coffee at an individual family level had been one form of resistance to the share-cropping arrangement. With increasing control over the labour process, strike action became more frequent. The largest strike occurred in 1913 and mobilized ten to fifteen thousand workers.

Politically, the family labour system was also relevant. The labourers

> did not adopt the system of head or leaders because this would have meant reducing to misery and persecution some of the most valuable members of this union. They acted in groups of four to five families in accordance with friendship within these groups, having not one leader for this group but rather one family in charge of transmitting the thoughts of the secret collective leadership which was the one that solved all problems. ('Um Socialista' in Pinheiro and Hall, 1979: 117; my translation)

Even so, there was a measure of upward mobility and social differentiation between the workers. Combined with other factors, such as movement to the newer coffee areas where planting rights were more favourable or marriage into a better-off family, family size and compositon were decisive in enabling immigrants to move out of the plantations and establish themselves on their own (for a similar process see Deere and de Janvry, 1981).

As the division of labour on the plantations increased, planters chose labour more consciously according to the labourers' family status and the specific requirements of the job. Single men were usually employed as *avulsos*, labourers recruited exclusively for the harvest or for special tasks, or as *camaradas*, workers in coffee processing and transport. *Camaradas* – a category that also often included young families – were resident wage labourers paid on a monthly basis. Large families were employed as *colonos* (Carvalho de Moraes, 1870: 66; Bollettino UCICA, 1903: 73; Domingos Jaguaribe Filho, 1877: 19, 32). Gangs of men contracted for specific tasks were called, significantly, *turmas de solteiros* (gangs of bachelors) (Ramos, 1923: 120). Having a family was an advantage for employability. In addition, *camaradas* were less secure in their jobs (Dean,

1976: 170–1). This factor must have made marriage all the more attractive. The labour system had already affected marriage, in that the initial indebtedness and the planters' efforts to recoup their investment curtailed marriage choices. Women usually followed their husbands in marriage, and parents, fathers in particular, tended to intervene in their daughters' marriage preferences. A child left the family upon marriage to set up a separate household. In order not to forgo their investment, planters would prohibit marriage with a girl from another plantation unless the employer of the bridegroom was willing to pay off her debt (Heusser, 1857: 48; see also Jaguaribe Filho, 1877: 32).

The extraordinary coffee boom at the turn of the century is proof that subsidized mass immigration and the *colonato* system, resting in part on the capitalist exploitation of the family, was most successful in solving the labour problem that had been posed by the abolition of slavery. A Prussian agronomist observed at the time that the *colonato* was 'the most perfect possible labour system', the product of Sao Paulo planters' 'untiring efforts and intelligence' (Kaerger, 1892: 333, 335).

Subsidized immigration continued until 1927, but planters recruited more and more national labour, generally from among those driven out of the Northeast by economic misery. At first national labour was contracted temporarily for specific tasks, but eventually whole families were employed as *colonos*. The change required some revision of the planters' traditional prejudiced view of the *caboclos* (indigenous workers) as idle, undisciplined, and immoral. As one contemporary observed:

> I still have to say what I have heard about the morality of the national laborer. It is good, very good. Well constituted families, mutual respect among the spouses, deference on the part of the children toward their parents. . . . Isn't it remarkable that in the wild *sertoes* [backlands] and distant lands, where civilization arrives only rarely, an institution such as monogamous marriage should have been preserved. . . . Isn't it extraordinary that an institution which is justly regarded as the flower of Christian civilization should have persisted in the nature of such a race despite the wildness of the environment in which they live? (Papaterra Limongi, 1916: 365–6; my translation)

The transition from family labour to individual wage labour

The inordinate expansion of coffee growing generated the first over-production crisis at the beginning of the century. By the late 1920s, government intervention and the recovery of the international market after the First World War produced a new coffee boom. The economic crisis of 1919 found coffee planters with the largest coffee harvest ever. Cattle, sugar cane, and cotton for the expanding textile industry were only gradually substituted for coffee, and large numbers of *colono* families were left out of work. An indication of the comparative profitability of the *colonato* system over straight wage-labour is the fact that the remaining coffee continued to be cultivated under this labour system. Only in the late 1950s did the planters increasingly recruit casual labour for work in coffee.

Coffee enjoyed a new, though brief, recovery in the 1950s when it expanded into the neighbouring state of Parana and returned to the older coffee regions in Sao Paulo. New, more productive varieties of coffee were introduced, and contour farming was used to prevent soil erosion. To increase the productivity of the soil, coffee trees were planted closer together and organic fertilizer was applied to exhausted soil. Intercropping of foodstuffs became less frequent as coffee trees were planted closer together; intercropping was also frowned upon because it reduced yields on poorer soils, especially undesirable at a time of rising coffee prices. At the same time, planters were increasingly reluctant to grant separate food plots – because they wanted to put those lands to other use and also because they hoped to increase the productivity of labour in coffee cultivation. Mechanization of coffee weeding, however, continued to be regarded as incompatible with the *colonato* system (*Agricultura em Sao Paulo*).

Even the limited innovations listed above altered the traditional annual labour demand cycle, accentuating demand peaks during the coffee harvest. By this time, planters recruited *colonos* mainly to meet the labour demand for coffee weeding, using additional casual labour for the harvest. The *colonos* themselves, deprived of planting rights and without compensation in wages, abandoned the plantations for better opportunities either in other regions or in industry.

A new decline in coffee prices in the late 1950s resulted in the eradication of almost half the existing coffee trees in the 1960s and the unemployment of many *colono* families. Finally, President Joao Goulart's enactment of the *Estatuto do Trabalhador Rural* (rural labour statute) in 1963 resulted in the dismissal of the remaining *colonos*. This new labour law repeated in part the ineffectual 1943 labour legislation; in addition, however, it granted to the *colonos* indemnity in case of dismissal and security of tenure after ten years' work on a plantation. This statute was a mere palliative to deal with growing social conflict in agriculture. Nevertheless, the planters saw these rights as a serious challenge to their freedom of contract and as a first step towards the loss of their land at a time when the debate over land reform was becoming increasingly heated. The most effective way to defeat the law was to dismiss the remaining *colonos* with or without indemnity and thereafter to work their plantations with *pessoal de fora* (outsiders), that is, casual labour recruited by *turmeiros* (labour contractors).

Other categories of resident labourers were similarly affected by the statute. The new system made labour supply more flexible and freed planters from any of the obligations stipulated in the labour statute. By 1970, of a total agricultural labour force of eighteen million in Brazil as a whole, over six million were casual labourers. In Sao Paulo in 1971, about 25 per cent of the agricultural labour force worked as casual wage-labourers, the so-called *volantes* (flying workers) or *boias-frias* (cold food). Note, however, that about 50 per cent of the agricultural labour force consisted of smallholders and their unpaid family labour. The labourers formerly resident on the plantations moved to the periphery of small towns in the interior of the state. In many of these towns homogeneous neighbourhoods of little self-built houses or huts sprang up during the 1970s. Workers who received an indemnity under the new law managed to acquire plots to build houses, but the majority had to pay rent.

These workers no longer have land or the time to produce their own subsistence. The *volantes* recall the *colonato* as the 'time of abundance'. With the exodus from the plantations the 'time of money' set in. Now it is only through the market that they can have access to use value, and they are entirely dependent on market forces. Because they are contracted individually on a temporary basis, economic uncertainty has increased. The end of the *colonato* produced the *turmeiro*, who recruits, transports and oversees the labourers and serves as mediator between them and the estate. Labourers are usually recruited on a weekly basis, though they may work in the same gang and on the same estate for longer periods of time. Women, and children from the age of about twelve, as well as men, have become casual labourers working in gangs. Roughly

25 per cent of casual labourers are women, though the women's participation rate varies regionally, depending on the supply of men and on alternative work opportunities for men. The additional burden of the rent and total dependence on the market for subsistence, coupled with the post-1964 wage freeze and inflation, have produced an almost continuous decline in real wages, even in regions such as Campinas, where employment opportunities exist for most of the year. Once again it takes contributions from all able family members to make ends meet. As one woman explained:

> We have to work; [the husband's wage] is not sufficient because we have to pay rent. . . . Before when we lived with our parents [on the plantation] it was better . . . everybody planted food; before there was abundance, we raised small animals; now we have to buy everything; in my youth the plantations were full of people; now they are empty.

Proletarianization and migration to the towns have altered the quality of social relations. Looking back, it is thought that the *colonato* enhanced solidarity not only within the household but between households. By contrast, individual wage-labour has generated great uncertainty among the labourers and is thought to have strained interpersonal relations in the neighbourhood, among kin, and particularly within the family.

Although these labourers have a keen awareness of their exploitation in a world that is seen as divided between 'us' (the 'poor') and 'them' (the 'rich'), they are very sceptical about the possibility of joint action now, not only because of the adverse power relations in society at large but also because *uniao* (solidarity), the recognized prerequisite for any collective action, is felt to be lacking (Martinez-Alier and Boito, 1977). Kin and friendship ties served as important links in the process of migration to the towns, and they persist in the new environment, though often with new content. Neighbourhood relations are now tenuous, and conflict can break out for the smallest reason. As one older woman noted:

> Before it wasn't the same . . . it was everybody together . . . the families all together, not like now, one here and the other there; for me it was better before; everybody was united, neighbours also combined well; we lived all together, combined well; now it is difficult to find anybody to do anything together, there is mistrust; first, there was no mistrust; one day you

would give corn flour and eggs to me, another day you trusted me and I would give to you; now nobody does anything together anymore; I don't know why this is so; first we were more united, now nobody gets on anymore.

In situations of rapid and profound change without any noticeable improvement, it is not unusual to idealize the past. Life on the plantations was far from idyllic. The whole family worked from dawn to dusk. Relations between households were not especially harmonious. Particularly during the harvest, competition between families could be intense. Those families who managed to complete the harvest of their own coffee grove before the others could earn additional money by helping families that were behind. Those who were behind resented having to hire this help, for it meant that they lost part of the income from their grove.

On the other hand, there was also co-operation (*mutirao*) and the exchange of days of work between *colono* families. The homogenity of working and living conditions, as well as self-provisioning, permitted exchange of food without monetary expense. Now it is *cada qual por si e Deus para tudos* (each one for himself and God for everybody). Although it is felt to be important to have neighbours, mutual aid and co-operation between neighbours is practically absent. Social relations have been totally monetarized, and nobody has enough to give to another. Nowadays, as one woman exclaimed, 'Without money nobody is worth anything.' Moreover, 'In the village everybody is the same; it is impossible to help anybody with that miserable wage.' Conversely, there is reluctance to ask a favour for fear of being unable to reciprocate and thus losing face in a situation where self-esteem is at a low ebb.

Permanent economic insecurity in a profoundly unequal society in which manual labour lacks any social prestige has eroded self-esteem and has made casual labourers extremely sensitive to the slightest offense. Mutual accusations, quarrels and even outright fights are not infrequent. In such a harsh and tense social environment it might be expected that family and kin would function as the last, but essential, source of support and solidarity. But the circumstances under which the transition to wage-labour has occurred have severely strained intra-familial relations as well. The quality of these relations appears to be more distant than ever from what is regarded as the ideal. The family continues to be coterminous with the household: 'The family are the people who live together in a house.' There is a resonance of the past: 'The family is a lot of people in a house, a crowd.' People not belonging to the family or household are *gente de fora, homems de fora, os outros* (people from outside, men from outside, the others), as opposed to *alguem da casa* (somebody of the house). But whereas *colonato* household members worked together, now family members are dispersed among different workplaces: 'The family are those who help us to work, whose wages belong to us.'

Households are predominantly two-generational, containing either both parents and their unmarried children or a mother and her unmarried children. Children are expected to remain in their parents' home until they marry and to contribute their entire earnings to the family income. Upon marriage they are expected to establish their own households. It is rare to encounter grandparents beyond working age within the family household. Married adults will attempt to live in their own households as long as they are able to earn their own living, often until they die: 'As long as one is able to work, one will work.' People regard going to live with their children as a very unattractive prospect.

If the necessity arises, however, it is the sons rather than the daughters who are expected to care for aging parents. The daughters have to look after their husbands, and the husbands are generally not willing to take care of parents-in-law: 'The daughters' husbands don't like to work for others.' A distinction is made between consanguines and affines: consanguines belong to one; affines are the others.

Relations with kin outside the nuclear family are quite fluid, and the boundaries beyond which any specific kin obligations cease are difficult to define. There is a certain amount of visiting between kin, usually between consanguines, unless it is a joint visit by a married couple. Visits by or to neighbours are rare. As one woman remarked, 'I don't usually go to my neighbour's house; I don't like to go to other people's houses.' Relatives, usually up to the second degree, are expected to help in case of need, and it is resented when assistance is not forthcoming. These expectations and obligations are also extended to ritual kin, by baptism or marriage, who have been and continue to be chosen among kin or acquaintances – the latter ideally of the same class, although people certainly do not always abide by this rule.

Interaction between kin is not only determined genealogically; both geographical and social mobility have produced social distancing. Contact is maintained only among those relatives who live within reasonable distances. Travel is expensive and takes time, so that it is impossible sometimes even to visit one's own parents. The older labourers are illiterate; they do not write letters. Thus, contact is very easily lost.

In addition, social differentiation between kin is a perceived obstacle to sustained contact. Whereas it is precisely the better-off relatives who could be helpful, they are often regarded with a mixture of distrust and shame. As one woman, the only one still working in agriculture, said of her brothers, who live and work in town:

They don't pay any attention to me and I don't run after them; since my father died [eighteen yeaers ago] I haven't seen any of them; they are better off than I, they have a car; I don't care if they don't come; let them stay there; when my mother and father were alive I would go there every week; when one has a father and a mother one has the obligation.' Moreover, one would not know how to behave in the home of the better off and would feel awkward. Another woman confessed: 'I'm ashamed to go to visit my daughter for lunch in Campinas; I'm ashamed to eat, to open my mouth, to cut the meat with a fork ... my daughter is a *grafina* [a fine lady]; her husband works in a bank; they have a car; they don't come to visit; the husband doesn't allow her to.'

In other words, social advancement tends to erode solidarity with parents, especially in the case of married daughters. Sons, as men possessing a status that can be shared with others, are more likely to maintain the ties with their family of origin and might even help their siblings to advance. Women, whose status is derived from their husbands, have no status to bestow on others.

As indicated, sons rather than daughters are expected to take care of their aged parents. This is also one of the reasons some parents adduce for preferring sons to daughters, who, in addition, are said to be more difficult to raise as respectable adults. This preference does not mean, however, that relations between parents and sons are more intimate than those between parents and daughters, provided they have remained at the same social level. Practical assistance tends to flow more frequently from mothers to married daughters than from mothers to sons. In the specifically feminine sphere of childbearing, a mother will assist her own daughter during birth but not her daughter-in-law, unless the latter has no female consanguines living close by. Such assistance, however, is rarely extended to childminding if the daughters work, because usually the mothers also work for a wage.

The nuclear family household constitutes a distinct social unit within which, ideally, effort and income are shared. Even in cases where married children continue living with their parents, or old parents reside with married children, each nuclear unit tends to have a separate economy with its own stove and shopping, cooking and eating arrangements.

Another category of kin – children by adoption – bridges the boundary between the nuclear family and extra-household kin. Unlike married children, who are genealogically close but residentially separate, adopted children are usually more distant kin but now a part of the household. Although the expected family size has decreased, it is still not uncommon to raise someone else's child or children, usually the children of some female relative who has died, along with one's own. This is a moral obligation that, none the less, has material implications. In a situation of grave economic uncertainty, no one can afford to invest effort without being sure of a return. Social relations with social equals, whether neighbours or kin, are governed by the imperative of reciprocity. Favours must be *reconhecidos* (recognized) – that is, acknowledged and repaid. Indebtedness means incapacity and inferiority and is feared also because it may mean no further help. Logically, the principle of reciprocity does not operate in the same way with social superiors. Favours do produce a feeling of obligation, but at least material repayment can always be relegated to a mystical agent: *Deus lhe pague* (may God pay you).

Kinship creates a moral obligation to offer help that may be cancelled out by other social factors, but once given it must be reciprocated. An adopted child is expected to pay back the investment made in its upbringing as soon as it is able to contribute to the family income. However, this right acquired by the household through teaching the child and caring for it is not uncontested. The surviving parent may reappear when the child has reached working age and, adducing parenthood, may claim it back to put it to work for him- or herself. In one such case a foster mother went so far as to go to court and was told by the judge that he would compute the cost of the labour she had invested in raising the child. The father was in no condition to pay, and the child remained with the foster mother. One way to prevent reclamation is to adopt legally, *com papel pasado* (handing over the birth certificate), a procedure that is said to *cortar a sangue* (cut the blood); but parents are not enthusiastic about this procedure. With married and adopted children, the articulation between kinship ties understood genealogically and material rights and obligations grounded in the household is often problematic.

From a formal point of view, the new socio-economic conditions have not threatened the nuclear family as the typical household structure and unit of social reproduction. In practice, however, the household has lost one of the central attributes that gave it cohesion, joint labour. The family has ceased to be a labour and consumption unit and has become a wage-earning unit. This transformation in the material content of intra-familial relations appears to have menaced its very persistence as a viable unit.

Under conditions of declining real wages and increased economic uncertainty, everyday survival depends more than ever on the pooling of effort by all members of the household and reciprocity over time. Life was hard on the plantations, but subsistence planting protected the *colonos* against market forces even if it implied a high level of exploitation. Now it is more important than ever that all household members contribute to the family income, for capital has been able to depress wage levels below the cost of reproduction even of an individual female labourer. The *colonato* labour system enhanced family solidarity. The transition to individual wage-labour at current wage levels makes co-operation imperative; on the other hand, it puts considerable strain on household cohesion by eroding the family morality that the *colonato* reinforced. Mutual dependence among family members remains, is perhaps even increased, but individualization of labour and individual aspirations often frustrate a consensus of needs. As one older labourer of Italian origin remembered:

As *colonos* the family worked all together; women and men did all the same work; where one went all the family went; the head, the father, contracted with the *fazenda*; the head received the money; it was he who arranged everything; the coffee *colono* is the same as the coffee *empreitada* [mixed task- and piece-rate system]; the harvest was done by everybody together; it wasn't like at present that only women harvest the coffee; we were paid every sixty days; each pay covered one weeding; the payment was calculated per thousand coffee trees; the number of coffee trees contracted depended on the size of the family and these had to be tended all year round; the harvest was paid by the sack of coffee the same as now; the family worked together, not like now in the gang; the gang scatters everybody now; one goes in one direction, the other in the other; we [the men] also worked *por dia* . . . women would go to weed rice, beans on the family plot; the *patrao* [boss] did not want to contract women *por dia* in order to protect the family plot; only the men would go and work for the plantation directly; and it wasn't like now either, everybody earning the same; the weaker [families] earned less; that was already set down in the contract book; . . . at the time things were bad because there was no money; you worked and worked and had nothing; the family was more united everywhere because at that time it was the family head who commanded; what he said was done . . . also there was no fighting because there was little money, we bought few things.

Now each family member is recruited individually by the *turmeiro*. Men attempt to decide changes of gang for their wives and children, to arrange jobs for them, but in practice the women make decisions for themselves and for the young children, who usually start working with their mothers. Ideally the wages of all family members should be pooled and administrated by the husband or father as family head, but sons in particular are often reluctant to hand over the whole of the wage, paying instead only for their room and board. Wives and daughters do hand over wages, but the husband does not always administer the joint income. As one woman pointed out: 'It is the family head who should control the money; in many places the head of the household is the man, in many it is the woman; if the husband is irresponsible, spends all the money on silly things, the woman has to take control.' The one who controls the money is the household head.

As provider, the husband should pay for the running expenses of the household, the *despesas*, that is food, rent, water and light bills. The wages of the wife and children should be used for occasional expenses such as clothes, a piece of furniture, doctor's bills, and so on. Husband and sons are entitled to spend money on cigarettes and drinks, and the girls should get something to accumulate a trousseau. The only one who is not entitled to any expenditure on herself is the wife or mother. Women constantly fear their husbands might divert more than their legitimate share to excessive drink or to other women, thus menacing the whole family's survival – 'robbing the innocent children of their food', as they say.

It is generally accepted as an undesirable fact of life that both wives and daughters must work for a wage. Because they no longer work under the direct surveillance of the husband or father, their work is cause for new suspicions and new friction between spouses. One man voiced the concern of many: 'The gang trucks have brought many novelties, they have brought the separation between husband and wife, quarrels between husband and wife, they have brought lack of respect; women have lost the fear of their husbands, they have brought the husband's distrust.' The labouring gangs are regarded as places of dubious morality, inappropriate for respectable women. *Turmeiros* have a reputation, not unfounded, for taking advantage of their position to seduce women workers. Men's suspicion is enhanced by the belief that women who lack the protection of their men will easily succumb to other men's advances. Mistrust derives from traditional morality that gave men control over and exclusive rights to their wives' sexuality, and from fear of the possible consequences for the survival of the household of women's contact wih *homoms de fora* (men from outside).

In earlier times there was surely no perfect fit between an ideal morality and practice regarding women's sexual integrity. Planters and overseers seem to have been a considerable menace for the *colonos'* women and cases of pregnant daughters having to get married did occur. Still, living and working conditions must then have seemed less of a threat to the men's power to exert control over their women. Also, the material implications of, if not the ideological motivations for control over women's sexuality seem to have shifted. During the *colonato* the procreative capacity of women was of prime importance to men and was duly recognized. Now procreation is far less important to men than is access to a woman's domestic and extra-domestic labour. Some women suggest cynically that men no longer marry women for their beauty, but to have them working for themselves. A man can obtain a woman's labour without pay only if she is his wife, either legal or consensual, or his daughter.

The husband's jealousy is a frequent cause of fights. Time and again stories are told of women who have run away with other men – stories that often have little basis in reality. There are constant complaints that the neighbourhood is no place to raise respectable daughters, that morals are not what they were. Men's fears that women might run off with other men, or that unmarried daughters will present the family with additional mouths to feed, are far less founded than is women's mistrust; an important element in men's fear is the feeling of loss of control. Women are justified in their misgivings about male alcoholism, which is a major cause of family instability and violence, and when a man becomes involved with another woman, family income is diverted accordingly.

At this point it is important to stress that it is by no means only the purely material consequences of the transition to individual wage-labour – the generalization of commodity relations, declining real wages and instability of work – that have strained intra-household relations. There is no immediate reason why economic hardship in itself should generate conflict rather than reinforce solidarity within the family or household. Rather, the meaning of socio-economic change for those concerned is compounded of material changes, previous socio-economic circumstances, and the ideological and cultural expectations implied in them. More specifically, the effect of economic individualization for household members has been mediated by a gender ideology that accorded specific attributes to the sexes, attributes that have been challenged materially and ideologically by the transition to individual wage-labour. The *colonos* have experienced proletarianization not as autonomous individuals but as social beings enmeshed in specific social relations with specific reciprocal rights and obligations.

In order adequately to evaluate the effects and meaning of socio-economic change as it affects gender relations, one must take into account at least three different, though related, levels of experience. First there is the most objective level of immediately material change in the individual condition of women and men with regard to work. Secondly, there is a relational level. Gender is a social relation; therefore, any change in the circumstances of one of the terms of the relation will necessarily produce a transformation of the relation as such, a transformation that will in turn have an effect on each partner to the relation. And there is a third cultural level. As suggested above, among the elements giving meaning to change are previous cultural and ideological expectations and norms of conduct. It is also this cultural dimension that, in a very material way, will shape the responses to change of those concerned.

Their transformation into casual labourers has affected women and men in fundamentally different ways. Men have been reduced to simple wage-labourers. They have lost the relative autonomy to organize work. There is no longer any possibility of their deciding the allocation of their own or their families' labour power. In the process, they have also often lost the right to control the family income. This perceived loss of significant elements of men's social identity has undermined their authority, producing a profound feeling of insecurity and an erosion of self-esteem that makes men all the more distrustful of their wives and children. Job insecurity and low wages have made it increasingly difficult for men to fulfil their ideologically constituted role as breadwinners. In view of all this, the danger that their wives may leave them seems all the more real. The transition to wage-labour has not affected women in the same way. During the *colonato*, women worked both at home and in the fields, but they were excluded from wage-labour for the plantation. They worked *para a gente* (for ourselves). Their incorporation into wage-labour has meant not a reduction but an increase in women's obligations. There has been no transformation of the domestic sexual division of labour or of the traditional definition of women's work as subsidiary to that of men: 'The one who has to maintain the family is the husband; the wife works to help the husband.'

Men work to maintain their families; women work to help their husbands. Motivations for working for a wage also differ between men and women. Women work for a wage reluctantly, driven by necessity in a context of general poverty; men work because they are men. As a consequence of this interaction between material and ideological forces, men have a stronger commitment to work for a wage and are more directly affected by the conditions of the labour market – the lack or insecurity of work. They will endeavour to leave agriculture and work in the construction industry where wages are higher and working conditions somewhat better.

Other work is available for women, but alternatives outside agriculture are less attractive. They could work as maids, but this work is regarded as undesirable because of long hours and greater dependence. Women do not only work in the fields. When they come home they still have to prepare food and do other domestic chores. When men come home, they change and either watch television or go to a bar. Women not only get up earlier now and work longer hours than men; their cultural definition as women makes them more submissive and less demanding at work, so that they accept any task: 'Those who work for a day wage have to do what they are told; if they tell us to quarry stones, to dig a ditch, we go.'

This is also the reason why women nowadays usually do those jobs that are paid piece-rate, like harvesting coffee or cotton. Working for a piece-rate means working with greater speed and intensity than for a day wage. Men refuse to do such jobs. As a result, not only do women work longer hours than men, but often their labour intensity is greater.

The transformation of the whole family into wage-labourers has affected the sexual division of labour in a complex way. For those women who do not go out to work, either because they are in the initial phase of the family life cycle and cannot leave their small children or because the husband has a better income and the wife does not need to work, the division of labour by sex has been intensified. For those women who work for a wage, the effect has been to redefine tasks by gender and create a new general division of labour between the sexes, with women doing the worst jobs. Agricultural tasks formerly done by men or by the whole family, such as weeding or harvesting coffee, are now done by women, and men are attempting, not always successfully, to move into new, better paid, and exclusively male occupations – construction work, for instance. The redefinition of tasks by gender proceeds in three steps. Men move out of jobs for better ones; women succeed them in doing what are inferior and worse paid jobs; finally, what have now become female jobs are typified as feminine on account of some alleged special female ability, such as the famous nimble fingers that seem to qualify women for the privilege of picking coffee and cotton. Men justify their advantages on the labour market ideologically.

Change has generated resentment in the women, and new misgivings towards men. As the women complain: 'It is a good thing to find a man who does not allow one to work; but working, it is no use to have a husband,' or 'We marry for sport; the husband does not take care of the wife; we take care of ourselves.' Two points need to be made, however. First, women resent having to work for a wage. The necessity is perceived as a result of the situation as a whole and as a failure of their husbands. Women do not resent the continuing responsibility for domestic duties. (See Hartmann, 1981) for a case where housework sharing is a source of conjugal conflict.) Secondly, though in different respects, both men and women resent the transformation in their mutual relations brought about by proletarianization.

If they could, women would stay at home, but domestic work is not paid. In fact, domestic work is neither invisible nor regarded as inferior by these labourers, though some women think it more entertaining to work in a gang (probably a sign of growing social isolation in the home). With the transition to wage labour, domestic labour has lost its value in a relative sense. During the *colonato*, a woman's work at home, and in the field when feasible, was regarded as the proper and sufficient contribution by women to the family income. Now a woman has to work more than a man to fill family needs and expectations. It is in this sense that domestic work has been devalued. Paradoxically, while on the one hand, 'The woman always is useful in the field and at home, she always works more,' on the other hand, 'The woman nowadays has no value anymore; before she had greater worth.' In this sense also the incorporation into wage-labour offers no more personal autonomy to women than did the earlier exclusion from it. Compared with men, women feel acutely that they have the worse lot now. All the same, men, when out of work, have nothing to fall back on and lose their male social identity; women, by contrast, not having been deprived of their essential attribute, motherhood, feel useful even if they do not work for a wage. Proletarianization has increased women's burdens, but it has not affected their social identity as women, that is, as wives and mothers.

Generalized wage-work has affected family size, though again the situation is contradictory. During the *colonato*, having a numerous family was a positive value. Small children were taken along to the field and left sleeping in the shade of the coffee trees, while the mother participated in the harvest or tended the food plot. Having several children of working age is still a distinct advantage for the family, for the more favourable the worker consumer ratio in the family, the better its economic situation. With wage-labour, however, a mother with small children cannot take her children to the fields and work for a wage, and a single wage is absolutely insufficient to feed a wife and several small children. 'For those who had many small children it was better before; those who had twelve, thirteen children could raise them easily . . . now, those who have only small children, for the father to work alone it is very hard.'

Not surprisingly, expectations about numbers of children have dropped. 'Nowadays nobody wants to have children anymore;' that is to say ideally a person should have two or three, but not more. Probably the most frequent method used to prevent conception is coitus interruptus, but some women, in particular the younger ones, take the pill or use the IUD, even though medical assistance is precarious.

The ideal number of children has diminished, but both men and women share the conviction that one should have children, and if one cannot have them oneself one should adopt them. One woman who had adopted a boy underlined the women's ideal of having children with the graphic proverb: *bananeira que nao da cacho merece ser cortada* (a banana plant that does not give fruit should be cut down). Motherhood is woman's essential attribute. Only by losing it will she cease to be a social being. Women's transformation into wage-labourers has not threatened their procreative role, however. For men, the consequences of the transformation in the relations of production, which deprived them of some of their fundamental attributes and made their role as providers so much more insecure, have been dramatic. One woman remarked ironically of her husband, who had been unable to work for some time: 'He was not meant to be a man; a man should not like to stay at home; women must like to stay at home; I don't like it . . . God made a mistake.' The husband revealed his own discomfort of cultural and material considerations: 'If I was a woman, nobody would find it wrong that I stay at home; being a man I think to myself that people are starting to say, won't he ever get better?' This sense of uselessness is intensified by seeing women working for a wage.

Women's greater versatility, while involving hardship, provides them with special resources with which to confront life. As women themselves often say, they have more 'courage' than men. Still, this greater resilience has contradictory consequences: women are stronger because they must confront hardship, but precisely because of that greater strength they also have a greater capacity to put up with it.

As we saw earlier, drunkenness among men is frequent, an understandable reaction to their demoralization. Deserting their families is another response to socio-economic hardship. (See Hagerman Johnson, 1978; Kuznesof, 1980; Roldan, 1982). About a third of the women I knew (seventeen out of a total of fifty-seven) lived with their children without a man in the household. Among those women who lived with their husbands, there were instances where the husband was incapable of working and/or drank. None of these women, however, thought of deserting the man. There are ideological reasons that make it much more difficult and thus unusual for women to abandon their families. Whereas men have to, literally, 'earn' their rightful place in the household, women's 'natural' place is in the home. Men might abandon the home when they feel they have failed. For women, the act of abandoning the family constitutes the failure: 'Many women who left their husbands ... did so with reason ... and still people would say that it was she who was wrong; women always get a bad name.'

A decisive obstacle discouraging wives and mothers from leaving their homes is the special bond thought to link mothers and children. As the saying goes, 'Mother you have only one; father, nobody knows who he is.' The physiological difference between women and men in regard to childbearing is ideologically marked to underline the special nature of motherhood. It is also for this reason that fatherhood depends on co-residence and exclusive access to the wife's sexuality, and that it is potentially more fragile. The maternal and paternal bonds are conceived of as differing in quality and intensity. Children are expected to respect both their parents, to obey them and not talk back. Yet their attitudes towards father and mother are different: 'They must respect their father and even more their mother because the mother suffers more; also, the mother feels greater love for her children; a mother will go without food in order to give something to eat to her children.'

Because the wife and mother is conceived of as the natural centre and agglutinating force of the family, a husband and father's desertion is much less of a peril for the persistence of the household than would be that of the woman: 'When the father leaves the home, the household trembles; when the mother leaves it, the house crumbles.'

Although it is difficult for women with children and without husbands to reconcile their domestic duties with the need to earn a wage, nevertheless they will do their utmost to succeed. Just as men are judged the natural providers of the family's material needs, women are conceived to be endowed by nature with special abilities to care for and raise the children. But whereas this special ability of women is not necessarily incompatible with wage-work outside the home, men are dependent on women for all domestic services. Thus, a man will make a great effort always to have a woman at his disposal. It is rare, however, for a widow or a deserted wife to accept another man.

The greater degree of individualization of men, at least in relation to their control over the income (Whitehead, 1981) and in work motivation, in fact obscures the consequences of the ideology of the male breadwinner in severely curtailing men's individuality. Casual labourers are probably the 'formally free' labourers *par excellence*. But it is precisely these male labourers who reveal most clearly the contradiction between individualization on account of capitalist expansion and the ideological constitution of men as family providers (which is, of course, another facet of capitalist expansion.)

However, this male gender identity is not a historical residue. It is permanently recreated in advanced industrial society. The new economic circumstances have not produced new definitions of gender roles. Rather, one is impressed by the strength and good humour of the women in contrast to the defeated look of many of the men. Women resent the added burden they have to carry, blaming both the planters for not giving them subsistence plots and their husbands for not providing for them. Husbands blame the socio-economic system as such for their difficulties, but frequently vent their frustrations on their wives and children. Domestic violence seems to have increased. Although it is difficult to know exactly, it appears that conjugal conflict ending in physical violence also occurred in the past. The new tensions, however, have certainly exacerbated conflict.

The victims of intra-familial physical violence are typically women and children. When men feel their inadequacy most keenly, they attempt to reassert their authority and domination through the use of physical violence. There are circumstances that are generally believed to justify beating, as when a child is disobedient or a woman has another man. But a woman gets the worst of both worlds: the husband is as likely to beat her up when he fears her reprimands for his infidelity as he is when she is suspected of being unfaithful. Drunkenness often precipitates physical violence and is justly feared by women.

Children, particularly sons, will usually come to the aid of their mothers in a fight. In one instance, a father shot his own son for trying to prevent him from returning to the bar where he had already got drunk (most men have small firearms or knives at home). In another case, a son stabbed his drunken father, who was trying to beat his mother. Another woman, with a number of small children, attempted suicide when she could no longer bear her husband's assaults. These are extreme cases. Still, they indicate one of the contradictions of a socio-economic system that with one hand endorses and permanently recreates a family ideology and structure implying women's subordination to the power of men (who do not realize that they pay a dear price for their pre-

eminence as the family providers) and with the other may undermine the family as one of its sources of profit by forms of extreme
exploitation.

Conclusion

The transition from the *colonato* to wage-labour was not a passage
from an idyllic life of abundance, personal gratification and happi-
ness to one of misery and demoralization. Such an impression would
be inaccurate. The *colonato* was a labour system based on the
extreme exploitation of family labour, and as such it reinforced the
nuclear family as a set of social relations and moral values. The
colonos were aware of their exploitation and resisted it when they
could. Under the present system of temporary wage-labour, because
of declining real wages, co-operation between family members is as
vital as ever. On the other hand, the new relations of production,
by individualizing labour and depriving the men of important
attributes, have had a disintegrating effect on personal relations
within the household and between households. These contradictory
pressures are particularly felt against the background of the *colonato*.

The transition from the *colonato* system to temporary wage-labour
on Sao Paulo coffee plantations is only one instance of the more
general operation in economic processes of detectable extra-eco-
nomic ideological and cultural forces. In this case, planters organized production on the premise of a specific family model and in so
doing created material constraints that reinforced this family form
as a set of social relations and values. The labourers' reaction to
economic change is, in turn, mediated by their belonging to a
family and by the social roles assigned to them within it. The
contradictions that mark this process are the compounded result of
economic pressures as they are experienced in the light of social
values and expectations.

As *colonos*, the labourers knew how to cultivate coffee and food
crops and had a significant amount of autonomy to organize the
labour process. This was surely a source of self-esteem. Now people
have to sell their labour and carry out whatever task they are
told to perform. The trucks that take the labourers to work are
called *pau-de-arara* (bird cages) in which they travel like birds sitting on a rod. The only thing expected of the labourers is that they
work as hard as possible at the lowest wages that planters can
impose.

There is an important political dimension to this transition. Wages are never determined exclusively by market forces. In countries like Brazil, political control is an especially visible factor in depressing wages. Thus, the incipient rural unions that grew out of the increasing mobilization of rural labour in the 1950s were either taken over by the government or simply closed down after the military coup of 1964. The labourers are well aware of the forces that are at the root of their poverty and exploitation, but power relations are seen as essentially adverse. There is also constant reference to the absence of *uniao* (solidarity). On one's own it is impossible to achieve anything, and yet people are still not united. There are at least two reasons for this lack of solidarity. People cannot stick their necks out because they would immediately be dismissed. There is also the socially disintegrating and demoralizing effect of the transition to wage-labour.

It has been shown that wage-labour has affected women and men in different ways because the transformation in the relations of production was mediated by former cultural values regarding sex roles and the sexual division of labour. Women also perceive the roots of their present situation differently from men. They share men's general interpretation of their exploitation, but also blame their husbands for the increased burden they have to bear. Women are keenly aware of their greater exploitation in comparison to the men. On the other hand, however, by demanding that their husbands fulfil the traditional role of provider, these women are endorsing those institutions – marriage, the family and the sexual division of labour within it – that are at the root of their exploitation and subordination as women.

It could be argued that this attitude is an indication of the women's basic conservatism (not to mention that of the men, who resent having lost part of their power over women and children), one of the consequences of the penetration of the dominant family values into the working class. But this system of values – the aspiration to marry, the pressure on women to stay at home, the expectation that men will provide for their families, the demand that girls be respectable – coexists with a considerable tolerance towards those who do not observe the community values. Here was one girl in the gang who was the lover of the *turmeiro*, became pregnant by him, lost the child, eventually had an affair with her mother's sister's husband, had a child by him, and went to live with him. Her aunt understandably was deeply affected by all this, but the women in the gang and the neighbourhood did not discriminate against her in any way. Of another woman, who had five children by different fathers and now lived in poverty with her aged parents, it was merely thought that she had been silly in getting herself into such difficulties. Beyond purely ideological constraints there are material pressures that enforce the nuclear family as the appropriate form of social reproduction. In a society in which all aspects of life are structured on the premise of the universality of the nuclear family, alternative forms of living are difficult to envisage and even more difficult to put into practice. Also, in societies such as Brazil, where social inequality is so overt, the complex articulation of the family with the socio-economic order is much more obscure than class antagonism and exploitation and the power relations that sustain them. Finally, emotional dependence among family members hides the underlying exploitation, but cannot prevent and even aggravates personal conflict.

There are a significant number of female heads of household. These women often have no desire to acquire new husbands. Even so, women do not often choose such households for everyone is aware that it is very difficult, at least materially, to get along without a male provider in the family. Both women and men are forced to live within an institution that is strained by deep conflicts and contradictions, and are often unable to escape from it. The result is the extreme exploitation of women and the further demoralization of men.

As indicated earlier, capital organizes its strategies of accumulation and the basis of existing social institutions, such as the nuclear family. Yet it may change and, in times of extreme exploitation, undermine them. In the particular case with which this chapter has been concerned (and which is similar both to the situation during the early decades of the English industrial revolution and to times of crisis in capitalism), generalized wage-labour has not only uprooted and demoralized the labourers but has also had a negative effect on the productivity of labour. In recent years, individual planters and the Brazilian government have made attempts to reorganize the labour system to overcome the widely felt deterioration of productivity. Labour-intensive crops such as sugar-cane and coffee require reliable and good-quality labour, and this is not provided by the temporary wage-labourers who now try to work with the least effort for the best pay, as a last form of resistance. One of the attempted solutions has been to resettle labourers on the plantations in order to revive the commitment to work that has been so greatly undermined by the general misery and disorganization of their lives.

4

MIGRATION OF WOMEN, FAMILY ORGANIZATION AND LABOUR MARKETS IN MEXICO

Orlandina de Oliveira

INTRODUCTION

Internal migration streams in Mexico, which clearly intensified from the 1940s onwards, have been analysed from a variety of viewpoints. There is a vast literature dealing with the characteristics of these population movements and their linkages to other macro-social processes such as urbanization, industrialization, urban-industrial centralization, the de-composition of the peasant economy and the family organization of labour. However, some modes of the geographic mobility of the population have not yet received the attention they deserve. One of these is the migration of women.

In some Third World countries with high levels of urbanization, there is a clear predominance of women's migration *vis-à-vis* men's; this trend can be seen at a still incipient level even in countries with low urbanization. In this respect, Mexico is placed among the majority of Latin American countries, characterized by a significant presence of women in the migratory streams to metropolitan areas and to big urban centres (Cabrera, 1970; Unesco, 1980; Oliveira and Garcia, 1984).

This chapter[1] demonstrates that women's migration is a relevant process in Mexico, due to its quantitative importance and, above all, to its economic and social implications. By referring to cities located in regions with specific demographic and economic dynamics, the aim is to illustrate the role of female migration in the formation of various sectors of the working class. For this, census and special survey information regarding Mexico City in 1970,

101

Villahermosa in 1980, and Ciudad Juarez in 1980 have been relied upon.

These three urban centres were selected because the nature and dynamics of their economies are good examples of the diversity of industrialization efforts in Mexico, showing specific features at different historical times. Mexico City has been the core of economic and demographic concentration, especially since the 1940s, when strong industrializing policies based on import substitution were enacted (Leff, 1976; Arizpe, 1978a). Villahermosa, capital city of the state of Tabasco, is located in a currently important petroleum-producing area in Mexico (Allub and Michel, 1982). Ciudad Juarez has played a key role in the industrialization programme of the Northern border, which has gained momentum since the 1960s (Carrillo, 1983; Fernandez Kelly, 1983).

Through reference to studies that analyse the family organization of labour inside domestic groups, the importance of the migration of women (and of men) in the processes of reproduction of the family and the peasant productive unit is stressed. Likewise, some of the specific determinants of female migration, linked to the subordination of women in their domestic groups, are pointed out. Furthermore, the study of groups of workers in Mexico City show that migrants and natives frequently participate jointly in the organization of the family's daily maintenance activities.

The specific objectives of this chapter are related to general considerations regarding the complex character, and the historical and structural foundation, of the migratory process. These should briefly be made explicit:[2]

1. Migration streams are the manifestation of a process of unequal development among regions, sectors and social groups. It is a population phenomenon closely linked to socio-economic, cultural and demographic transformations taking place within regional, local and family domains. From this perspective, several changes stand out as features conditioning migration: changes in the rhythm and degree of capital accumulation in various regions and sectors; trends in land tenure systems; changes in the technology and dominant crops; shifts in the modalities of exchange among regions, between urban and rural areas, and in the urban economies themselves; specific industrial policies. It should also be borne in mind that these macro-economic processes bring about other changes in the social,

cultural and political dynamics at the community level, and in the forms of family organization of labour. These, in turn, influence the volume and types of migration.

2. In general, female migration is a fundamental component of population movements. In order to detect its specific features, it should be compared with the migration of men. Furthermore, it should not be forgotten that, as in the case of other flows, it is a highly heterogeneous phenomenon, taking on specific forms at different historical times and places. The temporality of the movements, their origin and destiny, their social composition and their individual or familial character, are among the aspects that should be taken into account whilst analysing their causes, characteristics and consequences. Different combinations of these features reveal the presence of flows that result from the most varied social processes and may have very different implications.

3. In societies where different types of rural and urban organization of production coexist, the processes of labour migration may have diverse implications on rural or urban areas, on regional or national societies. From the point of view of the areas of capitalist expansion, the shift of labour from peasant economies is considered to be part of a process of production of the labour force, that is, of the formation of the wage-earning sectors employed by the capitalists. From the perspective of the peasant population, immigration is one of the mechanisms to which domestic groups may resort in order to enable the daily reproduction of its members and of the family productive unit. For the urban population, migration is an important component of growth and increase in young adult sectors. For the migrants, the fact of moving from the countryside to the cities may involve access to better living conditions.

Women's immigration and urban labour markets

In general, migration to cities is considered a mechanism for supplying the urban labour markets with cheap or highly skilled workers who, according to the needs of the urban economy, will enter industry or the service sectors. In the case of the migration of women to Latin American capital cities, what has been stressed is its contribution towards the increase in labour supply; its contribution towards the re-creation of the sector of independent workers (ped-lars, artisans) in the cities; its role in satisfying the high demand of paid domestic servants generated by the middle and upper classes of the big cities; its place in the expansion of non-manual sectors that grow with the expansion of health, education, management and commerce services; and the formation, though only for a minority, of an industrial proletariat (Jelin, 1977; Unesco, 1980; Oliveira and Garcia, 1984).

Mexico City is a very good example. There can be no doubt regarding the importance of women's migration in increasing labour supply in this urban centre. In 1970, 43·5 cent of the active female population was constituted by migrants (the corresponding figure for the total population was 38·4 per cent). Throughout recent decades, this urban centre has received important flows of female migration, especially from peasant regions. It also receives, though in smaller numbers, migrants from other urban areas (Leff, 1976).

The social composition of rural and urban migrants arriving in Mexico between 1950 and 1970 was very different: women coming from areas where high percentages of the population were engaged in rural subsistence activities (Oaxaca and Hidalgo) were, in more than half of the cases, daughters of agricultural workers; while those coming from urban areas (Puebla) were daughters of non-manual workers (professionals, technicians, administrative personnel), as well as of workers in the production sector (37 and 35 per cent, respectively). In both cases, women were predominantly single. The daughters of impoverished peasants prevail among migrants to Mexico City; though daughters of wealthy farmers also migrate to the city. The latter come to study, either with their whole family or on their own, whilst the former migrate in search of work (Leff, 1976; Arizpe, 1978b).

The migration of rural and urban women to Mexico City has had clear effects on its occupational structure (see Table 4.1). On the one hand, migrant women, especially those of rural origin, participate massively in manual activities in the service sector. In spite of the heterogeneity of the rural migrants, the most important flow is that of women who come on their own to work as domestic servants and live at their employers'. A smaller number of married women also migrate from rural areas to Mexico City, with their husbands and children. These women come temporarily to sell fruit in the city's streets, whilst their partners work in the construction sector or in other unskilled activities within the service sector.

Table 4.1 Economically active population by migratory status, rural and urban origin and sex by current occupation, metropolitan area of Mexico City, 1970

	MEN			
	Migrants			
	Rural	**Urban**	**Total**	**Natives**
TOTAL	100·0 (806)	100·0 (208)	100·0 (1086)	100·0 (1732)
Professional, technical	21·0	37·9	25·2	24·9
Administrative	7·3	6·8	7·2	11·5
Sales	7·8	11·1	8·7	9·1
Manual workers, artisans	29·0	29·6	29·1	33·5
Service workers	22·7	11·8	19·8	15·7
Construction	7·1	1·1	5·5	2·8
Street vendors	2·9	1·4	2·7	1·5
Others	2·2	0·3	1·8	1·0
	WOMEN			
	Migrants			
	Rural	**Urban**	**Total**	**Natives**
TOTAL	100·0 (560)	100·0 (129)	100·0 (689)	100·0 (896)
Professional, technical	10·0	21·7	12·2	22·5
Administrative	6·6	14·7	8·1	29·5
Sales	6·6	11·6	7·6	8·9
Manual workers, artisans	9·8	7·8	9·4	16·6
Service workers	63·8	41·9	59·6	21·0
Construction	–	–	–	–
Street vendors	3·0	2·3	2·9	1·5
Others	0·2	–	0·2	–

Source: Phase A of the survey on internal migration, occupational structure and social mobility in Mexico City

Arizpe analyses these migrant women in detail and characterizes the conditions in their places of origin in the Mazahua region: the greater availability of land and the opportunities of obtaining an income from local extractive activities make it possible for families not to rely on sending their daughters to work as domestic servants. Furthermore, for cultural reasons, some migrants prefer to be ped-lars rather than domestic servants, a position which is considered humiliating among certain ethnic groups. Finally, Arizpe also points out that many women prefer selling in the streets, either because they can 'look after' their children while working, or because they have contacts with people from their same villages living in the city, from whom they can obtain fruit and vegetables at wholesale prices (Arizpe, 1975 and 1977; Leff, 1974).

On the other hand, urban migrants, given their social origin and schooling levels, have other labour possibilities besides unskilled services: 47 per cent of the urban migrants participate in non-manual activities (as professionals, administrative staff, salesgirls). Although this figure is lower than that of the natives, it reflects the differential composition of the urban migratory flows *vis-à-vis* rural ones (see Table 4.1).

Urban migrants and native women carry out most of the non-manual tasks in the different branches of the service sector (public administration, health, education, finance), activities that have expanded noticeably in Mexico City with the intensification of industrial growth, starting in the 1940s.[3] The participation of migrants of both sexes in non-manual activities shows that urban economies also absorb skilled migrant labour when so required and when they can count on the necessary supply. The relatively higher presence of male versus female migrants in the professional and technical groups in Mexico City reveals the greater educational selectivity of male migratory flows in comparison with the female ones. In many cases, male youngsters come to the capital city to study and, once they have graduated, do not return to their places of origin.

The relative importance of female migrants in manual activities in the industrial sector in Mexico City was quite limited in 1970: less than 10 per cent of migrants (rural or urban). The industries in the capital city have absorbed mostly male migrants (rural or urban) and natives of both sexes (see Table 4.1).

In summary, the linkages between female migration and urban labour markets is complex and heterogeneous. In the case of Mexico City, female migration contributes its labour mainly to the unskilled sectors of the services, as is the case in other Latin American cities; it also supplies some non-manual workers and, finally, manual labour within industry. The relative importance of one or the other possibility depends on the historical period analysed and on the multiple economic, social, demographic and cultural aspects that intervene in the configuration of labour supply and demand.[4]

In Villahermosa, the modalities of incorporation of the migrants into the labour market (see Table 4.2) are similar to those of Mexico City, though with different nuances: on the one hand, migrant manual-worker women also participate in service-sector activities, though in lower percentages than in Mexico City. This is due to the fact that there is less demand for domestic and non-domestic services in Villahermosa, given its smaller size and the lesser complexity of its economic structure. On the other hand, it is traditionally the male population (migrants and natives) that carry out manual tasks. As shown by Allub and Michel (1982) for 1980, the more recent migrants to the *municipio* centro (chief town) in Tabasco (where Villahermosa is located) entered the most dynamic and productive industries, especially oil-production, construction and manufacturing. According to the figures in Table 4.2, 48 per cent of male migrants in this *municipio* were manual workers in 1980. It must be noted that the participation of women (whether migrants or natives) in the group of manual workers is minimal, as a result of the nature of the industrial activity carried out in this urban centre that traditionally hires males.

The pattern of female migration and of the incorporation of migrants into the economic structure of urban areas in the Northern border region has different modalities from those prevalent in Mexico City and in Villahermosa. Ciudad Juarez is an example of a specific urban-regional context where high percentages of women participate in manual activities in the industrial sector: in 1980, 37·9 per cent of working women were manual workers and artisans (see Table 4.3). Data for another border city – Reynosa – yield the same results (Margulis and Tuiran, 1984). Unfortunately, no data are available on the distribution of female migrants by occupational group or sector for Ciudad Juarez. Although the importance of female migrants' participation in the *maquiladora* (transformation) industries is known, it would be very useful to be able to analyse the dynamics of the labour markets in border cities, differentiating between men and women, as well as between migrants and natives at various points in time.

Table 4.2 Economically active population by migratory status and present occupations by sex, Tabasco, 1980*

| | MEN | | |
	Migrants	Natives	Total
TOTAL	100·0 (243)	100·0 (287)	100·0 (480)
Professional, technical	19·3	17·7	18·5
Administrative	5·4	11·8	8·5
Sales, commerce	14·4	22·4	18·3
Manual workers, artisans	48·2	39·7	43·9
Service (non domestic)	8·2	5·5	6·8
Domestic services	0·4	–	0·2
Others	4·1	3·0	3·5

| | WOMEN | | |
	Migrants	Natives	Total
TOTAL	100·0 (78)	100·0 (112)	100·0 (190)
Professional, technical	15·4	21·4	18·9
Administrative	25·6	27·6	26·8
Sales, commerce	23·1	25·9	24·7
Manual workers, artisans	3·9	2·7	3·2
Service (non domestic)	19·2	13·4	15·8
Domestic services	12·8	8·0	10·0
Others	–	0·9	0·5

Source: Socio-economic survey of Tabasca, CONAPO
* Data refer to urban areas (5000+) in the *municipio* Centro

In spite of the lack of this type of information, available studies (Carrillo, 1983; Fernandez Kelly, 1983) show what type of female migration is absorbed by industrial activities, and why the *maquiladora* industries prefer female labour, especially migrants. Likewise, the case of migration to a border city illustrates the close historical linkages between the movement of the female population to the Northern border and emigration to the United States.

Table 4.3 Economically active population by current occupation by sex, Ciudad Juarez, 1980

	Men	**Women**	**Total**
TOTAL	100·0	100·0	100·0
	(126,895)	(72,021)	(198,916)
Professional, technical	9·6	8·5	9·2
Administrative	9·7	15·1	11·6
Sales, commerce	12·5	8·1	10·9
Service workers	7·6	5·6	6·9
Manual workers, artisans	41·9	37·9	40·5
Domestic services	0·6	7·9	3·2
Others	18·2	16·9	17·7

Source: Xth Population Census, 1980

Since the mid-1960s, migration of women to the Northern border and the United States has increased; furthermore, patterns of migration to this region have undergone changes directly related to the establishment of *maquiladora* enterprises in the border cities and to the variations in their labour recruitment policies. Carrillo (1983) stresses that, whilst during the 1940s young women migrated to the border to work as domestic servants and in the 1950s they went to the United States to perform agricultural and industrial tasks, during the 1960s young women migrated to the border on their own or with their families in search of work in the *maquiladora* companies. Based on data from a survey carried out in 1978 in Ciudad Juarez, Carrillo describes the characteristics of the female population employed by the *maquiladora* industries: most of them are young (sixteen to twenty-four years of age); single, without children; with studies above the primary level and, in half the cases, migrants, predominantly from urban areas.

This latter result supports the results of other studies. Fernandez Kelly (1983), also on the basis of survey data, points out that most migrants working in the *maquiladora* industries came to the city from other urban areas when they were still small, with their families. Most of them live in the city with their families and share the responsibility of supporting their households. Women who work for the *maquiladora* companies usually contribute more than half their weekly salary towards family expenses.

109

To this pattern of family migration, Carrillo (1983) adds that of individual migration. Likewise, he calls attention to the sector of rural female migrants in Ciudad Juarez, who differ from the urban migrants in their pattern of labour insertion. Whilst the latter are mainly hired by large transnational enterprises that prefer young, single women, with high-school studies, rural migrants work for small contractor or subcontractor enterprises that, due to their unfavourable position in the market, absorb labourers with a lower educational level, over twenty-five years of age, and accept married women with children, or single mothers.

In spite of the variations in the recruitment criteria of different types of enterprise, it is important to note that the *maquiladora* industries prefer female to male labour. This pattern is common to several Third World countries, due to the presence of international capital and to the preference for low cost, more easily controlled labour, with high manual skills, to be employed in the labour-intensive industrial processes (Elson and Pearson, 1982; Fernandez Kelly, 1983).

Female manual workers constitute a sector of the economically active population that, due to financial or family needs, and bearing in mind the female condition of social subordination, is more vulnerable to exploitation and labour violations than male manual workers. Female manual workers in the *maquiladora* companies are especially subject to high rotation in their jobs. In the case of Ciudad Juarez, temporary contracts, constant dismissals and closing-down of plants bring about a small but constant stream of *maquiladora* workers who migrate to the United States to work in transnational plants. This implies the free transfer of labour with work experience, subject to an even higher exploitation due to lack of legal immigration papers (Carrillo, 1983).

In summary, the comparison of three urban contexts with diverse types of insertion in the social and geographical division of labour and with diverse linkages with various industrialization policies implemented at different historical moments, offers a clear picture of the multiplicity of forms in which female migrants participate in the occupational structure.

Female migration and domestic groups

The consideration of the domestic group as the basic unit of analysis makes more salient and visible the specific determinants of female migration and its implications for the process of reproduction of the labour force, both in the countryside and in the cities. Since the mid-1970s, students of migratory processes have stressed the importance of the domestic group as an analytical instance where the macro-structural conditions facilitating the migratory flows and the family and individual determinants converge. Stressing the social processes linked to the daily maintenance of individuals and families is, in turn, part of the anthropological tradition and, above all, part of the usual framework of studies of agrarian questions; they have been developed further in the analyses of the condition of women in the urban popular sectors (Yanagisako, 1979; Jelin, 1984; Garcia, Munoz and Oliveira, 1982).

The theoretical importance of the household is based on several analytical dimensions (Jelin, 1984; Martinez and Rendon, 1983; Garcia, Munoz and Oliveira, 1982; Zemelman, 1981). Those that are most relevant to the theme of this chapter are as follows. First, it is important to consider that members of domestic groups differ regarding age, sex and their place in the kinship structure; such characteristics mean that they participate in a different manner in activities related to production, reproduction and distribution. Second, power relations are established among household members; these relations, coupled with a set of ideological components, ensure the persistence of the domestic group. Furthermore, in so far as we are dealing with a set of social relations, domestic groups are not autonomous and isolated entities; their members participate in a network of interrelationships with members of other households and are subject to pressures arising from other social domains (the economy, the State, the school, the Church). However, this is carried out in an active manner; that is to say, people perform many types of action, although often in conflictive relationships, to attain the persistence or transformation of their collective interests. This dynamic character of households grants them relative autonomy *vis-à-vis* macro-structural processes and allows them to act as a mediating agency between the individual and society. Through the analysis of migratory behaviour, an illustration will be given of how forms of household organization condition their members' actions; special emphasis will be placed on the organization of family labour.

111

Peasant domestic groups and female migration

Among peasants, productive units are also domestic groups; several forms of organization of family labour are needed for the daily reproduction of the members as well as for the survival of domestic groups and productive units (Arizpe, 1978; Davila, 1982; Young, 1978; Salles, 1984). Martinez and Rendon (1983) stress the multiple possibilities of labour organization in concrete situations: intensification of family labour, task diversification, specialization in certain activities, supplying wage-labour within the community or outside it. From this point of view, migration is one of the concrete manifestations of the organization of family labour. It would then be relevant to ask why in some cases peasants resort to migration and in others do not. More relevant to the analysis of this phenomenon is the consideration of the contexts within which migrant labour is the only possibility available for members of a peasant group.

In order to understand why migratory labour may constitute an 'alternative' for female peasants, one must refer to a series of interrelated factors (economic, political, demographic and cultural) that shape the different modalities of women's participation in the rural family. Both female as well as male migration are subject to general processes of change in rural society, as a result of its insertion within the regional and national context. However, it is important to reveal, in concrete situations, what conditions of the rural exodus selectively affect the female population. Within this search for specific determinations, the importance of the social organization of domestic groups clearly emerges as a mediating mechanism between macro-economic processes and individual behaviour.

Thus, for example, when capitalism penetrates into the rural area through the introduction of industrial products that compete with domestic manufacturers, female migration may be encouraged.[5] But this is far from being direct and mechanical. The transformation of female labour into excess labour force for the peasant economy will depend on the changes that the destruction of craft production may bring about in the family organization of production and consumption activities. Since most frequently it is women who work in domestic industries, the competition of industrial products may have selective effects and free them to migrate (Arizpe, 1978b; Young, 1978).

It should also be considered that the penetration of industrial products into rural areas may take place together with the increasing incorporation of the peasant sector into the market economy and with an increase in the monetization of the rural economy. In turn, these processes may generate new forms of social differentiation within the rural community and weaken the community-based mutual aid mechanisms that contribute to the redistribution of the surplus among peasant households. The interrelationship between the economic, social and cultural changes may bring about a transformation in residential, kinship, inheritance and marriage patterns; alter the availability of resources and labour within households; lead to reorganization of intra-family division of labour; and necessitate the migration of members of peasant domestic groups (Martinez, 1980; Arizpe, 1978a).

The differential place and character of household members becomes relevant at this point. The division of labour among family members and the decision as to who will migrate are made not only on the basis of the availability of land, of the necessary resources for production, and of the global labour potential of the household; the age, place within the kinship structure and, above all, the sex of household members are key criteria for such decisions (Jelin, 1984; Martinez and Rendon, 1983).

The fact of being a woman is an immediate disadvantage: women's duties and obligations are different from men's; those of mothers distinct from those of daughters. Young daughters are more frequently faced with the opportunity or the option to migrate, while their mothers take care of productive activities for family consumption, do the necessary housework, take care of small children, and perform the agricultural tasks assigned to them within the peasant group. The place of destination and the duration of the move will depend on the opportunities of incorporation of the female labourer either in rural or urban labour markets.

Finally, stress should be laid on the importance that the authority structure and the ideological components of the domestic domain may take, mediating between the economic, social and cultural changes at the local level, the reorganization of the intra-family division of labour, and women's migration. In this respect, it seems important to know, in peasant domestic groups, who has authority and decision-making power regarding the division of labour within the family's production unit. Arizpe shows that by exercising his authority and using ideological means, the head of the domestic group, usually an elderly male, may keep surplus labour power on the land or release needed workers to engage in migratory work

113

(Arizpe, 1978a). The manner in which woman's subordinate position within the domestic group affects her possibilities of participating in migratory work should be analysed in specific situations.

In summary, the determinants of migration, as well as the relative weight of one factor with respect to others, vary from one historical period to another and among different structural contexts. However, family-level features are essential in understanding the meaning of peasant migration (female and male) as a reproductive mechanism both of the family and of the productive unit. Furthermore, authority relationships and the culturally and socially grounded subordinate role of women may act as specific conditions explaining the migration of daughters and the permanence of mothers. Finally, it should be stressed that the employment opportunities that arise for women in rural and urban markets (harvesting of certain products, domestic service, jobs in *maquiladoras* or in agro-business) may also induce female migration.

Women's migration and urban domestic groups

As in studies of the peasant economy, the introduction of the household as an analytical tool for the analysis of demographic processes in urban areas has broken down the dual vision of migrants and natives as aggregates of isolated individuals; frequently, both interact within the same domestic group. In 1970, in Mexico City, the most common case among manual workers was that of migrant parents and native children (Garcia, Munoz and Oliveira, 1979).

Studies that go beyond the conceptualization of the supply of labour as an aggregate of isolated individuals have contributed towards stressing the participation of migrant women, both in the market-oriented economic activities as well as in domestic and extra-domestic tasks related to the daily maintenance of individuals and families in the cities (Lomnitz, 1975; Garcia, Munoz and Oliveira, 1979).

Unlike peasant units, most urban households assure their economic reproduction through the wage-labour of one or several of their members (Garcia, Munoz and Oliveira, 1982). Nevertheless, the domestic and the economic spheres intertwine when members of the wage-earning urban groups organize themselves to guarantee their daily maintenance. Popular sectors, be they wage-workers in industry, service workers or self-employed, develop a variety of forms of production for self-consumption which, coupled with domestic tasks, give women an important role in the intra-family division of labour.

Although they cover a relatively small proportion of the total urban economy, there is a large number of family productive units; these units may be related in varying degrees to large capitalist enterprises. Such family enterprises, however, extensively use the labour of women and youngsters. Productive activities, domestic work and production for self-consumption are hard to separate.

On the other hand, households that rely on non-manual wage-work of one or several of their members are in a privileged situation when compared with those of the manual sectors. The 'middle-class' family may hire domestic servants and buy more goods in the market, which surely alters the forms of organization of their daily maintenance. The organization of households of non-manual workers shows how the insertion of rural women into urban domestic service gains new meaning when examined from the viewpoint of the organization of the family.

In fact, besides implying the transfer of cheap, unskilled labour from rural to urban labour markets, it becomes an integral part of the process of reproduction of the labour force for expanding capitalist activities. The migrant woman who works as a domestic servant frees part of the female labour force of the domestic group that was devoted to housework and may, in this way, contribute to increasing women's participation in market activities, thus increasing the family's income. Furthermore, domestic service may reduce the reproduction costs of the labour force of middle- or upper-class urban families; otherwise, part of the services rendered by the domestic servant would have to be purchased at a much higher price in the marketplace (Jelin, 1977).

So far the analysis has dealt with urban domestic groups, differentiating them according to social sector (manual or self-employed workers, middle class), as if each of them were homogeneous in social composition. However, in urban areas members of the same domestic group may have a diversified labour insertion according to age, sex, kinship structure position, and the type of labour demanded in the labour market: while some members of a household are manual or service workers others may be non-manual employees. And some have to devote their efforts to domestic tasks so that the rest may participate in the market economy. Little is known about the utilization of agrarian migratory labour by urban domestic groups in areas of population expulsion.

An illustration is given below of the social heterogeneity of domestic groups in urban areas and the shared participation of migrants and natives in the family division of labour, comparing working-class households with migrant and native heads in Mexico City in 1970 (Garcia, Munoz and Oliveira, 1979). The following results seem relevant to the present line of thought: a) in households where the head of the family is a migrant manual worker who receives close to the minimum wage, the situation of the migrant wife contrasts with that of a native daughter; the former works in manual activities within the service sector, while the latter enters the industrial sector; b) in domestic groups where the migrant head is better paid, wives devote most of their time to domestic tasks at home and native daughters work in non-manual administrative and commercial jobs; c) in most of the households headed by migrant workers, the sons, usually natives, predominantly join the industrial proletariat. In summary, men and women, migrants and natives, manual workers and non-manual workers, often share a common life strategy.

Many of the implications of migration (of men and women) on the formation and transformation of households in different social sectors in the cities are still to be studied. Likewise, little is known regarding the effects of labour diversification in migrant and native households on the processes of transformation of the urban social structure. Detailed study is also required of the modalities of linking rural and urban domestic groups; whether the authority and decision-making patterns in the organization of everyday life are different in both contexts; whether differential migration by sex leads to an increase in female-headed households or to the formation of extended households in urban areas. Finally, it would be interesting to analyse the consequences of the migration of families and of single women on fertility and marriage patterns and on the status of women, both in the countryside and in the cities.

Final considerations

In Mexico, the predominance of women in migratory flows to the cities can be seen since the 1930s, that is, before wide industrialization in the 1940s, a process that intensified rural–urban migration and accelerated the country's urbanization. This fact distinguishes Mexico from other Latin American countries, in which female migration surpasses that of males only when high urbanization levels are reached.

The comparison of cities with different economies allowed several outstanding modalities of incorporation of migrant women in the urban labour markets to be perceived: manual workers within the service sector, especially domestic workers in Mexico City; manual workers in the *maquiladora* companies in Ciudad Juarez; and non-manual workers in Villahermosa. Due to the type of information analysed (census and surveys), it was not possible to evaluate the relative importance of self-employment among temporary female migrants in different activities in the cities. Furthermore, since the only information available was on occupations, it was not possible to specify the percentage of migrants participating in wage-earning relationships in industrial and service enterprises within the different urban contexts.

In spite of the limited data, the analysis showed that generalizations attributing a homogeneous character to the participation of migrants in urban labour markets may be misleading. Rather, attempts to theorize should take diversified structural situations as their starting point, in order to discover the multiple factors that interact in determining the different modalities of incorporation of migrant women into urban economies. The following aspects have to be considered: a) the complexity of the urban economy, in terms of the characteristics of the industrial and service enterprises; b) the rhythm of creation of different types of employment, especially those which are typically female, within the capitalist economy, and the expansion of self-employed activity; c) specific policies for labour recruitment related to the expansion of national and international capital within a given region; d) population dynamics in the receiving cities, the composition of the native supply of labourers of both sexes, and of male migratory flows; e) some basic features of female migratory flows, such as duration, social and ethnic composition, age, schooling, marital status (it is of foremost importance to know whether migration is individual or in family groups); f) informal arrangements used in obtaining employment; and g) the participation of migrant women in domestic activities related to their own daily maintenance and that of their residential family, as well as contact maintained with relatives in their place of origin. It must be borne in mind that several of these aspects and their inter-relationships change from one structural context to another and through time.

117

Finally, it should be reiterated that the research projects reviewed show that the work of the migrant (and native) woman in domestic tasks, in production for self-consumption, in the family enterprise or in the labour market plays an important role in the economic maintenance of the members of urban working-class households. In addition to these tasks, women also participate in reciprocal and mutual aid networks, that are reactivated when difficult situations arise (unemployment, illness, death) and in community organizations to obtain public services, to defend land occupancy, and other activities that are frequent among the working class in the cities. Moreover, bearing in mind that women's work in agriculture and migratory labour is a source of monetary income for the peasant household, this provides a general framework that will allow the meaning of women's (migrants and natives) multiple activities for the reproduction of the labour force to be assessed.

Notes

1. This chapter is part of a project on urbanization and regional labour markets in Mexico, with the participation of Brigida Garcia (CEDDU) and Orlandina de Oliveira (CES), at the Colegio de Mexico. One of the objectives is to study in detail the modalities of women's incorporation in different regional urban markets.
2. The arguments briefly presented in the text have been developed by several authors in different studies: Arizpe, 1980 and 1983; Balan, 1981; CLACSO, 1980 and 1983; Martinez and Rendon, 1983; Oliveira and Garcia, 1984; Singer, 1977; Verduzco, 1982.
3. An analysis of the transformations of the tertiary sector in Mexico City between 1930 and 1970 can be found in Munoz and Oliveira (1976).
4. Changes in the incorporation of male migratory flows into the occupational structure of Mexico City are analysed in Oliveira (1976).
5. There are cases where the penetration of industrial capital into rural areas is carried out through the utilization of home production. For example, in the Yucatan, the peasant-based home-production of embroidery for the domestic market could explain part of the increase of female participation in agriculture in the 1970–80 period, contributing in this way to retaining female population in rural areas. Female labour incorporated into this form of production does not migrate definitively or temporarily; women go to the city to sell their products in the streets or to deliver them to contractors who employ them as disguised wage-labourers (Rodriguez, 1981; Garcia, 1984).

Section III

THE FAMILY AND KINSHIP NETWORKS

INTRODUCTION

Elizabeth Jelin

Even when households are daily occupied in maintaining and reproducing their members, the concrete practices involved imply a permanent relationship to other social institutions. On the one hand,
with the State, the community and other public organizations. On
the other, the boundaries of the household and its composition are
permeable and fluid; relatives and neighbours are part of everyday
life. In that sense, the isolated, nuclear family is a fiction. Even
when it exists in terms of household membership, it is part of a
wider set of social relationships, in which information, capital, goods
and services circulate. Furthermore, each of the household members
has his or her own network of kinship and friendship relationships,
at times compatible and at times contradictory to those of the other
members.

The chapter by Larissa Lomnitz and Marisol Perez-Lizaur shows
how the 'grand-family', that three-generational kinship group composed of grandparents, parents, children and collaterals, is the basic
unit of solidarity in Mexico, even when at the same time class
differences are highly significant in the ways in which this solidarity
is expressed. Upper-class families have seldom been studied in Latin
America. The formation and transformation of the Gomez family
network throughout one hundred years of Mexican history is a case
that allows the study of the relationship between historical times,
between family and individual or biographical time, between the
logic of entrepreneurial rationality and the logic of kinship obligations and rights.

Claudia Fonseca's chapter analyses the dynamics of solidarity
and conflict in a poor neighbourhood in Porto Alegre, Brazil. The
novel theme here is consanguinity. Recent literature on the subject
has led us to study households without men, the so-called 'female-

121

headed households', as a phenomenon that is growing in numerical importance and in social significance in Latin America. No doubt this is an unmistakable reality and studies such as this help challenge current interpretations. The fact that there is no adult male in the household implies that women have to take care of their children absolutely alone. Is it unmistakable evidence that men have abandoned their families? Does it imply the growing role of the 'mother–children' reproductive unit?

The culturally determined overemphasis of the man/husband/-father figure has led us to overestimate the importance of the absence of males in family life. Claudia Fonseca's chapter suggests an antidote: men/husbands/fathers may be absent, but women rely on and receive help from non-coresident males of their own consanguineal kinship network: their own fathers, brothers, sons. In fact, Western culture has over-emphasized the centrality of the couple. In actual concrete social relations it seems that consanguineal bonds between relatives of different sexes can become a significant criterion for the organization of reciprocity.

Here, as in the chapter by Lomnitz and Perez-Lizaur, women hold the centre of the stage. Even when they themselves are not the final decision-makers in the system of reciprocity and exchange relations, it is the women who transmit information and keep the system running.

5

DYNASTIC GROWTH AND SURVIVAL STRATEGIES THE SOLIDARITY OF MEXICAN GRAND-FAMILIES

Larissa A. Lomnitz and Marisol Perez-Lizaur

This chapter argues that the basic unit of family solidarity in Mexico is a three-generation descent group, referred to here as the grand-family. Research on households in a shantytown (Lomnitz, 1977) and among the upper classes (Lomnitz and Perez-Lizaur, 1978) in Mexico City suggests that the grand-family is a cultural structure that tends to reproduce itself and remain constant over time.

The material aspects of life, such as reciprocal exchange, vary in response to specific historical situations, economic factors and technological innovations. In contrast, culture, the basic code (or 'grammar') that makes society intelligible to its members, changes very slowly. In this chapter the *family* is used as a *cultural* category implying a set of norms governing expected behaviour between kin and, as part of the grammar of behaviour, reinforcing the economic, social and ritual aspects of solidarity. Such behaviour is grounded in repeated acts of exchange and is reflected in an ideology shaped by the values and beliefs of the kin group and its members.

A grand-family is composed of a couple, their children and their grandchildren, so that a person's 'meaningful others' include parents and siblings as well as spouse and children. There is no drastic change in parent–child relations when children marry and form homes of their own; solidarity and mutual assistance continue. Each person adjusts to the expectations of the members of the grand-family and expects their support in return. Basic family obligations include economic support, participation in family rituals, and social

123

recognition. The latter involves the impact of individual status changes on the entire grand-family and, perhaps more important, the corporate sharing of social networks – the social relations of all members form a resource pool to be tapped when the need arises.

The physical and social expressions of solidarity vary according to class, household arrangements and stages of growth within the family unit. Among peasant households the patrilinear grand-family often dwells in a family compound, with a separate home for each nuclear family, all built on the same property. Usually, at marriage, female offspring move into the husband's family compound and sons move away, leaving only the youngest son at home, together with unmarried children and daughters whose husbands do not own land. Each grand-family is an agricultural work unit based on any one of a variety of economic co-operation schemes. For example, men may support the household by regular cash contributions, while women share cooking and child-rearing duties; at other times, each nuclear family manages its own affairs (Nutini, 1968; Romney and Romney, 1966; Foster, 1972). Something similar is found among peasants in Peru and Ecuador (Escobar, 1980; Webster, 1980).

When a grand-family migrates to the city (usually in stages over several years), it is forced to reorganize residence patterns and redefine its internal forms of solidarity. The first migrant is often a bachelor, who lives among strangers. If he marries, he may move in with his wife's parents until he and his wife can set up an independent household. Should two or more brothers migrate with their respective nuclear families, they may establish an extended household, sharing cooking and expenses, if their wives get on well together.[1] Although the family's basic structure as a unit of solidarity remains the same, changes in residential arrangements lead to revised expectations of exchange and interaction between kin. To demonstrate how those arrangements vary according to the prestige and economic prominence of a grand-family, forms of inter-action in grand-families from two socio-economic strata of Mexico City are described below: shantytown and upper-class households.

The shantytown

The shantytown in question includes about 180 households (Lomnitz, 1975). Some 70 per cent of heads of household and their spouses have migrated from rural areas since 1940. Virtually all residents have marginal (or 'informal') socio-economic status, a stratum of the working class not integrated into the modern economic sector or into the state apparatus, and plagued by chronic job insecurity and extremely low wages. Typically, they are not entitled to social security or other welfare benefits, they earn incomes below the legal minimum, and they work intermittently as manual labourers in the construction industry or hold similar non-union jobs as street vendors, domestic servants, waiters, janitors, craftsmen, repairmen and proprietors of informal home enterprises. This stratum includes 50 per cent of the working population of Mexico City (*Secretaría de Programación y Presupuesto*, 1979).

Household formation in shantytowns is a dynamic process of random factors (housing vacancies or the availability of kin ready to move in when a vacancy occurs). The various types of household are the result of these unforeseeable circumstances interacting with three basic variables: kinship, residence and domestic function:

1. Kinship: a household is either nuclear or extended.
2. Residence: the house is under a single roof, on a single plot, or semi-detached. A single-roof household shares one residential unit. In a single-plot household, a series of dwellings share one plot of land. The semi-detached household occupies two or more adjoining residential units not originally built for one household.
3 Domestic function: the household members choose whether or not to share expenses.

Single nuclear family households are in the minority, and about half are waiting for a vacancy near relatives elsewhere in the shantytown. Only 15 per cent are nuclear households with no relatives in the shantytown.

Thirty-five per cent of households are semi-detached: members of the grand-family share neither cooking duties nor household expenses; each nuclear family apparently leads a separate economic life. There is, however, an intense reciprocal exchange system that includes a variety of domestic functions: the grand-family shares a common outdoor area used as a laundry, kitchen and children's playground. The semi-detached household provides the security of co-operation between close kin while allowing its component nuclear families a certain amount of autonomy and privacy.

The major portion (50 per cent) of shantytown households are single-roof or single-plot extended households, usually containing three generations: husband and wife, their children, and some of the children's nuclear families. Single-roof grand-family members frequently share household and cooking expenses, whereas among single-plot households, only a minority share such expenses.

In studying the residence changes of married couples from the time of their migration or marriage, it was found that 16·7 per cent began as neolocal households, 22·8 per cent settled initially with the wife's kin, and 37·6 per cent lived first with the husband's kin. Nearly a third of neolocal households were older couples who had taken up residence with children already established in the shanty-town. Thus, only 11·7 per cent of all couples had actually founded independent households upon marriage or arrival in the city.

Instances of patrilocality are not substantially greater than those of matrilocality. Furthermore, in 8 per cent of cases, the marriage partners met in the shantytown and, belonging to neighbouring households, settled with the kin of both husband and wife. These statistics support both the expected impact of bilaterality and the conclusion that preservation of the grand-family structure is the basic consideration in determining residence.

Few nuclear families remain in their initial residences for long. The trend is instead one of frequent change, depending on economic and social circumstances, stages in the family life cycle, housing vacancies, personal relationships among kin, and so on. The initial choice of residence is often primarily an economic consideration, despite the potential problems of crowded living conditions or con-flict between affines. Anticipating such problems, couples who can afford to do so establish neolocal households. However, maintaining such a residence becomes increasingly difficult: succeeding child-births, economic problems, job losses or the defection of a husband force many nuclear families to seek the shelter and protection of the grand-family. This factor helps explain the increase in semi-detached households, both matrilocal and patrilocal, from 27·4 per cent (upon marriage) to 35·4 per cent (at the time of the survey).

The typical shantytown couple begins married life in an extended household formed by the parents of the husband or wife. A hus-band's other relatives may also shelter the couple, or if the husband lacks relatives in the city or has relatives who cannot offer shelter, the wife's relatives may do so. Occasionally the wife's relatives offer land or other inducements to keep the couple nearby; indeed, matrilocality seems to sustain greater family harmony, especially among the women interviewed.

The upper and middle class: the Gomez family

An investigation of the opposite end of the economic spectrum studied 143 upper- and middle-class nuclear families in Mexico City, interrelated by a network of some 350 consanguineal kin descended from Don Carlos Gomez (1820–71), the son of a *criollo* (native white settler) small landowner, who settled in Mexico City in the 1880s.

The Gomez 'family' is not merely a kinship group based on specific descent: it is also an economic interest group, a loose conglomerate of business interests linked through kinship ties. Though entrepreneurs are in the minority among recognized family members, they dominate the kinship network: private enterprise is the organizing principle of the family structure. As historical conditions change, the mode of operation of private enterprise changes and so does the kinship structure.

Leopoldo Gomez, the first in a line of Gomez entrepreneurs, began his career in Puebla, living and working at a cousin's house. His cousin Maria had married an older Spaniard, the owner of a fabric, lace and ribbon store in Puebla. Young Leopoldo immediately began working as an all-purpose attendant at his cousin's store. During the Porfirian period the business atmosphere was frankly favourable to the development of liberal capitalism: many *criollos* as well as *mestizos* (half-castes) began to transfer their investments from agricultural holdings to industry and commerce (Hansen, 1974; Furtado, 1973; Calderon, 1965). By the 1880s Don Juan Miranda, Maria's husband, moved to Mexico City, and his store became one of the foremost downtown establishments. Don Juan died in 1887 and was succeeded by Leopoldo Gomez, who had become the manager, director, major shareholder and trustee of the firm. In addition, Leopoldo was the trustee of Don Juan's estate and took charge of his widowed cousin's interests.

By 1906, Leopoldo owned textile factories, lumber mills, tobacco manufactures, mines, clothing industries and retail stores, and was a shareholder in banks, finance corporations and insurance firms. Though a *mestizo*, he was admitted into high society and became a member of the exclusive Jockey Club, where 'the most beautiful ladies and the wealthiest gentlemen met' (Gonzalez Navarro, 1973: 400).

Earlier, during the 1890s, Leopoldo had bought a large house in the Mexico City suburb of Tacuba, where he settled with his mother, his brothers and sisters. He eventually married a woman of European origin and moved; Mama Ines and the unmarried sisters lived downstairs. Several of his brothers and brothers-in-law started working in his enterprises.[2]

The Mexican Revolution (1910–20) was a period of economic chaos and stagnation (Cordero, 1977; Hansen, 1974), but was followed by a period of economic reconstruction Leopoldo and Mama Ines became the central figures in an extensive kinship network. Leopoldo contributed through jobs or aid either partially or totally towards the economic support of several kin households, while Mama Ines was the emotional focus of the network. Leopoldo visited his mother every single day, in the company of his children, and so did most of the other relatives. Major family affairs such as birthdays, first communions, welcome and farewell parties, dances, private theatre performances and indoor mass during the years of religious persecution were all organized at the home of Mama Ines, and anyone who reckoned themselves members of the 'family' were expected to attend.

As already stated, Leopoldo lived very close to his mother and sisters, thus establishing at that time a pattern that still holds in the present in 80 per cent of the better-known Gomez's, three-generational families live in the same block, street or neighbourhood. This spatial distribution fosters social, economic and ritual interaction. One result of this trend is the formation of family 'branches' known by the neighbourhood in which they live or have lived – the Popotla Gomez's, the Anzures ones, and so on.

Leopoldo died in 1925, followed by Mama Ines in 1927 and by his sister Cecilia in 1928. Subsequently the extended family branched out into four distinct clusters: Leopoldo's direct descendants (upper class); the households of two brothers (Saul and Roberto, middle class); the households of another two (Modesto and Rosalia, middle class); and the four sisters' households. Each cluster comprised a set of mutually congenial relatives of similar socio-economic level, living in close residential proximity. The total family network retained the imprint of Leopoldo, who in his lifetime had maintained a certain aloofness from his middle-class relatives while cultivating friendships among his peers in Mexican high society. The present social stratification within the kinship network may thus be traced to status-conditioned behaviour among members of that generation.

Leopoldo's sons also started to form their own branches, choosing to buy lots and houses in various neighbourhoods. As their offspring married, they received a piece of land close to their parents' to build their own houses. The result shows up in the prevalence of three-generational residential compounds: grandparents, sons and daughters, and grandchildren living in a restricted area of the city, with very frequent interaction among themselves. Cousins play together continuously and grow up as if they were siblings. Some domestic functions are shared by relatives, especially rituals.

As the older generations died, the social relations between the various branches became more distant, being limited to compulsory attendance at funerals or invitations to christenings and weddings, and the economic differences more relevant. Contacts were renewed and information exchanged on the occasion of such gatherings, but the family had grown to nearly unmanageable proportions, making it impossible to keep contact with the whole network.

In between major social occasions, face-to-face relations have been largely replaced by telephone contact. In each branch information is centralized and transmitted by certain female figures who may be called *centralizing women*. These self-appointed keepers of the family tradition appear to fulfil an important role in channelling, switching and storing information pertaining to the entire kinship network.

There is a strict separation between male and female roles. A male member of the family wishes ideally to be his own boss, that is, to become an independent businessman/entrepreneur. In the context of family ideology, it is unseemly for a man to work for an outsider, and particularly for the government. Those unable to stand on their own feet would be given employment in a family business. Thus, an entrepreneur expects his sons to follow in his footsteps, to work from an early age under his direct supervision, and to take over a preassigned share of his business interests at his death.

This hard-headed competitive ideology was tempered by a strong feeling of *noblesse oblige* towards relatives, in order of social closeness. The elderly, widows, spinsters and other relatives in need were not to be allowed to seek charity outside the family bounds. This feeling of responsibility often extended to faithful servants and employees: after they had been with the entrepreneur for a long time, they would be treated like poor relatives. Women frequently provided the basic information which enabled the family entrepreneurs to channel resources to relatives in trouble. The typical centralizing woman was forever organizing parties and get-togethers of every description; she was a living calendar of birthdays, saint's days and other memorabilia. She also kept wayward relatives in line through sollicited or unsollicited advice.

The Gomez family entrepreneurs in each generation had been the repositories and, as it were, the living symbols of family tradition. They were unready for the economic changes in the 1960s. Big Mexican industrialists had become accustomed to operating in a situation of virtual internal monopoly, as sole claimants to government support and without serious competitors of any kind. By the 1960s, they were no match for highly efficient foreign-based competition. Their best chance of survival lay in forming conglomerates: thus, a certain number of independent family enterprises began to merge under unified professional corporate management which virtually excluded old-style family management (Aubey, 1977). The rugged individualism so carefully nurtured by the family was now an obstacle to mergers, at a time when business alliances with related interests were essential. The idea of the modern executive who makes technical decisions of an administrative nature without himself controlling the capital was entirely alien to the family ideology. After some years of trying to recoup his losses and to build up new independent enterprises of his own, the entrepreneurial leader of the family finally gave up. In 1975 he entered into partnership with a major multinational corporation, relinquishing exclusive control of his business and accepting the fact that his own sons would henceforth be working for business enterprises in which he did not have a controlling interest.

The economic pattern of the most recent generations reflects the economic evolution of Mexico. A rise in economic status became increasingly difficult for those who attained maturity after 1960. Some born into the wealthiest families continued being wealthy family businessmen, while those born into middle-class families without capital tended to retain their original economic status. The sons and daughters of medium and small entrepreneurs married into the professional middle class; very few eventually became independent businessmen.

The tight system of patron–client relations which had emerged between 1930 and 1960 resulted in social and economic stratification within the family network. Today the sons of big entrepreneurs are sent to college to obtain a degree in business administration and later given a chance to enter business at a suitable management level; not so other relatives. The 'family business' pattern subsists only in the smaller, traditional and technologically backward enterprises. Family ideology survives in the form of mutual assistance among relatives. Family affiliation alone is no longer sufficient to assure a comfortable living; the resources afforded by reciprocal aid, which exists potentially in the kinship network, have to be cultivated through conscious effort. Family pride, solidarity and tradition remain as important as ever; but the rugged individualism and anti-political bias of previous generations have been tempered by an acceptance of the new realities of Mexican economic life.

Conclusions

The analysis suggests that the notion of the grand-family presented here extends to other areas of Latin America and perhaps to the Mediterranean, although it is not yet proposed to argue this point. The findings do suggest that, in Mexico, the grand-family is the basic unit of solidarity in all social classes, and that variations in structure are, in part, socio-economic adaptations of the same cultural riddle. The system implies that an individual belongs initially to two grand-families, that marriage involves an implicit rivalry between the parents of husband and wife for the allegiance of their offspring, and that this rivalry is resolved when the couple heads its own grand-family. The dialectic of co-operation and conflict within the grand-family helps explain residential trends in the shantytown and among the urban upper class. It also clarifies the reciprocal exchange network in the shantytown and patron–client relations among the urban bourgeoisie. Finally, it illuminates the pervasive use of ritual and intense social interaction among kin.

In the case of the bourgeoisie, there is a tendency to construct a family ideology which rationalizes solidarity among relatives by emphasizing a certain set of characteristics as distinctive and supposedly unique family values. Members who conform to the requirements of the family ideology have access to family resources in terms of personal, economic, political and social advancement; those who fail to conform are penalized by withdrawal of kinship recognition.

To the extent that kinship translates into social interaction, it may be understood in terms of networks or fields of exchange among socially recognized relatives. Kinship relations need to be activated through relations of exchange in order to develop and persist. The exchanged items vary greatly according to social class. In the upper class, solidarity is defined in terms of loyalty to the family enterprise and economic responsibilities between parents and children. While a settler in a shantytown expects shelter, food and clothing, an entrepreneur would expect a dowry, a house, a job in an enterprise, or an inheritance. However, in both cases consanguineal groups face the world as a tightly-knit economic, social and moral co-operative unit.

While it may be appropriate for analytical purposes to separate the social and cultural recognition of ties of consanguinity and affinity from the exchange relations which typically occur between socially recognized relatives, in practice it is found that exchange determines the cognitive map of the kindred. In the Gomez family, until about 1960, the economic activities of members of the kinship group were largely conditioned by patron–client relations among kin: an example of the manner in which kinship can be used as the basis of entrepreneurial activities. After 1960, the family enterprises gradually lost their exclusive kinship base, but the non-unilineal descent group continued to provide an essential organization framework for economic exchange and status maintenance. The type of exchange evolved from predominantly patron–client towards reciprocity relations, but the intensity of exchange and its determining influence on kinship recognition remained unchanged.

The intensity of exchange between kin is not random. It is conditioned by a set of physical, economic, ideological and psychosocial factors, as well as by the implementation of previous exchange relations. In other words, the implementation of an exchange relation not only places a relative on ego's cognitive map of kindred: it also situates the relative at a greater or lesser social distance in relation to ego. Exchange may be carried even beyond ego's death, through the bequeathing of legacies and indirectly through the incorporation of decreased members into the family lore.

Notes

1. Such variations among shantytown residents in Mexico and other Latin American countries have been reported by Lomnitz, 1975; Browning, 1971; Arizpe, 1978; Leeds and Leeds, 1970; Kemper, 1976; and Butterworth, 1962.
2. The genealogy of this family, as well as the narrative of their one-century history, are presented in Lomnitz and Perez-Lizaur (1978).

6

SPOUSES, SIBLINGS AND SEX-LINKED BONDING: A LOOK AT KINSHIP ORGANIZATION IN A BRAZILIAN SLUM

Claudia Fonseca

The study of non-standard family patterns in Western society represents a special challenge to the ethnologist. The full force of this challenge was felt during the 1981–3 field study of the Vila, a Porto Alegre (Brazil) slum. Initial data indicated that family relations in the group studied followed a distinctly different pattern from that of the middle classes – a pattern characterized by the scarcity of formal marriage (roughly 10 per cent of couples), a high rate of conjugal instability (20 per cent of the couples went through some sort of conjugal dissolution during the two years of observation), nearly 25 per cent of stable mother–child units, and a high rate of child circulation (50 per cent of women over twenty had, at some time in their lives, placed a child in a foster home).[1] In an attempt to understand these data, reference was made to the principal concepts associated with conjugal instability among lower-income groups: 'female-headed household', 'matrifocal' family system, and 'survival strategies'. But the material obstinately refused to fit into these paradigms.

Because it diverges from the principal models set forth in contemporary literature, the case studied raises a series of questions about family patterns adapted to conditions of extreme poverty. Why do certain poor, urban dwellers appear so attached to legal marriage and conjugal stability (Lomnitz, 1975; Bohman, 1984), while the people in this slum show other tendencies? Why do women in this case redistribute their children among neighbours and kin upon remarrying? Why, instead of remarrying, do they not establish female coalitions (assuring a practical division of domestic labour) which would permit them to live with their children? Even if the irreplaceable character of a *masculine* presence in the domestic group were accepted, why, it might be asked, must the man present be a husband and not, as in certain places in the Caribbean, a brother? In other words, how is it that we find Caribbean-style conjugal instability side by side with a patriarchal pattern of domestic authority which inhibits matrifocal tendencies?

The complexity of this material casts doubts on the very terms of the analysis. Can one justifiably speak of *one* family model in this slum? Are the men really absent from the homes classified as 'mother–child units'? Does it make sense to treat the couple as an analytical focus especially when (as is the case here) conjugal instability comes hand in hand with tremendous consanguineal solidarity? A shift of focus from conjugality to consanguinity gave the surprising result of highlighting the *males* in this family system. The recent upsurge of literature on men in matrifocal families has brought out intriguing ideas on patrifiliation (Smith, 1973), the possible psychic pay-offs men derive from the system (André, 1982), and the non-resident male's contribution to the mother–child unit's survival (Stack, 1974b). By emphasizing the role of brothers and sons in the family system of the Vila, it is hoped to continue in this vein, thus undermining the myth (propagated by men themselves) that 'family is a subject for women'.

Concepts revisited

The term 'female-headed household' has been variously used to designate residential units composed of mother and children only (Blumberg and Garcia, 1977; Barroso, 1978), and those where the male spouse is present but because the woman earns more (Figuei-redo, 1980), has other consanguineals living with her (Whitehead, 1978) or simply runs the show through affection and mutual-aid relationships (see Kunstadter's misappropriation of the matrifocal-ity concept, 1963), she is considered by researchers and perhaps the people involved to be the *de facto* focus of family decisions. This plethora of definitions, symptom of a certain uneasiness among researchers, demands some consideration.

A great deal of the confusion surrounding lower-income family structure is due to the static nature of the 'household' concept. Already criticized for being overly rigid (Goody, 1972; Bender,

1967), this concept is especially inappropriate among the urban poor, where residential units appear to metamorphose three or four times, not in a life cycle, but in a single year (Morris, 1981; Fonseca, 1983; Bacelar, 1982). Since people, when asked to describe their household composition, have a tendency to enumerate 'normal' conjugal family members, one-shot surveys easily over-look the variety of kinship and social ties operating through residence.

In the Vila, the overwhelming majority of households are nor-mally nuclear (children, their mother, and eventually the mother's husband). Yet frequent and abrupt changes are not uncommon. For example, when the researcher first met Arminda (fifty years old), she was living with her eleven-year-old adopted daughter in a one-room shack. A leaky roof and the fear of being alone forced her into the nearby home of a 'married'[2] daughter, who was living with her husband and two children (one child from each of the daughter's marriages). Soon afterwards, this entire unit returned to Arminda's home-town, 150 kilometres from Porto Alegre. A month or so later, Arminda, together with her adopted daughter and oldest grandchild, surfaced at her son's in the shack he had planted next to his new father-in-law. The following month, Arminda's daughter (now separated from her husband) and her baby joined them. Faced with such cases, the classification of households into neat categories ('female-headed', 'extended', 'conjugal') was found to be of little use.

Such typologies blur the distinction between family system and household unit because they give the impression that a given per-centage of the population lives and reproduces within a 'nuclear', 'extended' or 'female-headed' pattern. The consequences of such confusion may be seen, on the one hand, in the literature which, on the basis of an observed mother–child residential unit, extrapo-lates a whole kinship system (Blumberg and Garcia, 1977), and on the other hand, in the literature which tries to reduce the matrifocal system to one of its parts (see Smith's criticism of Gonzales in Smith, 1973). It is essential to recognize that the diverse residential categories complement one other. The investigation of *how* they complement one another, how and why a domestic group is trans-formed from one category into another, is to focus on the family *system*.[3] Having brought out the difference between these two levels of analysis, it becomes clear that apparent similarities in the dome-stic organization of two groups do not necessarily indicate similar systems. For example, a high proportion of domestic units classified in the 'mother–child' category may be found, as in the case studied, in a system where the patriarchal, conjugal unit is still prevalent. In this case, these households represent a *transitional* phase between two conjugal unions; they are precarious units liable to be dismantled at any moment upon the mother's remarriage. The same high proportion may elsewhere be imbedded in a system where, as in the Caribbean, the domestic unit, centred on consanguineal kin, is relatively stable and self-sufficient, and where the sporadic presence of the mother's sexual partners alters but little the fundamental organization of the group.

The domestic unit (which is here designated also as 'household', 'residential unit' and 'family') is a key category in the analysis. While criticizing typologies, it is evident that here too terms have to be used to define the different sorts of domestic unit. Each term, however, has its own implicit premises. The use of 'mother–child' unit for example, instead of simply 'female-headed family', opens the way for a discussion of masculine and feminine power in the domestic domain which, in the area of lower-income families, has best been elaborated by the literature on matrifocality,

Precisely because it does not hinge on household composition, R. T. Smith's concept of the *matrifocal kinship system* represents a considerable advance in the discussion of family patterns among lower-income groups. Originally drawn from the observation of Creole families in British Guiana, the matrifocal paradigm is built along the following lines: the 'priority of emphasis [is] placed upon the mother–child and sibling relationship, while the conjugal relationship is expected to be less solidary and less affectively intense' (1973: 141). Because of a pattern of strict segregation of conjugal roles which, among other things, allots childcare to women, 'it is women *in their role as mothers* who come to be the focus of relationships rather than head of household as such' (Smith, 1973: 125). 'Whereas the woman had previously been the focus of affective ties, in the increasingly matrifocal unit, she now becomes the centre of *an economic and decision-making coalition* with her children' (p. 125), 'The expectation of strong male dominance in the marital relationship and as head of the household [is] coupled with a reality in which mother–child relations are strongly solidary and *groups of women, daughters and daughters' children* emerge to provide a basis of continuity and security' (p. 129, emphasis added).

The problem arises when one tries indiscriminately to generalize the use of this model in lower-income groups. Although the first principle, the conflict between consanguineal and conjugal ties, may hold, several questions arise thereafter. Is the mother's intimacy with her young children carried into their youth and adulthood? Does a woman reside with her children? Even when she does, what is there to guarantee that she will become the centre of an economic and decision-making coalition? And why should male–female consanguineal relationship not assume just as much importance as female–female ties? Because child-raising activities are easily observed through ethnographic techniques and because ethnographers have traditionally given child-raising an important space in their analyses, is it not possible that in some cases female-bonding in kinship networks has been overemphasized? It should be remembered that early hypotheses on female-bonding within working-class families were based on extensive network analysis (Bott, 1957) and on the careful observation of a wide range of activities (Smith, 1956). Researchers should be wary of taking short cuts to arrive at the same 'matrifocal' conclusions.

For many years identified with specifically black populations, where they were seen either as a remnant from original West African matrilineal tribes (Herskowitz, 1941) or as a result of family breakdown due to slavery and/or abrupt emancipation (Frazier, 1939), patterns characterized by conjugal instability have in current analyses shed most of their racial connotation and social pathology stigma.[4] Now, however, they have been subsumed in a new sort of determinism, wherein the 'female-headed household' is explained as an *adaptive survival strategy* to be expected in conditions of extreme poverty. In particular, serial monogamy is held to widen a woman's network and potential sources of aid. While not wishing to refute an economic-based analysis in general, this study takes issue with the simplistic versions of such an approach which harbour an implicit premise on the 'naturalness' of the conjugal unit (as though it were not itself a survival strategy), as opposed to the functionality of the mother–child unit (as though it were not also fruit of a historically determined set of cultural options).

A commonly held hypothesis is that a woman's status within the family varies proportionately with her economic value; that, in turn, depends on conditions in the larger socio-economic context. Blumberg and Garcia's article on the political economy of the mother–child family is the clearest argument presented so far along these lines. Briefly, they posit poor conditions for the emergence and prevalence of female-headed families: a) 'that the unit of labor, the unit of compensation, and the unit of property accumulation be the *individual*, independent of sex'; b) 'that females have independent access to subsistence opportunities (through viable jobs for themselves or their children, inheritance or welfare)'; c) 'that subsistence opportunities open to females be reconciled with childcare responsibilities'; and d) 'that the woman's subsistence opportunities from all sources not be dramatically less than those of the men of her class' (Blumberg and Garcia, 1977: 109).

This model proves useful in various settings where the female-headed household is common: in the United States, for example, where poor, unmarried mothers receive government aid (Stack, 1974a), or in certain agriculturally based settings where women grow subsistence products in their own fields while men circulate either as itinerant cash-earners (Gonzalez, 1969; Brown, 1975; Johnson, 1978), as fishermen (Figueiredo, 1980) or as hunters. The mother–child unit is not an automatic outcome of poverty. For example, Blumberg and Garcia foresee situations of extreme deprivation in which the mother–child unit would not be viable. Perhaps the group studied here falls into this exceptional category. Precisely because this population is virtually destitute, having little access to property, cash income or opportunities for material accumulation, it offers a contrasting group in comparison to cases where 'property' appears to be a decisive factor in family structure.

The ethnographic case and methodological problems

The Vila do Cachorro Sentado is a small squatter settlement four kilometres from downtown Porto Alegre, Brazil (**circa** 1,000,000 inhabitants). The terrain (about 100 metres by 200 metres) belongs to a neighbouring state mental hospital, and has been alternately occupied by and then cleared of squatters over the past two decades. Although one or two single men claim to have been there longer, the older families date their arrival to 1975. Since then, as in surrounding neighbourhoods, roads have been widened and other squatter settlements torn down to make way for apartment buildings. Landlords and (it is said) even city officials have hired trucks to help move their unwanted tenants, bringing successive waves of new residents to the Vila.

Between March 1981 and February 1983, research was carried out on women, some of their husbands, and some children, in seventy households. Five bachelors living alone, and a dozen or so teenagers (nearly all boys) living variously with neighbours or in make-shift shacks of their own, completed the 'sample' – which probably included somewhat more than half the households established in the Vila during the period of research.

There is no way of knowing whether this sample is 'representative' or not. Most contact was made by knocking at doors, or rather, by pouncing on women out washing clothes or cleaning their front yards. Only three families consistently declined to be interviewed. By sometimes working at weekends, it was intended to detect 'working-class' families which might otherwise have gone unnoticed. Few houses, however, remained empty during the week. Even the several people who held more or less regular jobs eventually become accessible, either because of sick leave or a change of job. It is possible that, by working through networks, a disproportionate number of households were found to be interrelated. Finally, the researcher obviously had an influence on the 'data'. Since her husband and two children occasionally accompanied her on fieldwork, her marital status was obvious. Even before research began, her house was on the route of many of the Vila's *'pedintes'* (literally, 'askers', here meaning beggars); the research brought an increase in the number of visitors as well as reasons for the visit. The ethical dimensions of this relationship as well as the rewards and tribulations it brought are material for another entire article. Here, suffice it to point out that the similarities and differences between the researcher and her informants were well-known to all, and the influence of this 'intersubjectivity' was a constant factor in the analyses.[5]

Except for three family heads, the men who depended on salaried employment (typically as night-watchmen or construction workers) spent as much time looking for jobs as working. The income of the 'self-employed' of the Vila (about a third of the adult population, working as shopkeepers, junk-dealers, gardeners, carpenters and construction contractors) was scarcely more stable. Approximately one woman in five had, at some time during the two-year study, held a salaried position (in the 'domestic services'). In contrast to women described in other urban ethnographies (Machado Neto, 1979; Haguette, 1982), very few supplemented their income by peddling their services as seamstress, cook, hairdresser, or washerwoman to neighbours.

In contrast to Sao Paulo and other metropolitan areas in Brazil, industrial jobs are rare in Porto Alegre. Due to an economic slump in 1983, job opportunities were fewer than ever. One of the female informants had worked at a nearby jam factory; another had at one time been employed at an industrial loom; one man had participated briefly in the shoe-making industry, working for piece-rates at home. And about a third of the adults had experience in agriculture. Yet, during the two-year study, apart from the relatively prosperous shop owners, the Vila inhabitants were confined to the worst paid and least reliable jobs of the tertiary (or 'services') economy. Activities of the 'informal' economy, such as begging (a task relegated mostly to women and children) and petty theft (apparently limited to men under twenty-five), were a logical supplement to many a family income.

Economic theory would have it that the distinction between proletarians and sub-proletarians blurs with the fluctuating needs of industry. None the less, the researcher believes that one may speak of a 'core group' in each category which carries a certain class (or subclass) tradition. The distinction is important especially in terms of social structure, as it has been suggested (and the researcher tends to agree) that each 'class' contains its own evolving patterns of kinship organization (Poster, 1978; Schneider and Smith, 1978).[6] Although during the 1970s most research on lower-income groups was carried out among proletarians where family patterns appear radically different from those found in the Vila (Macedo, 1979; Bilac, 1978; Durham, 1980), more recent studies (Barroso, 1978; Woortman, 1987; Figueiredo, 1980; Bacelar, 1982; Neves, 1982) would suggest that the social organization observed in the Vila is not entirely unusual. In this chapter the individuals in question are called 'subproletarians', in order better to conceptualize the specificity of group-sanctioned practices and values.

Sex-linked bonding in kinship networks

What is the relative importance of men and women in a kinship network? Is female bonding the logical outgrowth of the interest women share as mothers? In this sample, mothers regularly sharing childcare responsibilities with another woman were to be found in one out of every five households. In all but two cases, the collaborating females were mother and daughter – either living in the same extended household or sharing between nuclear households. But in every case of mother–daughter sharing, the older woman was living in a stable relationship with the younger woman's father. In a sample where close to 70 per cent of the women between thirty-five and fifty-five are *not* living with their first husbands (i.e. the fathers of their daughters of childbearing age), the unanimity of fathers present in the mother–daughter sharing relationship is significant. In the two cases where sisters shared childcare responsibilities, the mothers were uncommonly well-off: one was the wife of the neighbourhood's wealthiest shopkeeper; the other was being supported by her non-resident civil-servant lover.

Not one case of female bonding for childcare involved people who were typical of the Vila in terms of poverty or marital instability. And in every one of these 'exceptions', the mutual aid was contingent on a behind-the-lines *male* presence.

Residence is another possible measure of the relative importance of each sex in family networks. Ethnographic field techniques allowed a study to be carried out of the presence of kin living at some time during the two-year study in the same Vila, and a check on the sporadic presence of living-in guests in the household to be made:

Table 6.1 Incidence of inter-household kinship ties in the Vila

Nature of tie	Number of cases
Father/son	2
Mother/father–son	4
Mother–son	8
Brother–brother	11
Brother–sister	16
Mother–daughter	8
Mother/father–daughter	6
Father–daughter	4
Sister–sister	8

Two thirds of the households studied were linked through blood ties to another household in the Vila. But these links depended as much on men as on women. The extreme importance of the *sibling* bond should not be surprising, given its frequency in the literature on the Latin American poor (Lobo, 1981; Gonzalez, 1969; Lomnitz, 1975). However, in this case, the number of male siblings involved should cast some doubt on the idea that females always constitute the principal links in kinship networks.

Due to a certain father–son antipathy (and not, it is thought, to a general bonding between women), the overall number of female

– female cases is greater than the male–male. However, this edge dwindles as the individual age and the primary attachment to the parents is gradually transferred to siblings.

The above data includes all the adults, married and single, in the sample. If scrutiny is confined to couples, the importance of male contacts in establishing the place of residence is likewise confirmed:

Table 6.2 Incidence of consanguineal kin in the Vila

Kin present	Couple in which woman is under 26	Couple in which woman is 26 or over
None	2	10
Kin present of both husband and wife	7	3
Husband's kin only	9	4
Wife's kin only	7	1

As to ascendants and collaterals lodged temporarily in the couple's domestic unit, husband's kin outnumber the wife's two to one: guests are normally female relatives (mother or sister). Were non-relatives to be counted, the husband-sponsored would outnumber the wife-sponsored visitors four to one.

The mother–child decision-making coalition

In the typical matrifocal family, a woman's importance, perhaps dwarfed by her husband's dominance during the first years of marriage, *grows with her children* (Smith, 1973: 129). This could very well be the case in the Vila do Cachorro Sentado: a husband's domination of his young wife (including choice of residence, etc.) would not necessarily preclude her eventual ascendancy, due to a privileged relationship with adolescent and adult children. Indeed, a mother-centred pattern of authority was found in seven households: three maritally stable and relatively prosperous older couples, and four single, working women living with their children. (The four cases in which an elderly woman lived with an unmarried adult son did not fall into the 'matrifocal' category, as the younger member's sex and economic input appeared to counterbalance the older's status as 'mother'.) None of the other households was particuclarly matrifocal, either because the mother did not have adolescent and adult children, or because she did not live with them.

Marital instability and a lengthy period of childbearing, spanning a woman's life from the ages of fifteen to forty-five, means that for much of her life she will likely be dependent on a man (the father of her small children) who is not related to her older children. Of crucial importance to the testing of 'matrifocality' is the disposal of these older children. In many Caribbean societies and espeicially in cases where women have independent access to means of subsistence, the mother and her children commonly form the core of the household unit despite changes of spouse/father. Here, however, upon each new union, there is a definite rupture in the household unit, symbolized by a new house. It is extremely rare for a man to move in with his wife or even vice versa. Houses here may be built with scrap lumber for next to nothing, and resold for between $50 and $100. Although the man takes pride in considering that he is the provider of the house, disputes over ownership frequently arise when spouses separate. ('He may have built it,' says one woman, 'but I'm the one who provided the lumber.') Significantly, the 'compromise' solution often results in the demolition or abandonment of the house, as though the symbol of conjugality were destined to crumble along with the marriage.

Remarriage often represents a greater rupture in a woman's life than conjugal separation, since it is at this moment that she not only changes residence, but also may be obliged by her new companion to disperse her children by previous liaisons. Fully half the women over the age of twenty had already given out at least one child to be raised by others, either to consanguineals (23 per cent of the total number of cases), in-laws (12 per cent), acquaintances (22 per cent) or FEBEM (32 per cent). (The destination of 11 per cent of the children 'in circulation' was not discovered.) This dispersal does not necessarily imply a lessening of the mother–child affective ties, but *it does reduce the growing children's and therefore the mother's influence in the household*. Although in two or three newly formed couples, a man was supporting his wife's infant by a previous union, only one woman in the Vila could boast that her second mate had raised his stepchildren to adulthood. The consensus is that although a suitor may make a great deal over his girlfriend's baby, 'once you're living together, he gives you a choice – him or the kids,' since, according to a local saying, 'a man would have to be a fool to support another's offspring.'

Interdependence between spouses: income and honour

Why is it that women in Vila do Cachorro Sentado are not more active in social networks? The first hypothesis which comes to mind is economic: men have priority access to the means of subsistence. In fact, female informants complained that men hold the family's purse strings. In many households, a wife never even sees the money her husband earns. He opens a credit for his wife at one of the Vila stores and pays the account at the end of the month. Some women have only a vague idea of what the men earn: 'One month he says they made special deductions, another the boss paid late – he [the husband] has one story after another'.

In case of need, a woman's female relatives cannot help in the same way her male relatives can. Because the former do not have control over money, they cannot give much support without their spouse's assent. L, a seventeen-year-old mother of two, seeing her husband becoming daily more abusive, decided to take her children and flee. First, she went to her mother's home, but the latter, although she had visited her daughter regularly over the past few months, providing her with clothes (acquired at charities) and moral support, could do nothing. According to L, 'It's because of my mother's husband. He's wicked and he's never liked me. If it were up to him, she'd never give anything to us [children by a former mate].' L then appealed to her married sister but encountered the same essential problem: her brother-in-law flatly refused to take on the (even temporary) burden of three extra, non-related, mouths to feed. So L returned to her husband. . . . Another woman told of her brother's role in her marital relations: 'Last time it got too much for me, I just left [my husband]. I went to live with my brother who was married and living in another city. Now what do I do? My brother is separated and living with me. I have nowhere to go. My sister? She and her husband think they're too good to associate with the likes of me.' There were also cases of young, even single, girls complaining about being rejected by mothers and aunts whose husbands were 'against' them.

Economic dependence no doubt partly explains why women are so often forced to sacrifice their alliance with female kin and young children to a husband's wishes. Yet one wonders to what extent his male financial superiority is due to the larger economic context (the job market, etc.) and to what extent to a particular cultural configuration wherein women are discouraged from working. Furthermore, there is no obvious reason why the economic superiority of men should obviate social and mutual aid links between a woman and her consanguineals. In other cultures men are happy to help out their in-laws and so imbricate themselves in the affinal network. Why not here?

According to Blumberg and Garcia, (1977), Vila do Cachorro Sentado is a propitious setting for equity in male and female earning power. Whereas the job market is restricted and unstable, with mediocre pay for both sexes, women could theoretically supplement their income through non-formal activities – babysitting, sewing, washing clothes, selling bakery goods, etc. Although in other studies of the Brazilian working class such female activities are common, in the Vila they are of minor importance.

Among fifty-three couples, only four women had regular jobs: two shop owners' wives who assisted their husbands, one street cleaner and one luncheon counter cook. The others worked on a sporadic basis as cleaning ladies, seamstresses, washer women, etc., but they seldom worked more than three or four days a month. True, men, when they find jobs, are normally paid more than their wives. But when, as is frequently the case, the man has no job or refuses to share a minimum with his spouse, why don't the women seek work on a more regular basis?

The most common explanation given by women to middle-class survey-takers is that they don't work because of their children: 'Who would take care of them?' D, a woman whose husband was out of work and whose children had gone hungry for the past three days, turned down an offer of work as a cleaning lady: 'It's true. I said I was wanting work. But, you know, my husband went out to his aunt's last Tuesday and hasn't come back yet. If he'd come back, I would have gone to work on Saturday, but as it is, I didn't have anyone to stay with the kids.'

Ironically, this woman lives in the middle of a cluster of in-laws with whom she has not hesitated to leave her children in other cases. One wonders to what extent the children are really an impediment. Husbandless women, many of whom work, manage to find a solution, even if they have to pay a neighbour to look after their children. On the other hand, most of the married women remain jobless even after their children are grown. D, continuing her commentaries, provides another clue as to her refusal to work: 'Once before, when my husband was out of work, I found a job. Well, he just put his feet up and quit even looking!'

A woman who works to support husband and children can only lose in the bargain. First, she will continue being responsible for all the household duties. (Only one husband, a semi-invalid, regularly helped his working wife with household tasks.) Women report that when they take outside jobs, their husbands – as though embittered by this affront to their honour – become even more exacting of their domestic services. Second, and perhaps more important, a married woman will not dispose freely of the money she earns. Her husband's authority, with or without his wife's agreement, will include control of all her belongings. The story of N, a 36-year-old beggar/-part-time cleaning lady, is not atypical. According to her neighbour, a friend of twenty years' standing, 'Her husband is finishing her off. She never sees his pension money. He won't support her sons. She lent him money to buy the house and now he's after the two lots that her first husband left to their sons.'

V reports how the father of her fourth child insisted on selling all her furniture (acquired before she met him) to buy new, different things: 'The only thing is that when we broke up, he claimed everything belonged to him. One day, while I wasn't home, he came and moved all my things into his new girlfriend's house.' Power over a woman's belongings extends to her earned income. E, now single, tells of how her ex had been outraged when she spent her money on a 'new' (used) set of kitchen table and chairs: 'He was so furious that he took an axe and split the table into two.' At least three women complained of husbands having raided their secret money cache. The pittance they manage to save is nearly always earmarked, apparently, for basic necessities (children's shoes) or possible emergencies (medicine, etc.) The men, according to their wives, spend the money on partying ('na farra') and noise ('na zueira').

Such behaviour, although common, is not condoned. The greatest criticism that can be made of a man is to say that he 'sent his wife to battle for him'. This expression originally referred only to a man's inciting his wife to prostitution, but it has come to include any situation in which he lives off her income. A man stakes his honour on his wife's virtue. Thus, as boys and even married men meander about the Vila with cronies, attend, unaccompanied, the local dance, and generally enjoy an intense social life, their wives theoretically stay at home. They are not exactly cloistered. On the way to and from the water tap, they may stop and chat at length; borrowing a sewing needle or a cup of sugar is sufficient excuse to stay hours in a friendly neighbour's house. But several women claimed their husbands did not allow them to venture unaccompanied as far as the street-front stores. One husband jealously stopped his wife, mother of their seventeen children, from getting regular physiotherapy because it took her out of the sphere of his authority. Other, more subtle men simply grumble: 'Of course the baby's sick – his mother is always out. . . .'

Needless to say, for a woman to have an income, she needs some independent contact with 'bosses' or 'clients' – contact which, it is presumed, would bother her husband. Dona L, who at the age of forty-five occasionally sews shirts for Vila neighbours, lives with her husband's constant threats: 'He gets furious when he finds out I've had a customer here to try on clothes. He keeps saying he's going to wreck the sewing machine.'

Thus, ironically, a woman's increased contribution to the family finances, fruit of extra-domestic paid employment, does not increase her status at home. On the contrary, the man's public image is besmirched and he becomes an easy object of contempt. The contempt internalized into self-loathing, he projects his frustrations onto wife and children. Her husband may be a bad provider, but unless a woman is willing to assume the pimp–prostitute implications, she had better make sure that he be the sole socially recognized provider of their home.

As if these circumstances did not suffice, there is still another element in the husband–wife relationship that discourages a woman's desire to work. If she acquires an income, she will lessen her dependency on her husband, alleviating the one strong moral responsibility that ties him to her: to feed their children. When he occasionally works, he will no longer feel constrained to spend the money at home; he will have more opportunity to make financial investments in other affective ties, in other women. In fact, few men in the Vila had full-time mistresses (of whom their wives were aware); one may suppose they couldn't afford to. Significantly, the only wife who complained of her husband's philandering was married to a regularly employed mechanic and had, herself, a relatively good, although irregular income: 'I know he has another woman,' she confided, 'because for the past five months, he no longer gives me his payslips to keep. . . . He knows the girls and I aren't going to starve, so he takes advantage.' If the wife's financial independence does not throw her spouse into the arms of a lover, it may well narrow his ties to women in his kin group. According to one girl, while she had worked to support the couple's children, 'All my husband's money went to his mother.'

The tie that binds: blood rather than marriage

Despite previous abandonment, mistreatment, years of separation, there is a tremendous institutionalized sentiment binding blood relatives together. Parents (both father and mother) evoke the blood tie to reproach ill treatment by their children: 'How could he [or she] do this to me? Her own blood?' An elderly woman is confident that she can discern which baby was fathered by her grandson: 'I recognize my blood when I see it.' Children's first words are their siblings' and uncles' names, their first numbers the birth-dates of close relatives. From babyhood, they learn to see and expect their parents' brothers and sisters occasionally moving in. And they learn to distinguish blood relatives from relatives by marriage. One eleven-year-old girl, helping the researcher out on the genealogy in a neighbourhood full of her brothers, sisters and cousins, clarifies the status of a certain R: 'He's nothing of ours – just my sister's husband.'

In other studies, it has been seen that legal marriage does not necessarily mean conjugal stability, nor does 'mere' concubinage necessarily lead to marital instability. But here, in the Vila, one has the impression that consanguineal ties are so valued exactly because they are considered the *only* lasting ties. As one elderly matron put it, 'You can have fifty husbands, but a mother is for life.'

In the same way that middle-class girls dream of being movie stars, it may be true that young women in the Vila dream of being married in a white dress and veil. However, most women seem to have assessed their possibilities in such a way that these dreams in no way influence their strategies or behaviour. Fewer than 10 per cent of the couples interviewed were officially married to each other. Despite mild protest against prenuptial sex, in practice, courtship is synonymous with sexual relations and 'marriage', or official recognition of a liaison, coterminous with co-residence. A fellow who says he is 'getting married' on Saturday specifies, when asked, that by then he will have finished building the shack where he and his pregnant girlfriend will be able to live together. In a setting where easily half the adults do not possess all required legal documents (birth certificate, electoral cards, work pass) and where many young spouses have not yet reached legal majority, an official marriage represents untoward bureaucracy and cost.

Whether by rationalization or real lack of interest, women often claim they do not want formal marriage: 'If you're married, a man thinks he owns you – even after you're separated'; 'He has claim over the children', etc. Rubbo (1975) and Brown (1975) report similar attitudes in other lower-income Latin American groups. Concubinage is legally recognized and, rightly or wrongly, women feel that as concubines, they have the same advantages as a wife. Legal marriage may even complicate life. One woman couldn't get her second husband's pension after he died – not because they hadn't been legally married (their two children were ample proof of long-term concubinage), but because her first husband to whom she *had* been married was still alive. Another woman mistakenly believed that, since she had never married the father of her two children, she, unlike her married sister, would be entitled to a lifelong pension after her father's death.'

The kin–allliance opposition takes on special importance in the study of the power women wield in a given group. K. Sachs has suggested that anthropologists have regularly assigned women an inferior status because they have been viewed primarily as 'wives', while their status as 'sisters' has been underplayed (1979). Indeed, in Vila do Cachorro Sentado, such a shift of optics brings out an entirely different dimension in the man–woman relationship. A companionship seldom expected in the married couple seems to blossom between adult siblings. Brothers and sisters almost never live together for long and thus do not suffer the tensions of co-residence, the worries due to the daily division of domestic tasks. A man need not stalk his sister's every move since her behaviour does not reflect on his honour. The lack of regular, defined material obligations enhances a relatively unstrained tenor to their relation-ship. And finally, the woman need not worry lest another usurp her place and terminate her hope of receiving the man's support. The link between brother and sister is a lasting one. Many brothers and sisters visit each other regularly into middle age; social norms value such mutual affection which, incidentally, does not appear to conflict (as does marriage) with peer group solidarity. A seventeen-year-old member of one gang admiringly commented: 'S is really

devoted to her brother. She's counting the days till he gets out.'
Pointedly, this woman faithfully visited her brother once a fortnight
during his nine-month jail sentence when his wife had long since
disappeared.

The importane of male clout

As mentioned above, brothers not uncommonly aid their sisters and
mothers on a sporadic basis. However, to reduce the brother–sister
solidarity to a strictly economic dimension would be misleading.
Only four households (all mothers with bachelor sons) could measure up, for example, to Gonzalez' definition of the 'consanguineal
household'. And it appears that even the occasional financial gifts
a man may give his sister are played up for their symbolic rather
than their practical value – serving more to point out a husband's
inadequacy than to better a woman's material conditions: 'He's a
real bandit, you know,' comments one young mother about her
brother, 'but he's good to me. He's never let me down – not like
some people I know' (an obvious reference to her husband). A
male consanguineal's prior importance, then, lies along other-than-
economic lines.

In Vila do Cachorro Sentado, it is necessary somehow for each
household to provide its own security. Mugging and robbery within
the Vila (notwithstanding the persistent refusal by idealistic
researchers to recognize such occurrences) are not at all uncommon.
Although women occasionally bring in the police to settle their
marital disputes, residents claim a person would have to be suicidal
to resort to the police against local hoodlums' aggressions. A man
in the household, especially a brawny man, is a useful deterrent to
such aggression. Thus one old fellow, to explain his residence in a
distant relative's house, offers the plausible explanation: 'Since my
compadre [the head of the household] is out all day, he asked me to
come look after the womenfolk.' An old woman whose living-in,
middle-aged son is in hospital, begs that his absence be kept a
secret: 'I don't want anyone to know I'm alone here at night.'

Lest these comments mislead the reader, it should be added that
violence does not run rampant here. The use of physical force, for
example, against small children or pregnant women is considered
shocking. Ganging up on a victim or beating an old person are also
roundly criticized acts. Even for a man to beat an unrelated woman
is considered somewhat cowardly. But wives are another matter.

Whereas battered women may well be common to all classes, here a husband's use of physical force is socially condoned. A woman threatening to end her twenty-year marriage because her spouse recently gave her a black eye is cajoled by a sympathetic neighbour: 'Come on. It happens to all of us. You should have seen the shiner my husband gave me last month. But that's no reason to separate.' An atmosphere reigns where a young husband arriving early one morning in a group of friends can jokingly say, 'I'm late because I had to give M [his wife] her daily beating'; or where a boy can tease his married sister, 'A woman needs to be beaten occasionally – it fans the flame for her husband – at least it seems to in your case.' One girl, indignant at being accused of theft by her employer, pointedly (and, it is suspected, incorrectly) told the woman she had been beaten by her husband because of the accusation.

Against physical force, women must somehow defend themselves. They may use their own physical prowess. (The only woman who claimed she had never been beaten by her spouse was, significantly, a head taller than him.) They may use slander or threaten to attack a third party (Fonseca, 1984). They may even call in the police to redress the balance of power.[8] But perhaps the most effective protection a woman has against her husband is the nearby presence of male blood relatives.

Whether because of his physical brawn or his male honour, a male consanguineal's presence is expected to attenuate the husband's absolute authority over his wife. This protection, although not always effective, is a theme which recurs in the researcher's ethnographic notes far more often than any economic facets of the male–female consanguineal relationship. D is a good example:

> I wasn't at home when O [her husband] started to drink and get bitter, so I didn't know. My father had come by that day and saw what was in store for me. He told me later that on his way out, he'd stopped to drink in a bar at the front of the Vila. He was hoping to head me off. But since I didn't come, he left. My brother? Oh, he had gone out as soon as he saw what was coming. He knew the others were there to help me and that if he stayed around, he'd have to stop O. Then one or the other would for sure have ended up getting killed. I thank God he left.

A brother's protective role was brought out in the comments one woman made after her neighbour was knifed during a marital quarrel. Although the victim had an older sister and brother-in-law living nearby, everyone looked to the younger, seventeen-year-old brother to take action:

> She was badly hurt, but no one wanted to get involved. I collared her brother and told him, 'It's up to you to do something. You can't let *your blood* die like that'. He's seventeen but he's really just a kid still. The girl's husband would have killed anyone else who turned him in, but her brother . . . well, he had the right.

The protection accorded by male relatives does not normally take the form of intervention in petty squabbles. (The active intervention of one man in his daughter's domestic life resulted in his nearly being blinded by the son-in-law and in the dissolution of his daughter's marriage.) It is rather a latent threat, an *entente* between men, that blood relatives have a stake in a woman's well-being and therefore the husband's authority and violence must respect certain limits. Women who have no brothers or fathers to give them weight in the domestic power play emphasize the maleness of their half-grown sons. 'He's my life,' says one mother of her twelve-year-old boy, a child unrelated to the woman's present companion. Another woman makes the triangular relationship of mother–son, wife–husband, stepfather–stepson even clearer:

> D [her husband] went out drinking yesterday with that group of his. When he got home early this morning, he threw me out on the street, in the rain and all. . . . None of this would have happened if C, [her fourteen-year-old son] had been here. He doesn't get along with his stepfather. But D respects him, more than he does me. When my son is at home, D doesn't dare treat me badly. My boy says that when he gets bigger, he's going to get even with D for all the wrong he's done me.

The importance for a woman of finding alternative males to side with her in domestic quarrels was demonstrated by one middle-aged lady, Dona L, who lived far from her siblings and had no sons. She systematically befriended the homeless, adolescent boys in the Vila, giving them frequent plates of food and generally opening her house to them. At first, it was believed she did this to assure protection (or immunity) for her teenage daughter – and no doubt her system had that effect. But the importance of the pseudo-adoption of these boys also worked to her advantage in her marital relationship. One boy who had come slightly drunk to share the sudden profit of a business transaction with Dona L and her daughters, proudly explained his role:

Señor H [Dona L's husband] respects me. When their oldest daughter got pregnant, he was going to throw her out of the house – but Dona L got me and I sat down and talked to him for hours – till things worked out. Once I was here when Señor H started to beat his wife, but I stopped him. With me, he listens to reason.

The female consanguineal's role

What do women offer in return for their male blood relatives' material support and tacit protection? Men do not appear to need financial support as often as women. Their earning power is greater and their financial responsibility for children much less. Thus a woman, when she is able to, may discreetly 'lend' money to her male relative or even shelter him from time to time; she may, as does the 'pseudo-mother' of the preceding paragraphs, simply offer an occasional meal or cigarettes. But her major contribution to male relatives is the performance of needed feminine tasks in the absence of or in competition with a wife. These may include certain domestic services such as washing clothes, but the most common and important services she renders are supplying affection and moral support, running administrative errands, and providing a potential home for her brother's offspring.

Moral support from relatives is almost unconditional. When, for example, one teenage boy killed another, the victim's mother practically enshrined her defunct son as a hard-working, obedient boy who preferred staying home (with her) to partying. The aggressor's mother referred to the murder as 'that accident my son had', and, while paying out a fortune in lawyer's fees to keep her son out of jail, quietly implied that the belligerence of the victim and his family were the real culprits. In the case of separation, mothers and sisters repeatedly side with their sons and brothers. For example, one woman proudly comments on her son's recent separation:

When his girl had a baby, he brought her here to live – it was the first I knew about the romance. But she was paralysed – with one leg deformed from polio. And it looks as though it deformed her character as well. She was infernal. My son sent her away. What he likes best is to stay at home with me. No one takes care of him better.

D has seen her two brothers through their two marriages, strongly approving when they abandoned their wives; one spouse she considered 'slovenly' (because she 'let' their baby die), the other, simply dumb-witted. The need for female affection (as opposed to sexual favours), is believed to be great; the importance of this offering which women bring to their relationship with close male kin should not be underestimated.

Women also vie with wives in running diverse secretarial errands for their brothers, fathers and sons – procuring everything from cheap prescription medicine and identity cards to laywers' certificates and (for jailed men) *habeas corpus*. Finally, in the event of a separation from his spouse, if a man wants to keep control of his children, he will certainly call on a female relative to help him, since new wives are generally no more willing than new husbands to raise unrelated children. A man who wants to hang on to his children will probably simply place them in a household (his sister's or mother's) where he can maintain some control. Altogether, men were instrumental in some eleven out of fifty-six placements of children in non-maternal homes; children were either raised by a remarried father (four cases), a patrilineal relative (five) or they were adopted due to the man's insistence (two). There were another two cases where a man and his relatives tried to kidnap a child against its mother's will; and cases of women temporarily taking in or babysitting grandchildren long after their father (the woman's son) has separated from their mother are quite common.

Just as sisters tacitly proclaim their prior loyalties to brothers, so a man repeatedly demonstrates that the moral sway held over him by female consanguineals is superior to that of his wife. One woman boasted she had stopped her brother from beating his wife to death. Several people, including the young man's father, had watched the fight, but she implied she was the only one with sufficient authority over her brother to stop him.

The most patent case of 'blood' prevailing over the husband–wife tie was that of Dona Maria, her three sons and one daughter, all married (the mother remarried), all with infant children, living with their respective spouses in houses side by side. When the wife of one son, through gossip, caused a scandal among her in-laws, her husband moved in with his mother, declaring he preferred separation to beating his wife. Shortly afterwards, a second brother was jailed, leaving his wife and two children to fend for themselves. The two ex-sisters-in-law temporarily set up house together, while Dona Maria's daughter (having fought with her husband) moved in with and became supported by her now single brother. The third and youngest brother entered a period of vacillation during which he would repudiate his young wife only to ask her back three days later. She at one point explained that he was at the same time regularly buying groceries for the jailed brother and paying medical expenses for the sister's sick baby. His own wife and child had to eat on whatever was left over from his minimum wage.

In this same family, there was a maternal aunt considered highly meddlesome by the brothers' wives. When one brother lost his job and had no more money, he simply moved out to his aunt's for ten days, where he ate comfortably while his wife and two children starved. The aunt was a widowed, childless woman with a regular income, and repeatedly criticized her nephews' wives as lazy and unfit. One wife summed up her resentment thus: 'O [her husband] is like a doll. His mother and aunt pull the strings and he dances.'

The significance of husband-absent households

In Vila do Cachorro Sentado, nearly 25 per cent of the mothers of the sample (seventeen out of sixty-nine) remained 'husbandless' for the entire two years of the study. This fact, however, says very little about domestic power. Delving further into the matter, it can be seen that there is a marked male presence in most of these households – the nature of which varies radically according to the woman's age:

Table 6.3

Age of woman (years)	A: Number of husbandless women	B: Total number of women in sample	%A:B
Under 26	3	26	15
26–45	6	32	19
Over 45	8	11	73
TOTAL	17	69	25

Of the women under forty-five years old, two were supported by lovers, two lived close to an ex-husband, two received periodic support from the father of their children, and two were living very close to an adult brother. In every case, the man in question publicly assumed the role of household 'protector'. It is not so much conjugal residence that predominates here, as the conjugal relationship or at least the conjugal *status*: the great majority of these women had a man, tutor of their sexual favours and their reproductive potential. If not, they were actively engaged in the marriage market in search of such a patron. Only two women aged forty-five or under could be considered to be exceptions: R, whose reputation as 'crazy' and 'drugged' was so bad that she continued, despite every effort, husbandless; and J, thirty-seven, mother of three adolescents, who had to move out because neither she nor her children were willing to participate in the social life of the Vila. Pursued by rejected suitors and their jealous wives alike, J sighed in exasperation: 'It's impossible to raise children decently in this place.'

The case of older women is different. Three-quarters of those over forty-five lived in husband-absent domestic arrangements. Could this situation be explained by a lack of elderly men, due either to out-migration or a higher mortality rate among adult men[9] In this age group, the slight excess of women over men is not enough to justify this hypothesis. (In all other age groups, the sexes are equally matched.) A demographic explanation probably only scratches the surface of the problem – and the cycle of sex-linked activities, in particular the end of a woman's reproductive phase, and the concomitant change in her status and in her relation to men, is much more central to the issue.

Domestic organization is no doubt facilitated by the presence of individuals of each sex, but for older women this presence is satisfied more often by sons than by husbands. Seven of the eight widowed or divorced women over forty-five lived with or near an adult son. Single women of all ages claimed they lived 'alone' not because they lacked opportunities, but by choice:[10]

I didn't want to marry again. Husbands are a bother. As it is, I go to bed and I sleep. With a husband, I have to get up, make coffee, do all those things he ordered me to.

L, a widow of sixty, goes into greater detail:

Yesterday when I came home from work, I went over to G's.

It was her birthday. She had made a cake and we opened a bottle of white wine. We spent the evening giggling like teenagers. Do you think, if my husband were alive, I could have done that? Now, sometimes, I only come home at 11 o'clock. My kids may worry, but who cares?

The fact that these words are repeated as much by young divorcees (who no doubt are going to 'marry' again) as by 'false' spinsters (trying to hide the presence of a new mate from the ethnologist's indiscrete gaze) leads one to suspect that conjugality is not the pariah they make it out to be. None the less, the complaints are not without significance.

To be married, although practically obligatory for young women, is not necessarily considered an enviable condition. The norm is sometimes reinforced by coercive measures. The case of J, expelled from the Vila for having refused to conform to the conjugal norm for her age group, has already been discussed. Informants always had one story or another about a neighbour who only puts up with her 'brute of a husband' because of his threats of what he would do, to her or her kin, if she dared leave. Let there be no mistake. A woman is not exactly coerced into accepting a husband or lover. During her productive years, she is a willing partner in the conjugal pact – hoping, through marriage, to attain status, a certain physical and material security, and some affection. Experience, however, slowly eats away at these aspirations. After the menopause, a single woman no longer represents a taunt to male virility; having gained a moment of respite in the battlefield of the sexes, she considers her options from a new vantage point – and, not uncommonly, her choice falls on sons rather than husbands.

Suggestions for future research

It is not hard to pick out the 'self-sustaining' elements in the Vila's pattern of kinship. Property has a symbolic rather than practical value. A woman never has much, but her husband is expected to take control of what she does have. He is to provide a house and assume responsibility for her and the children she bears him, but her children by a previous marriage do not enter into the bargain. Since the conjugal relation is not considered of lasting value, to invest in stepchildren would be foolish – worse than foolish, by putting a woman's allies in the house, it would destroy the man's domestic authority. Teenagers who, because of their mother's remarriage, have no home establish their own conjugal units early, thus re-initiating the cycle. But even if the system is, to some extent, self-sustaining, it is not self-generated.

This writer would suggest that the direct and indisputable influence of economic and demographic factors on family orgnaization is mediated through a cultural heritage of sex-linked authority. The failure of the various synchronic approaches to explain differences between poverty-stricken urban populations indicates the need for more historical research – to scrutinize the influence of Church, State and regional economic patterns on emerging family patterns.

Admittedly, ethnographic material cannot answer these questions. For example, a superficial estimate puts the average number of marriages for women today much higher than that of their mothers. Older informants claimed that, 'In the olden days, people didn't get married so young, at fourteen or fifteen like the kids today.' One grandmother mumbled in mirthful disgust, 'It looks nowadays like kids think the sooner they marry, the sooner they can get divorced.' But it is very possible that these older women had themselves unconventional marriage careers and that the apparent difference between them and their daughters is merely the result of the embellished re-elaboration of distant happenings. Even if their words were to be accepted as faithful accounts of past reality, they wouldn't be able to go back more than forty to forty-five years. 'Oral history' is thus not a cure-all for the problem.

Freire, Costa (1979), in his description of the evolution of middle-class families, clearly states that slaves and poor people were excluded from the dominant norms. And, in fact, there are certain indications that the working-class family in Brazil followed quite a different course from the stable, conjugal model. In many regions, well into the nineteenth century, legal marriage was the privilege of only about a third of the population (Ramos, 1978; Samara, 1981 and 1983). Inquisitors, sent by the Church from the sixteenth to the nineteenth centuries, left records on the widespread occurrence of consensual unions (Luna, 1982; Mott, 1983). And the first census-takers in Sao Paulo, at the beginning of the nineteenth century, turned up a surprisingly high number of 'female-headed families' (Kuznesof, 1980; Dias, 1984).[11]

The historical material is still scant. To complicate the issue, it must be remembered that Brazil is a vast country with several regions, each with its own distinct social and economic history.

These restrictions do not justify, however, the dearth of theoretical speculation on the evolution of family forms in the country. The comparison of historical and ethnographic studies certainly represents a major hope of going beyond more empirical findings, advancing theoretical debates, and thereby beginning to understand the specificity (regional and socio-economic) of the diverse family forms among lower-income groups in Latin America.

Notes

1. The place of children in the family organization of this group is considered in other articles (Fonseca, 1985 and 1986).
2. This chapter uses the words 'married', 'wife' and 'husband' in the same way the Vila dwellers do: to designate all couples, whether legally married or not.
3. Meyer Fortes, writing on 'developmental cycles in the domestic group' (1958), suggested an analytical framework capable of linking the various household forms. However, this vision, by relying on an average of diverse life trajectories, runs the danger of belittling significant differences between individuals and families within the same group (Hareven, 1978).
4. For studies on kinship organization among Caribbean populations, see R. T. Smith, 1956; M. G. Smith, 1962; Greenfield, 1966; Gonzalez, 1969; Rodman, 1971; for those on North American blacks, see Hannerz, 1969; Lieboew, 1967; Martin and Martin, 1978; and Stack, 1975. Worthy of note are the efforts of certain scholars (many themselves black), who, refusing to attribute all the 'qualities' as well as 'faults' of the Black American family to mere economic poverty, are arguing in favour of a 'cultural variant' analysis (Mathis, 1978; Allen, 1978-).
5. Researchers who are overly worried about their presence altering 'routine' behaviour can be assured that old-fashioned participant observation (i.e. spending hours in apparently aimless small talk) brings out situations where such 'interference' is minimal.
6. See, for example, L. Stone lamenting the failure of scholars to note certain developments among the 'lower-income groups in eighteenth-century England: . . .
the [working] class was itself being split between the 'respectable' and the 'rough' with different patterns of behaviour, concepts of honour, and aspirations to life. Whereas the former tried to follow the code of the middle class, the latter preserved its own working-class cultural values regarding work habits, drink, kinship, domestic violence and sexual behaviour' (Stone, 1984: 46).
7. Historians of European concubinage put forward that legal marriage was always present among working-class aspirations; that, in general, the consensual union was simply a state in a life cycle that usually culminated in marriage (Berlanstein, 1980; Frey, 1978; Levine, 1977). Before drawing hasty conclusions from superficial comparisons, stud-

ents of the Latin American family should take full stock of contextual differences.

8. In three of the four cases recorded in the field notes, the police did no more than scold the aggressing husband; in the fourth, the husband, much to his wife's chagrin, turned out to be a wanted thief and was arrested.

9. There is much debate about whether or not a female demographic excedent contributes to a high rate of female-headed households (Marino, 1970; Manyoni, 1977; Charbit, 1984). Empirical research on relevant themes in Latin America tends to support this hypothesis: Ramos (1978) and Kuznesof (1980) have both suggested that the long-colonized areas had more mother–child units than frontier areas, since men were migrating to the latter. (See Johnson, 1978 for similar observations in Chile.) See also Chapter 4 of this volume.

10. In the Vila, elderly women are not considered (as generally happens in middle-class milieux) asexual. More than one youth dreamed of 'snaring an old lady' as the most likely route to an easy life. (See Potash, 1986 for a cross-cultural look at elderly women's social life.)

11. A recent study conducted on Judicial Archives from 1900 to 1926 showed that practices such as concubinage, serial monogamy and child circulation were not at all uncommon among certain working-class groups at the beginning of this century (Fonseca, in print).

Section IV

SOCIAL CLASS AND LIFE STYLES

INTRODUCTION

Elizabeth Jelin

The organization of consumption is a theme where intra-domestic dynamics and the public world intersect each other. Household organization of consumption consists of assigning its diverse resources to tasks, goods and services, to the benefit of some of its members or of the group as a whole. In that decision-making process, all internal contradictions are at stake as well as all the conflicting external networks of each of its members.

A significant part of household consumption and maintenance activities – especially in urban areas – is carried out through its access to public services and state benefits, more than access to goods and services bought on the market. Thus, urban infra-structural services and utilities, education and health, retirement payments and pensions, access to day-care facilities, and so on, in many cases do not respond to the supply and demand in the capitalist marketplace. Rather, they respond to social policies that are the historical result of the process of widening social citizenship rights. This is one of the ways in which family and domestic organization are molded and shaped by the public power sphere and the state.

Above and beyond their manifestation in the realm of production, the specificities of each social class, its lifestyles, its value system and its representations, are revealed in the modalities of the organization of reproduction and consumption. The two very different chapters in this section point to two types of evidence of the relationship between domestic organization and the public world. Jelin centres her chapter around the intra-domestic dynamics of expenditure, and around gender and generational relationships in the process of negotiating a family lifestyle. It is based on a research project carried out in Buenos Aires (the same families as in Ramos' study, ch. 7). It shows how different members of the domestic group, according to gender and generational lines, have to negotiate their specific desires and wishes. By focusing on families that are homogeneous in terms of class, it allows a study to be made of patterns of behaviour in the public realm of extra-domestic social relations defined in terms of family position.

The other chapter deserves special mention. It is the only chapter dealing with a reality outside Latin America: family and social class in the United States, from the point of view of the organization of everyday life in the various social classes. Rayna Rapp's chapter is included because it constitutes a major contribution to the analysis of the relationship between the individual (especially the gender dimension), family and class, taking into consideration not only the material aspects of class condition but also the symbolic-ideological dimension. In that sense, the author states that the notion of the family is charged with ideological content that varies according to class and gender: 'families mean different things according to social class and also according to gender, because classes and genders are located in differential material relations.' By including information based on numerous studies of the family in various social classes in the United States as the basis for her empirical analysis, Rapp elaborates a model for the analysis of secondary materials; at the same time, she offers comparative empirical materials which may help in understanding findings in Latin America.

7

SOCIAL RELATIONS OF CONSUMPTION: THE URBAN POPULAR HOUSEHOLD

Elizabeth Jelin

The study of the dynamics of consumption at household level can be approached from at least two different perspectives. In the first place, the household can be considered as one of various social institutions and organizations. Both in production and in distribution, there are mechanisms for assigning tasks and responsibilities (with the corresponding conflicts) among institutions. The duties of the State, of private enterprise through market mechanisms, and of extra-market domestic production have been a focal point of permanent social struggle between various socio-political forces. In this struggle, household units are very weak. Faced with the State and its social services and with the market, the household is not in a position to protest: it just adapts itself to given conditions. Transformations are slow, resulting from substantive modifications in the social organization of production and distribution, and in state functions. In the short run, besides the influence of economic conditions, it is also subject to the social policies of specific political regimes.

A second analytical level concerns intra-domestic dynamics, and is the focal point of this study.[1] The internal dynamics of the household, expressed in decisions concerning the maintenance and reproduction of its members, is based on the pattern of intra-household division of labour and responsibilities on the one hand, and on the distributive struggle among its members, that is, on the organization of expenditure and the family budget, on the other. To this end, gender differentiation between men and women will be examined, as well as the differentiation between generations: parents and children.[2]

The project was carried out in Greater Buenos Aires, Argentina, at the time of a neoliberal authoritarian government, the objectives and ideology of which were aimed at the virtual elimination of State-distributed social services. The results presented here are merely an indication of some behaviour patterns of working-class families during that period. Due to the relatively high degree of social homogeneity in the sample, and given the period covered by the study, it is impossible to identify to what extent the patterns of behaviour encountered are typical of a social class: no comparable information is available for other social sectors. Neither can it be determined whether these patterns were the response of working-class sectors to the conditions they faced after 1976 or whether they correspond to stable modes of the everyday behaviour of this social sector.

The socio-economic context

Classical analyses of income and expenditure, or family consumption, start with an ideal-typical nuclear family, in which the husband is the only or principal supplier of monetary resources, usually on a regular basis (monthly or fortnightly). It is also assumed that there is rational organization of expenditure, which takes into account the monetary resources available. The actors know what their income is; they can foresee monetary flows and thus make the necessary budgetary allotments for expenses. For several reasons, this pattern does not correspond to recent Argentine reality.

In the first place, labour market conditions and real wages have undergone abrupt and sudden changes. The study (1979–82) began during a period of full employment, although wage levels were relatively low. This situation had deteriorated remarkably after the military coup of March 1976. Wages then recovered somewhat between late 1978 and 1980, but conditions changed with the intensification of the recession in 1981: greater unemployment, and a decline in real wages.

At individual and family level, between 1976 and 1979, households were able to make up for the low level of real wages by increased participation in the labour market of several family members, as well as by increasing the number of hours worked. The most common complaint at that time was fatigue. with low wages, the prolongation of working hours allowed some families to maintain the level of consumption to which they were accustomed and even to continue accumulating durable consumer goods. Governmental economic policy, calling for an opening of the economy, implied the opportunity to acquire new goods, such as colour TVs and cassette players. Gradually, hours of work (overtime, odd jobs) decreased; those that for one reason or another lost their jobs were not able to find other employment; wages did not increase and even started to decline; a rapidly accelerating process of deterioration of consumption patterns was initiated, which worsened during the following years.

In the second place, with high and unpredictable inflation, budgetary allocation of expenses becomes irrelevant. The logic of consumption has to follow other criteria. The rational watchword seems to be to spend the money as soon as it is obtained (if not before). In low-income families this implies permanent indebtedness; current income being used to pay debts. Beyond the general effect of inflation, it should be borne in mind that the prices of products do not increase at the same rate or at the same time. Not only are there important incongruities between income and expenses (all inflationary periods bring about a redistribution of income, some groups benefit and others suffer); there are also changes in the relative prices of goods and services. In so far as the demand for some is more elastic than for others, people may adapt to these shifts and decrease consumption of certain goods; but even though they may suffer greater price increases, some goods cannot be eliminated from the consumer's basket. Thus, the dynamics of consumption is related to a logic of debt (where and when can credit be obtained; for what kind of goods and services) and to a logic of substitution, following the changes in relative prices.

Need satisfaction and the family budget

There is no single criterion to determine the needs that will be met within a household. Needs vary, they are historically and culturally determined, in constant flux. At an aggregate level, the quantitative measurement of the relative welfare of various groups is seen in terms of the degree of satisfaction of certain consumption needs, according to standards that are administratively fixed, such as housing levels and degrees of overcrowding, nutritional levels measured in calory intake and 'adequate' nutritional distribution, maintenance of certain health standards, and so on (Altimir, 1979). A micro-social analysis must include the subjective outlook of the actors, starting with the recognition that living conditions are assessed by the subjects themselves according to what is 'expected' by reference groups, as they vary for different stages of the life cycle and for different historical moments. To study this subjective outlook, explicit critiera cannot be established in advance. The methodology used must be inductive (Jelin, Llovet and Ramos, 1986).

This general reflection is important for the selection of the analytical framework for the study of the distribution of family expenditure. What seems 'basic' or 'superfluous' to some may not be so for others. 'Priorities' with respect to norms, aims and desires may be established verbally during an interview, but the concrete behaviour might differ.

The Moreira family[3]

At the time of reference (1982), the Moreira family is composed of Rolando, sixty years old, shoe-shiner; his wife, Hebe, forty-nine years old, housewife; and their three children: Norberto, twenty-six, Claudia, twenty-one, and Sergio, sixteen. The oldest son is a policeman, the daughter is an administrative employee in an insurance company and the youngest has, for the last few months, worked as an unskilled labourer in a tennis shoe factory.

Whilst the father's daily income varies according to the number of clients requiring his services, the children receive monthly or fortnightly wages and maintain a stable working relationship that allows them to know in advance when and how much they are going to collect for their work. Every evening, when Rolando gets back home, he gives his wife almost all the money he has made shining shoes. With that money Hebe must pay for food, toiletries and cleaning products, and for every other item related to the daily maintenance of the unit (for example, kerosene for the heaters, gas cylinders for the kitchen stove). In turn, Norberto and Claudia (who earns the highest salary of the three siblings) give their mother a certain portion of their salaries at the beginning of the month. Sergio does likewise. He collects every fortnight and as soon as he is paid he hands it all over to his mother. In a sort of implicit family 'contract', the children's contribution goes towards two types of expense: the rent, which is paid monthly (but adjusted by the rate of inflation every three months), and the monthly credit payments for furniture and household appliances.

In this family, the most variable and erratic income is used for daily expenditure, the most 'secure' income is assigned to taking care of fixed monthly commitments.

Hebe: Claudia and Norberto give the money to me. A fixed amount, yes, because the rent went up and the TV set, they wanted it, so they pay for it jointly. My husband takes care of the rest. This means toothpaste for all of us, alcohol for the water-heater, soap for the bathroom. He is everything. I just tell them, 'The day you have no more father . . .'

When the money from Rolando's shoe-shining is insufficient, Hebe is faced with making choices: replacing certain products with cheaper ones, restricting purchases, or using up the money she usually manages to save. For example, when Rolando has a bad day when few clients request his services, or even worse if it rains and he has to give up until the weather gets better, he comes back home with very little or no money at all. Hebe is then forced to change her plans for food, replacing expensive foodstuffs by cheaper ones:

Hebe: Because perhaps let's say today, the weather is bad, he'll make four million.[4] He knows that if he brings me four million we might rough it. Instead of buying meat, I'll buy a kilo of potatoes, half a dozen eggs. I'll make an omelet and that's it . . .

When it is impossible to find substitutes and there is little money, they have to restrict the amount purchased:

Hebe: Norberto bought the stove. Since my husband brings money every day, we can afford the five litres of kerosene. If he earns a little less and I can't buy the five litres, if I don't have enough money, I just buy two litres. They are quite confident, they are pretty sure that they won't be left without since Rolando works . . .

When Rolando earns relatively well, Hebe administers the money in such a way as to save some. She keeps accumulating, setting aside whatever she does not spend, keeping it for various purposes. Among these, the purchase of household goods:

Rolando: I always try and spend the least possible, I give my wife a certain amount and keep some money, just in case. At this moment I'm earning an average of three million per day. She says she spends more or less two million. So I give her that. She is very frugal, and from what I give her she holds some money to pay for credit. She buys things for the house like blankets, a set of coffee cups, a set of plates. It's she who saves for all that, from what I give her. I always ask her, 'Do you have any money left, *vieja?*' 'No,' she says. But she sets money aside. And before I realize it, she shows me new blankets. Right now she's spent about nine million on blankets. We really needed them . . .

With these savings, Hebe also pays the utility bills:

Hebe: We agreed that the kids were going to pay the electricity bill, but they don't make enough to pay that for me. So then I've to get the electricity from my husband, from what Rolando brings in every day. . . . Next month, the electricity bill is due and along comes Christmas. I find it hard to save for Christmas and New Year, because it's precisely on the 26th that I have to pay, and I have to gather the money to pay the light. I don't know how much it will come to. So I try to save a million a day, or five, eight, six [hundred] thousand. And I don't touch that.

The contribution of the children towards the family budget is more regular; they know in advance the amounts, their specific destination and when the money will be coming in. Hebe knows exactly what she is going to pay, with what, even before receiving the money at the beginning of every month. Thanks to the children's contribution, not only has Rolando been freed from sole responsibility for the maintenance of the unit but, even more important, the Moreira's have been able to improve their condition by moving into a bigger house and acquiring new furniture and all kinds of household appliances. It was not by chance that this shift in their standard of living took place at the time when the gradual entry of the three youngsters into the labour market allowed them to avail themselves of sums of money previoualy unattainable. A good proportion of that income was directed to purchasing consumer durables such as a new refrigerator, a TV set, a sofa bed, etc. Hebe admits the crucial role of her children:

Hebe: As I've already said, it's thanks to the kids. Because if the children were small I would have nothing. Because, just imagine, my husband is probably earning the same as last year. Because people don't shine their shoes so often, because people look after their money . . .

Even though Hebe administers the children's money – in so far as she is the one who receives it and pays the bills – the decisions regarding purchases are not always hers. The acquisition of the TV set, the cassette player or a cupboard were urged by Norberto or Claudia, in some cases even against their mother's will. Furthermore, these goods are rarely paid in cash, thus creating the obligation of paying monthly instalments.

The considerable amount of money that the children are willing to contribute towards the family budget may certainly seem surprising. For example, both Norberto and Sergio socialize their income to such an extent that they are obliged to resort to Hebe for their daily personal expenses; their transport and recreation expenses depend on what she gives them, following her own calculations, usually in small doses. Why are the children contributing so much so regularly to the family budget? Beyond the solidarity and affective bonds that may lead them to show this attitude, there is a family agreement based on the parents showing their children that what they do is no 'sacrifice' of any sort, but rather the logical counterpart of the benefits they receive for remaining attached to the family:

Hebe: When we had to move out of downtown we talked to them. They are not giving the money to the household. That's what we want them to understand. Because one day Norberto said, 'You take every peso away from me. I'm left without. . . .' 'No, just a second, you are paying for the roof you are living under and for the food I prepare. And for the washing and the ironing too, darling. What you give me is for your own consumption. I don't charge you. What you give me is all spent in paying the rent, instalments, things for everybody's welfare.' That's what they've always been taught. If they are not satisfied, we've already told them a thousand times. 'If you are not satisfied. . . .' When we were going to move we told them: 'Well, we are going to rent a place, you have to contribute so much. If you agree, then come with us.' Because in the end, if you work it out, Rolando is the one who is working exclusively for all of us. Because Norberto can't live anywhere with seventy million; neither can Claudia with eighty, and forget about Sergio. You see? They can't go too far. . . .

The figure of the mother as a prudent and accurate administrator is another important aspect of the economic functioning of this family. She collects the income of all the members and controls most of the expenses.

Hebe: My husband used always to handle the money. Only now I'm doing it. I always used to tell him that the money had to be handled by the wife. Besides, he used to say: 'When the kids go out to work, they'll give me the money. . . .' And I said: 'Listen, the kids have no reason to give you the money. When children start working they must give the money to their mother. And their mother is the one to decide what to do with it. As you know, unfortunately it is the woman who is first left alone. It's always the man that goes first. And if you don't get the children accustomed to giving you the money, today or tomorrow I'm left alone and they won't bear me in mind if they're not accustomed to giving me the money. So you've got to allow them to give me the money. . . .'

But the basic reason for Hebe becoming the focal point lies not so much in her role as mother, but in her role as housewife; according to her, that places her in a better position than anyone else – in other words, better than Rolando – to know what is needed in the household and how it can be obtained.

Hebe: I think men get frightened, because before my husband used to do everything by himself, he would administer the money, he'd give me some and I'd have to account for it. Now no, now it's me. He wouldn't go beyond the refrigerator, the blender, the fan. But new things are always being created, things are innovated, renewed. I'm a progressive person. But in that sense, after the furniture, he wants what is necessary and nothing more. I think men don't realize, they come home and want to have everything; how it came, they don't know. Men don't pay any attention to the details in the house. When he married me, he continued with the same attitude as before our marriage. He would decide, he would buy, he would do everything. Not now. Now I can say: 'Look, I bought two pairs of sheets.' 'And were they necessary?' 'If I bought them it's because they are necessary.' Besides, when there was any problem, Rolando would go and sell things immediately. He wouldn't find another way out. Whereas I'm more conservative. . . .

The Pintos family

Luisa Pintos, mother of six children, lives with five of them (aged between two and eighteen); a six-year-old niece, her grandmother, who brought her up after her mother died when she was only two, and her husband, Cesar, who works out of town and comes back home only at weekends and during the first week of each month. Family income is very regular: Cesar's salary at the end of each month, an additional *per diem* allowance he receives according to the number of days he is out of town, and the grandmother's pension, which she handles for her own needs, contributing to the family budget when she wants to or when Luisa asks her, in order to meet emergencies.

Both Luisa and Cesar think that, given Cesar's job (he works for the National Highway Department and is in charge of a travelling laboratory that tests highway materials), they 'should' live better than they do:

Cesar: In my 'outside' family, everybody is concerned with my salary. I'm away practically the whole month and I collect a *per diem* allowance, but this is an additional effort, isn't it? . .?. So they are troubled about the place I live, not *how* I live, but *where* I live. Because according to my family I should already have a ten-floor fancy town-house, three cars, one for each of the older kids. But that's their problem, not mine. I'm happy living here with my family, and if I agree to live here I don't care about what people say.

Luisa: I live happily. The house is poor but I'm happy here.

Cesar: Besides, it may be poor, but for me it's big inside. Which is what counts, because it is my home. Isn't it? With my wife and children. So the rest . . .

When Cesar gets paid at the end of the month, he puts aside a small amount for his personal expenses and gives the rest to Luisa, who is in charge or organizing daily expenditure. The family budget is arranged in a way in which many current purchases are made with a *libreta*, an informal credit system that regular customers have with various neighbourhood stores or suppliers (the grocer, the butcher, wine delivery, and so on). It is based on registering in a notebook each transaction and settling part of the debt periodically, with no formal deadlines or penalties. Formal instalments for the purchase of household appliances, as well as utility bills (electricity, city taxes), are also paid on a regular basis, monthly or bimonthly. Luisa uses the monthly wage to settle such accounts. Cesar also regularly collects the *per diem* for the days he is away during each month. The family relies on that income as a stable and predictable part of the budget. Hence, Cesar's fear of illness and his reluctance to take any holidays or leave.

> *Luisa:* At the end of the month I get the money. I pay every-thing I owe, and if something is left, that's OK ... I can manage with no cash ... I would rather pay my debts and remain without cash for the rest of the month. Once I've paid everybody, if I'm left without money, bad luck! Anyway I know I can go to the grocer's and 'take' what I need, and they won't say anything to me, but if I owe money I feel bad. ... And what I like even less is for them to come to collect. At times, I can barely make it. I keep estimating all the time. Every day I look into the *libreta* to see how much I have spent, trying to 'square' and make ends meet. If I spend one more million, that's nothing. Besides, everything is going up in price. This month everything went up again, almost double its price. ... I already said that we will have to eat less, and I still don't know how we will manage, because here they can't live without meat. It's as if they'll starve. They do not know how to eat vegetables. ... I don't worry. Money won't kill me. ... If there's no money, bad luck, next month he'll get more. The only debt I have yet to pay is the butcher's, for that I'm expecting the *per diem* money.

Does she usually get to the end of the month with some cash?

> *Luisa:* No, I barely make it, tightly. If not, the *abuela* [grand-mother] will rescue me with her pension, but just now she is getting her pension late. ... Before she used to collect on the 21st or 22nd, but now she collects on the 28th or 29th. She would help me out with the children's bus fare.

Luisa oganizes her shopping daily:

> *Luisa:* Since we buy on credit it turns out to be the same to

buy every day or in bulk. My son buys in big quantities for his mother-in-law. He'd say, 'Mum, I've got to go to the supermarket. I'll bring you oil, potatoes, canned food, tomatoes.' I spent six to seven million. And then the grocer's bill was as if I hadn't spent anything. So I decided to buy directly at the grocer's. Everything I need. Each day I look up what's running out, what's needed, and make up the list.

Maria, the sixteen-year-old daughter, does the shopping:

Luisa: I give Maria the list of things she has to buy. She goes to the butcher's twice a week. It's a bit far away. To the grocer's, she goes every day.

Maria buys what's on her mother's list, although at times she buys things that are not on the list:

Maria: For instance, fruit or mayonnaise. Mom doesn't complain. The kids ask me for lollipops, and at times I bring them chocolates or other sweets.

The arrangement is that Maria is in charge of doing the shopping every day of the week, but never at weekends. Daniel, her twelve-year-old brother, must then take over the shopping. On Saturdays, Maria runs other errands:

Maria: This morning I went to buy bread and then to pay the credit at the store; then I went to buy some spare parts for the heater. . . . Then I went to the optician's to ask for an estimate to have my glasses made. At the store I paid the instalments for the washing machine, the iron and the plastic pool bought for *Reyes*. I paid eight million; the iron was bought this month and the washing machine was bought about three months ago.

Luisa sees daily cash expenses, the 'pocket' money, as residual. She always tries to have some money in the house, at least for the children's bus fare to school. But it is always possible to walk. . . . If there is any money left after paying credits and debits, it is used for clothes, especially for the adolescent children.

Luisa: I stretch as much as I can. For the smaller children, I fix whatever I can find. I have to buy for Daniel and Marcela because they go to school. We don't go out much, so it really doesn't matter, unless there is something special. A couple of months ago we had a wedding, and Maria didn't have a nice dress to wear. We bought her a pretty dress; trousers for Daniel and a dress for Marcela. . . . They have enough clothes to wear around the house. From Marcela, cloths pass on to the two younger kids. Both wear the same size. . . . Maria and Carlitos buy their own clothes. First they ask if they can buy something, they check prices. Now Maria wants a pair of boots; I say they are too expensive, so she is looking around to see where she can get them cheaper; but cheap sometimes turns out expensive. She won't buy the ones that cost eight million, but the four million ones, yes. She says they are good quality.

The Medina family

The flow, rhythm and volume of the income and expenditure of the Medina family – a couple, Nicolas and Rosa, and nine of their twelve children – clearly reflects an unstable situation. Their daily life is based on uncertainty. The only income the family receives on a regular bais is the father's rather meagre monthly wage. Since he arrived in Buenos Aires eleven years ago, Nicolas has worked as a labourer in a construction material yard. His salary never reaches home at a specific time of the month, because of advances he has to ask for. Also, seldom does he receive any of the bonus attached to regular job attendance; rather more frequent is loss of income because of his absences. His drinking weekends have a profound effect on Nicolas' income:

Rosa: You know, this last week he missed work three days, any money he could lay his hands on went on wine . . . and you can imagine what he loses there? It annoys me when he misses work like that, because on top of his earning very little, he loses money for having missed . . .

Occasionally, other income is added to Nicolas'. Rosa tried to palliate the critical situation by getting herself a job as a domestic servant, working by the hour, and his daughter Isabel (sixteen) at times works as a salegirl in a market. Rosa's daily income goes towards buying food: milk, bread and potatoes, whilst Isabel's income tends to be in kind:

Rosa: Sometimes Isabel doesn't bring any money . . . because instead of getting cash she brings something to eat . . . even at

times she takes more than what she has earned . . . so we're
always in the same boat . . .

Stability and durability of both incomes is highly doubtful.
Although mother's and daughter's occasional entries into the labour
market may contribute to ease various crises, they have always gone
back to the unstable situation of depending on the 'ghost' income
of a father who is each day more indifferent to his family responsibilities:

Rosa: You know, the other day we had nothing to eat and any
money he got hold of went to buy wine. . . . It seemed as
if thirst invaded him. You know, he collected the bonus for
childbirth, and also what he inherited from his sister . . . but
I don't know what he did with the money; I swear I didn't see
a peso . . . this happened during the summer holidays. He went
to Santa Fe and, you know, the chap brought money from
there, but he didn't stay here . . . he must have spent it going
out somewhere, wandering from place to place . . . and he had
told me that the money was going to be to fix the house that
is falling to pieces . . . and then he told me he paid what he
owed for the record player . . . but one won't change him . . .

With limited income, expenditure is obviously very limited, not
only in terms of how much is spent but also the timing of it. There
is no organization of the distribution of expenses according to type
of income; the money available always covers the most urgent
expense. If the day Nicolas brings some money home the electricity
bill is due, very likely it will be paid, even though it may be hard
to find something to eat the following day. If when Nicolas collects
his Christmas bonus, the salesman at the neighbourhood store offers
him a luxurious record player to be paid in instalments but with a
high down-payment, Nicolas decides on the matter right then and
there, and the money is gone, with the added commitment of instalments to be paid for several months. his unilateral decision-making
is coupled with a sort of compulsiveness. The consumption pattern
of this family responds to unconnected decisions made by the father.
When there is some money, it is spent – without taking into consideration the impact it may have on the future income or development of the household.

The daily functioning of the household, except when one of the
older daughters has a job or when Rosa goes out to work, depends

first on whatever food is left in the cupboard from a previous purchase. When she cannot resort to the kitchen cupboard, Rosa attempts the complex and not always successful purchase 'on credit' as the neighbourhood grocery. More than once, money found lying around the house has come in useful making up lunch for the children. When these possibilities have been exhausted, the only thing to do is to wait for 'Nicolas' return':

> *Rosa:* I don't know what we are going to eat tonight. . . . If he can ask for money at work, or ask his brother for some, we might eat. If not, we'll have *mate* with milk . . . just anything . . . the truth is that everything is in a mess and now they say that meat is going up again on Saturday . . . and then what? We poor won't be able to eat any more meat.

If we had to convey in a simple image the uncertainty of the daily life of the family, where even meals are uncertain, Rosa's words in one of the first interviews suffice:

> We always wait for him to bring something . . . and if he doesn't . . . we'll see tomorrow . . .

Categories of expenditure

With high inflation and deterioration in real wages, consumers face a chronic instability of prices of basic commodities which, coupled with instability of income, creates great difficulties in budget organization. It is impossible to keep up to date as regards the relative magnitude of changes in incomes and prices. Consequently, adjustments in consumption patterns take time and tend to be irregular; indebtedness becomes chronic.

One way of facing this apparently chaotic situation is by establishing a direct relationship between types of income and types of expenditure. Rather than an overall budget, people organize small 'packages' of income–expenditure. Obviously, this can only be done in households where there is more than one source and type of income. The most stable and predictable income goes towards paying 'fixed' expenses; the variable income towards the more elastic expenses. The Moreira's example is eloquent in this respect.

A basic distinction in budgetary organization is between daily or 'pocket' expenditure, for which one must have cash; monthly expenses, that are billed periodically in a regular way (rent, credit instalments, electricity, taxes, and so on); and purchases in 'open accounts', where payment is more elastic and may be delayed or negotiated until the necessary cash is available.

Daily expenditure is incurred in a very large number of small transactions. One must have some cash every day to pay for transport to and from work or study, when one is outside the home, and cigarettes. These are essential expenses for a person's daily functioning. Thus, it is usual for wage-earners individually to reserve a certain amount of their income for these expenses, before contributing to the family budget. But the daily expenses of those members of the household who do not earn an income (housewives, students, elderly people) must be covered with money from the common budget, normally handled by the woman/housewife. These expenses are rarely budgeted or accounted for and it is frequent to come across situations in which there is no cash available for them.

Food for the family is sometimes a daily expense paid in cash; in other cases, the whole or part of it becomes a monthly expenditure through the system of local credit, the *libreta*. It is unusual for a family to use this system of credit for all food expenses. Normally, families may have *libretas* at one or two shops (for example, at the grocer's and butcher's), whilst the rest of the shopping is paid in cash (bread, vegetables, etc.). When there is no cash, consumption is reorganized in order to include only goods purchased at the stores where a notebook is held. The use of the *libreta* converts daily food into a monthly expenditure, to be paid together with the rent, taxes, the electricity bill and commercial credit. 'Paying the *libreta*' is added to the payments to be made at the end of the month. This credit system is preferred by the households that primarily receive stable monthly incomes, such as the Pintos. Their basic principle is not to get behind with the payment of debts:

Luisa: I prefer to be left without a peso before owing somebody money. If I owe the grocer, I pay him, I still owe five million, so now I give him sixty and five when I'm paid. 'Sure, Madam'. Let's suppose that Cesar's salary gets delayed one more week; I get desperate and I often go along and say, 'Luigi, they've got behind with the payment, it's not that I don't want to pay you.' 'And who asked you to pay?' That's how things are . . . when it was Carlitos' birthday my husband hadn't collected his per diem; it was over a week's delay. I wanted to get meat but I hadn't paid the butcher the twenty million I owed him.

179

So I went along to Ruga's and said, 'Ruga, I'm going to ask you for a favour. I still haven't paid you but I need some meat.' 'Did anybody claim for anything?' 'No, but as I still haven't paid you', 'I didn't say anything'. Everything I pay, I write down, because if not I forget. The wine merchant . . . I wasn't quite sure whether I'd paid him or not, because he is the first one I pay. When the milkman comes, I pay him, when the wine merchant comes, I pay him . . .

How much did she pay for milk this month?

Luisa: Only four million and a half. The baker's bill doesn't add up to much either. One and a half kilos of bread per day. So then, I wasn't quite sure whether I'd paid the wine merchant; so the following Friday I asked him: 'Tell me, did I pay you this month?' 'No, Madam.' 'Please forgive me; if you wish to leave me the wine do so, and I'll pay you everything next month.' 'Don't worry, Madam.' When I collected, the first one I paid was the wine merchant. It's different if I forget. . . . Besides I always check how much money I have left . . .

The Arias family

The Arias family is a good example o a different strategy. The household is composed of five persons: Nilda works in a private school as a kitchen assistant, with a monthly salary; in addition, she works overtime doing some cleaning which she collects every week. Angel works at a meat market; he also does some extra work within or outside the company. Moncho, a thirty-year-old nephew, drives an urban passenger bus, and usually works overtime. Their two children, Patricia who is fifteen and Luis Alberto, twelve, are both students, although Luis Alberto has also had some temporary working experience. Everyone's income is 'pooled'. Both parents and the nephew contribute towards the pool. As a general rule, the Arias do not agree with the *libreta* system:

Angel: Thank God, we buy everything in cash. We don't want to ask for a *libreta*. When one has a *libreta*, it's easy to say, 'Go and get it with the *libreta*' and then when you have to pay. . . . On Friday or Saturday we go to the market and buy meat and other merchandise. Or if not I bring meat for the whole week.

With the money she earns working overtime, Nilda buys the food for the weekend, when they all eat together and try to have better food:

> *Nilda:* Food is what we spend most on. Depending on the money I have, I go and buy. We spend most on meat.

The organization of expenses changed when Angel started collecting on a monthly basis instead of each fortnight:

> *Nilda:* Now he collects monthly . . . but I think he earns very little because he only gets a hundred and something per month . . .

Does the change from fortnightly to monthly salary help?

> *Nilda:* I really don't know, because when he collected every fifteen days we never bought anything on credit, but now there comes a time when I have to buy on credit in order to have money for the bus fare, for me or for the kids.

Where does she buy on credit?

> *Nilda:* At the greengrocer's, but I'm careful. I don't buy that much. . . . Sometimes I spend twenty-five; the other day I thought I'd spent more than ever and it only added up to fourteen, and I was having fits because I thought: 'The salary isn't going to be enough.' But I don't buy much. There are people who, since they can buy on credit, then 'bring, bring stuff, afterwards you'll pay for it', but I'm careful, it has to be something I need, then I go and buy it on credit. . . .

Credit in neighbourhood stores is limited and depends on the occupational and income stability of the client. When family income is scarce, unstable and unpredictable, it is almost impossible to have access to any type of credit. This is the case with the Medina family; several times their *libreta* has been cancelled due to lack of payment.

Credit and the creditor

At times of recession and scarcity, people ask themselves: 'What can be postponed or eliminated?' In general, repairs to household appliances are postponed, no medicine is bought, improvements to the house can wait for the future. Less food, or food of lower quality, might also be bought, and fewer clothes. Daily consumption is based on an accumulation of discrete, unrelated decisions, rather than on a planned and co-ordinated budget.

When resorting to credit, payments follow an implicit logic: in principle, payment, or delay of payment, does not depend on the urgency of the need satisfied by the goods or services concerned but on the characteristics of the lender. Payment is delayed if the lender can 'wait': when credit is established on the basis of a personal relationship; when the parties concerned are immersed in wider networks of relationships where the affective-emotional bonds are important – as sometimes where the grocer is concerned and almost always in the case of debts with relatives – or when 'for pity' the lender will not penalize the debtor.

A common figure in popular neighbourhoods is that of the 'Turk' or 'Russian' who sells clothes, sheets, blankets and towels. He is a door-to-door salesman who peridocially visits his clients, offering goods according to the season – school clothes when classes begin, blankets and warm clothes in winter. The sales are made on credit, with the tacit agreement that it is licit to 'stretch' the debt beyond the agreed period, should this be necessary. The interest for the risk run is, of course, included in the price.[5]

Hebe: I bought this tablecloth at my doorstep. And, logically, a tablecloth sold here is always going to be more expensive: two million two hundred to be paid in monthly instalments of four hundred and fifty. I paid the first month and the chap never turned up again. I've bought several things like that. They sell glasses, sheets, blankets. I tell you I bought everything here at my doorstep. Because for me it's easier to buy here than to gather all the money to buy three blankets, because I just don't have the cash. When I buy here, I sign documents. The first thing I bought here was the quilt for my bed. The second time I bought three blankets for which I paid seven million each. And I don't have 21 million to pay in cash, so I pay a million a month for each blanket. And then came another chap and I bought two sets of sheets and three bed-covers for the summer which I still haven't used, but I bought them because I thought the more I wait, the more expensive things get.

It may also happen that the debt is cancelled before it is due. Formal credit, for which the contract establishes penalties in case of delays, is paid more carefully and punctually: the rent, taxes and the electricity bill, instalments for the purchase of a lot, and house-hold appliances. When people decide to delay these payments, they are aware of the possible consequences: confiscation or loss of the goods.[6]

In summary, there seems to be a certain logic in periodic expenditure, in terms of the lender; a different one for cash consumption. In the case of the former, the formality of the relationship and the potential penalities are more important factors than the nature of the goods or services. The latter depends on how essential the expense is and how long can it be delayed. On other occasions, there is a certain urgency to spend when there is money available. Furthermore, there doesn't seem to be a clear way of establishing priorities between one type of expense and another. Instalments may be paid even before knowing whether there will be money to buy food.

Within this dynamics of expenditure, the degree of control that the various members of the household have on income and expenditure is important. Fixed expenses are covered by the income of members with stable jobs. The power that arises from earning money tends to be translated into decision-making power and the ability to make commitments: deciding on the rent of the house, purchasing land or consumer durables, assuming responsibility for the corresponding credits, generally formalized in contracts. These decisions are taken by the husband/father, or sometimes by the working children. When, as in the case of Hebe Moreira, the wom-an/housewife handles the overall budget, she does it as a result of explicit struggles. In general, food and daily expenses are left to women. Somehow they manage to get what is needed. Women also handle less formal credit (at the 'Turk's', at the grocer's) and are the ones who have access to and maintain networks of mutual aid and informal relationships (among relatives, neighbours, and with the social services in parishes and municipal hospitals, etc.).

The dwelling and household equipment

Any observer interested in the standard of living of working-class sectors from a 'rational' perspective that privileges 'real' consumption needs, will be concerned after visiting the homes of these families. It is not unusual to see people going hungry when there is a (broken) high-fi in the home; and in dwellings where there is broken glass in a window and no running water, there will be a

colour TV set. If one were to rely on a parameter of administratively
defined welfare, based on scientifically constructed priorities of
needs, household over-equipment would be absolutely out of proportion with other areas of consumption, especially the quality of
the house itself.

Working-class sectors have great difficulty in gaining access to
housing (Feijoo, 1983). The costs involved are enormous and cannot
easily be included in the regular budget of a worker's family. The
'great' decisions imply many years of commitment: land to be paid
for in endless instalments; the slow process of building the house,
starting with just one room and then enlarging and improving it
little by little; the purchase of construction materials that are gradually accumulated to allow future enlargements and improvements.

There is a remarkable difference between the situation of families
who own their house and those who pay rent. When the family
rents, the monthly expenditure is fixed and may be calculated in
the budget, whilst owning the house means continual repairs or
improvements. However, leasing is often considered a transitory
stage, and thus payment of instalments for the plot of land and
savings for future construction are added to the budget. Having
one's own dwelling is viewed as a definitive solution to the housing
problem, even though the efforts may be excessive compared to the
quite unsatisfactory results obtained. When a family gives up hope
of having its own dwelling, it may allocate these resources to other
objectives, either to other investments (in one case, the purchase of
a station-wagon to enter the transport trade as a second job) or to
improving the standard of living or the level of consumption.

Maria and Pedro, rural–urban migrants, live with one daughter
(the second was born in 1980) in an apartment that goes with
Pedro's job as a janitor in an apartment building. They were asked
whether they had plans to buy anything:

Maria: Well, a piece of land to build a house, or if not to
look for a house, because if one looks around one might find
something not too expensive, but I'd have to do the searching
because he can't go far from here. It would have to be on
Sundays, Saturdays. . . . I would go to my sisters' . . . so one
of them can accompany me. Where my sisters live, the area's
very nice.

Maria's cousin (present at the interview): Do you remember
Pedro didn't know whether to buy the station-wagon or the

plot of land? So I tell him he'd better buy the piece of land, because you're not going to take your things there in the truck. 'But it's much better,' he says, 'maybe I can go to the country-side . . . I've got the things in the truck. . . .'

He has these two alternatives, either the truck or the piece of land?

Maria: Yes, but he also prefers to buy the lot first. Anytime they might kick us out of here.

Cousin: Besides that, you can start building the house, because you are not going to move there in the conditions we did; our house wasn't finished, the roof was missing and we had to go and live there because we had to hand in the house. . . .

Eight months, the station-wagon bought by Pedro came to inter-rupt Maria's dream of buying a piece of land. With this station-wagon, Pedro does odd jobs to supplement their income:

Maria: He wanted the truck first. And he won. He won because my brothers defended his position. They'd say, 'If it's to work why won't you let him buy it?' We thought so, but now with this . . . [She refers to the temporary breakdown of the station-wagon that doesn't allow him to do his odd jobs.]

Domestic equipment is another story. With some exceptions, there is a considerable gap between the variety and quantity of domestic appliances and the quality and variety of furniture. Physi-cal space is limited and the pieces of furniture tend to be old, worn out, bought second-hand or inherited from relatives. In turn, household appliances are plentiful and new ones are added almost constantly.

These goods are bought on the market. Only in cases of emer-gency (a broken iron or a sewing machine urgently needed) may they be borrowed or transferred through informal networks. Neither are they a part of the public services or goods to be obtained as social rights or through charity. In other words, they are goods bought privately, for family use. Undoubtedly, each one of the household appliances has a certain use value that contributes towards family welfare, either by helping with the domestic tasks (refrigerator, washing machine), or by increasing the level of infor-mation, or by contributing to the family's recreation (television sets, record players, cassette players). This potential use value influences the decision to purchase the goods. But there are additional factors to explain their massive presence in working-class homes.

Here it is necessary to distinguish two time periods during fieldwork. From 1978 to 1980, economic policies opened the market and flooded it with imported household appliances, including articles that were new to Argentina (especially audio equipment and colour TV). Working-class families were active purchasers on this market. The deep recession of the subsequent period led to a considerable decrease in the sale of this type of product.

Domestic appliances are bought because the supply is right there, aggressively attacking the potential consumerg, offering credit and flexible payment conditions which are tailored to each family's income pattern. Purchases are often made on impulse:

Nilda: We were walking by with Patricia and I didn't even look that way, and Patricia says to me: 'Look, mother, what a beautiful piece of furniture.' Well, I took a look at it and said: 'You're right, it's very nice, let's go in and find out the price of it,' but without the intention of buying it. We did so and were told: 'Fifty, to be paid in two instalments.' So right then and there I came and paid the first half and said: 'Well, I'll speak to my husband and perhaps come back tonight,' and he said somebody else had ordered it for the end of the month. Well, that evening I took my husband and showed it to him, and I left a down-payment.

In general, families have a credit account in a neighbourhood household-appliance store. It is not an impersonal credit line in a big store, but a personal relationships with the salesmen, who use it to induce buying. The credit line is continuously active, being renewed when the outstanding debt for the previously bought goods is about to be cancelled. People talks about 'drawing' (*sacar*) the objects from the store. The dealer keeps an inventory of the objects each family-client has and what they 'could' want or need, showing them these objects to create the need and demand. For example, one of the families interviewed started talking about cassette players, including references to the tape recorder used during the interviews; a few months later they had 'drawn' one; not long after, the conversation included the advantages of a colour TV set. They then showed a brochure that their dealer had given them when they went to pay the instalment for the cassette player; just a few months later a colour TV set entered the family room.

Credit of this type is part of the lifestyle of these families. Goods bought in this way are not always useful and usable. A floor cleaner polisher given as a Mother's day present has been sitting in a corner for the last two years without ever having been used; such a device is totally unsuitable for the floors of the house. The family had plans for improving the floors at some time in the future so that they would be able to wax them. In another house, the record player (out of order) takes up so much room that it is clearly a nuisance in the small space available in the dwelling of a family with ten children. Besides, household appliances may easily break, since the instructions for their use are not simple to follow and the conditions of installation (including the electrical wiring of the house) are often inadequate. And even if the payment of the monthly instalment is included in the ordinary family budget, repairs are not. A large number of broken household appliances wait months to be repaired.

An alternative used by households with lower and less stable incomes is the purchase of second-hand household appliances, sometimes out of order. The price of an out-of-order second-hand object is very low compared to the original price; people carry out such an operation in the hope of fixing the device and being able to use it. As the reader may imagine, repairs carried out at home hardly ever work and commercial repairs are very expensive and may be deferred, thus increasing the number of appliances that are out of order.

During the interview carried out in August 1979, Ramona tells how they bought a used refrigerator. They paid little for it because it had some parts missing. They bought it from a relative who had bought it to get married. As he didn't in the end get married, he left the refrigerator at a brother's. Ramona and David paid for it in cash. A month later when asked whether they had fixed the refrigerator, they said they hadn't: it cooled a little, but the self-starter didn't work. Their plan was to have it fixed by a nephew who 'is very busy'. Four months later, in December – at the height of summer:

Ramona: We still haven't done anything about it. We still haven't had it fixed. The man who came to see it says that the service will cost twenty-five million to be paid in two instalments. . . . I use everything as I buy it, because if not you just can't manage, it all goes bad. . . . I go and look for meat in the afternoon because I almost always cook in the afternoon; at midday I just buy anything and in the afternoon I cook so we can all eat.

In March the following year, the story continues:

Ramona: He took it to be fixed across there but now there's something else missing. ['Across there' refers to the workshop where Luis works] The coiling burnt out; it heats up a little, it doesn't quite work.

In May, the refrigerator hadn't yet been fixed. There was a similar story with a second-hand black-and-white TV set, a huge old model. The image lasted for a couple of weeks. After that, they used it only for listening.

The great emphasis placed on the purchase of household appliances has a symbolic meaning, besides obvious use value. In the first place, given the difficulty of access to more adequate housing and the very high cost of housing improvements (for example, the cost of installing running water or a bathroom), people with low incomes may choose to buy more accessible small goods, but 'first-class' ones. These are novel goods that can be shown off and help make the family more presentable, not only in social relationships in the domestic domain but also outside it, in public life. Especially for adolescents, the possibility of talking with friends about colour TV or about the latest cassettes opens up a field of definition of 'integrated' social identities, not marginal to the 'advances' of the consumption world.[7]

With respect to the purchase of household appliances, as well as in relation to clothes, the desires and aspirations of the youngsters play an important role, even though the final decision lies with whoever is going to sign for the credit. Since the basic household appliances (refrigerator, gas stove, radio, sewing machine) have been incorporated into the lifestyle of the Argentine working class for some decades, the additions in the last few years have been made in the area of goods related to the youngsters' free time: cassette players, colour TV sets, record players.[8] In a way, access to these new consumer goods, not long ago 'luxury' items reserved for the rich, must have acted as a compensation mechanism as regards the deterioration of consumption in other areas of basic needs (for example, health and education).

Household appliances are overloaded with symbolic meanings,

all of them related to hiding inferiority and deterioration in the standard of living. They may be taken subjectively as evidence of the existence of a margin for selection and choice, indicating living conditions that are less deplorable and dead-end. For the adult who takes the decision to buy, usually the father/head-of-the-household, they are the evidence of his power as a consumer on the market and as a supplier of satisfaction for his family. For the adolescent who enjoys them, household appliances help his public image of a relatively 'privileged' social condition (or at least make his position less hopeless).The most pragmatic view of the acquisition of this type of object seems to be expressed by mothers, who consider household appliances an investment and may voice the opinion that whenever some money is available, it should be invested in consumer durables; if not, the money disappears, spent on goods that leave no trace. Even when such objects are not used, should there be an emergency in which no money is available to buy food for the children, they could be sold or pawned for cash. Situations of this type experienced by the people interviewed endorse this perception.

In macro-social terms, the presence of household appliances cannot be conceived from the perspective of a theory of 'basic human needs' that studies the specific historical and cultural 'satisfiers' of these needs. It indicates rather that the nature of human needs cannot be understood without an explicit reference to the actual daily modalities in which these needs are met within specific social systems (Leiss, 1976: 8). In so far as these objects are the prototypes of the consumption society within which the individuals orient their needs towards a type of satisfaction identified with an increasing number and variety of goods, these objects have a privileged position in the basic consumption needs of the masses.

Adolescents' consumption

The contrast in the quality of clothing of different members of a family is enormous. Smaller children, who don't yet go to school, may be dressed in rags; the mother, whilst she is at home, wears old clothes, but if she works, she does have a 'respectable' outfit to go out in; and the father dresses a little better, given that he spends more time outside his home. There is no doubt that the best dressed ones are the adolescents. Not only do they wear clothes that are clean and in a good state of repair, but they are also always dressed in the latest fashion.

Adolescents' clothes constitute a permanent subject of discussion within the family. They ask, demand, and seem to have power, since (within certain limits) they obtain what they demand. They do not control the money directly but demand it from their parents who, after voicing more or less opposition, finally give in to pressure. Mothers complain most often about their children's requirements. As has already been pointed out, the desires and needs of youngsters also prevail in the purchase of household appliances.

How is it possible for adolescents to have such an influence on decisions regarding expenditure? Not the youngsters who work and have their own income, but those who have no personal income and at times neither contribute towards collective domestic tasks nor study (Jelin and Feijoo, 1980).

Why do the parents give in so often? One can accept that they have altruistic feelings that are satisfied when they see their children happy with the goods they want. One can also accept that the advertising media orient their messages towards youth, since they are aware of their influence on family decisions concerning expenditure. Family interaction in this area, however, seems to be more than 'giving in' to pressure. There seems to be an acceptance of the 'need' of adolescents to be well dressed, to have money to go out dancing with their friends, to have a soft drink or to go to the latest rock concert. Isabel, mother of four, was asked whether the children argue about clothes:

Isabel: Sure they do. They want to buy the clothes themselves. The other day the eldest was going to buy himself a pair of trousers. Well, said his father, I'll give you up to seven. No, no, he said, I don't want a pair of trousers that costs seven. I saw one at ten million. I'm going to buy that pair and I won't bother you people any more until the summer. . . . When they buy things they go in for the latest fashion! When they were small I used to buy them what I wanted. Now one can't buy them anything because they don't like it. They have to go themselves and they go in for what's expensive. Adolescents express themselves through their way of dressing; a boy may not have all the words to speak to a girl, so he dresses well so the girl will look at him. . . . As they don't have a well defined personality, they give great importance to the way they dress. Afterwards they get over it.

If this line of reasoning about the symbolic content of goods is carried a stage further the operation of a family mechanism of 'public presentation' through adolescents may be detected. They are the ones who participate the most in commercialized leisure activities, the ones who go out the most, who have most contact outside their kinship network (except, of course, for contacts related to a labour situation), more contacts among their peers, selected by affinity. Consequently, the family image for outsiders is explicitly expressed in the presentation of these youngsters to their friends' world. For a son or daughter 'not to have anything to wear', or not to be able to go out dancing because of lack of money, would be an admission of failure, not only on the part of the youngsters but also their parents who were not able to give them what they needed.[9]

In this respect, family pressure on adolescents to go out to work and earn their own income is not exerted primarily with a direct contribution to the family budget in mind, but rather so that they can buy more and better clothes and do what they like without stretching the family budget:

Nilda (referring to Patricia's work): I would like her to work because then she will get accustomed to working and, at the same time, will be able to buy what she pleases. We buy her things, but maybe not all she would life. If it were for me, I would dress her in the latest fashion, today she goes out with one, tomorrow with another, that would make like me very happy.

In another family, going through a period of economic hardship, including a decline in real income, the mother complains that her son makes demands but does not seriously consider looking for a job (not in order to contribute to the family budget but to 'do what he likes'). The day the job-hunting discussion between Marcelo and his mother was witnessed, he was dressed in the latest fashion, as usual. As his mother pointed out, even though they didn't have enough money for food, there was a tape recorder on the table, an element ever present in the culture of urban adolescents. Marcelo is the second son. His elder brother studies and can only do odd jobs at weekends. Marcelo has finished a short technical career and now faces the problem of how to meet his daily needs, that revolve around clothes and money for his own expenses. That day, Marcelo had just returned from an unsuccessful search for work. His attitude, however, was not one of frustration, since more than earning a living, he wanted to get a 'respectable' job. When he arrived, a very tense conversation took place between his mother, who repeatedly expressed her anguish, and Marcelo, who seemed to express a relative lack of interest in the family problem:

Isabel: And meanwhile we have to eat and pay the telephone bill and he has to dress and buy himself tennis shoes, because he wears them out, because he uses up shampoo, and he uses up the soap in the bathroom, he uses up everything. . . . I always brought them up to appreciate their environment. . . . But what happens is that now, like in Marcelo's case, they don't have their feet on the ground; he doesn't say, 'Well, the old folk need dough – excuse the expression, the vulgar language – the old people need dough so I'm going to do just anything until I manage to get a job.' . . . But he's a sixteen-year-old boy and is thinking of his looks. . . .

Another adolescent, Maria Pintos, seems to be more 'family-oriented'. She wants to work to buy herself clothes, but also to buy things for the house and presents for her younger brother. With her first salary, earned in a temporary summer job, she bought a set of coffee cups for the house. Perhaps, as she belongs to a family that enjoys a slightly higher socio-economic level, her ambitions as regards the family's 'presentation' go beyond her own clothing and include some 'small luxuries' in the house.

Some final comments

In the daily intra-domestic dynamics, interactions and decisions regarding consumption and budgeting are not separate from other dimensions of domestic relationships. Not only do they happen simultaneously but they are also interdependent. Decisions on expenditure are part of a complex system within which the division of labour and the criteria that yield authority and control are discussed and decided on at the same time. All this happens in an area in which love and affection, mutual duties and obligations, are also at stake.

The rest of this chapter shifts the level of analysis from consumption and expenditure to a consideration of conflicts and alliances as an expression of intra-domestic dynamics.

Given the chronic scarcity of monetary resources, decisions concerning distribution of expenses cause recurring intra-family conflict, though these are not necessarily central to everyday domestic life. The dynamics of expenditure covers an area in which decision-making is a daily and recurrent fact, following a logic that depends on the type and amount of income, on changes in the price structure, and on the 'needs' and desires of family members.

Other areas of domestic discussion and decision-making are relatively more stable and do not require such frequent negotiation. The intra-domestic division of labour, which implies deciding when members change from 'dependent' to worker, is not permanently questioned in daily life. In general, there are strong social norms that differentiate roles according to sex, with minor adjustments and negotiations based on the acceptance of those principles. Changes are only decided in crisis situations (illness, loss of a job) or at times of transition in the life cycle (children starting or graduating from school, births, passage from schooling to the search for work). This does not mean that there are no conflicts regarding the division of labour. On the contrary, these exist and may be severe, based on the opposition of deeply-rooted values and principles. Whether women 'must' or 'may' go out to work is a clear example.[10]

There are two basic areas of intra-domestic conflict and alliance: the distinction between gender and the distinction between generations. In the adult couple, the division of the main responsibilities is not challenged: the woman/mother/housewife is in charge of domestic work and the man is the supplier of monetary income for the family's maintenance. Problems may arise when women work outside the home or complain that the working men – husbands and sons – do not help sufficiently in domestic tasks. A woman is in charge of housework simply because she is a woman, before being a wife or mother. Single women also do housework, and mothers expect their daughters to participate in these tasks. This may generate an area of conflict between mothers and daughters who do not necessarily accept the gender typification of roles. And it generates tensions between daughters and sons, in that the former demand that their brothers have equal domestic responsibilities. (Jelin and Feijoo, 1980).

With regard to consumption, the distinction between generations is always important. Sons and daughters, especially when they reach adolescence, demand personal items and consumer durables as well as cash for their recreational activities. The demands of girls and boys, however, are different. The girls seem more family-oriented, ready to place the household's collective needs and those of their parents before their own.

Claudia Moreira is an example of this. Unlike her brother, who also contributes to the maintenance of the household but under pressure and permanent insistence on the part of his parents, she seems to do it of her own will, in collaboration with the group, setting aside to some extent the satisfiaction of her own likings and preferences. Besides the agreed contribution she makes to the family budget, under which she and her brother pay the rent and some credit instalments, Claudia regularly buys other things for the household and its members:

Hebe: She started working at the age of fourteen and earned very little. But with what she earned, paying with great sacrifice, she would dress us all. We have the house full of things thanks to her, there are lots of second-hand things, because we lost everything when we went to live in the countryside. Norberto takes care of purchasing what he likes. The stereo. But, of course, all this is secondary. Claudia thinks a lot more of things for the house than the oldest. . . . She gives me first and then starts spending. For example, last month she gave me a set of cups, with a coffee pot and sugar bowl; she gave me a centrepiece, poultry shears, things that I sometimes say: I have to buy such and such a thing, and time goes by. Well, Claudia turns up with that . . . because Claudia knows how to administer her money well. First of all she is going to make sure that I lack nothing. With the peso that's left over, she knows I would like such a thing, so then she keeps what was left over and the following month pools it. . . .

This type of behaviour promotes understanding between mothers and daughters. For mothers, it is part of their role-definition as protectors of the household's and the smaller children's consumption. No doubt the cultural norm that identifies the role of mother and that of a woman is important in this respect, since it inhibits the expression of personal interests that could be regarded as 'selfish'. Consequently, the mother's struggle (sometimes allied to her daughters') is aimed at controlling resources, in her capacity of protector of the 'collective interest', and is identified, in the first place, with feeding and caring for the smaller children and, secondly, with the maintenance of satisfactory domestic equipment. Conflict arises with her husband when he 'neglects' these priorities and diverts resources for his own wishes or for the needs of other relatives, especially his family of origin.[11]

In summary, gender and generation are present in a highly dynamic manner in the micro-social process of family decision-making regarding consumption and, through it, regarding the life-style of the household.[12] An in-depth analysis of the daily life of some working-class families shows that these areas of intra-family confrontation are always present, and constitute the axis of the articulation of everyday intra-domestic dynamics.

A different question concerns the macro-social meaning of the intra-domestic dynamics. At the level of hypothesis or conjecture, the existence of conflict and alliance is related to the perception that individuals have of their alternatives and options. Of course, the range of options is not endless, it is structurally framed and limited. Continuous discussions and decisions in daily life may have the appearance of a constant renewal of options and selections, while hiding the structural limitations. This is particularly visible in the expansion of manufactured goods in the basic working-class shopping basket, especially fashionable clothes and household appliances. Can one talk about freedom when playing a game in which the participants elaborate strategies and affect results, but where the rules are totally outside their control? Under such conditions, playing implies accepting these rules and regulations.

Notes

1. The paper on which this chapter is based is part of a research project on 'Households and living standards among the urban popular sectors: labour force participation and consumption in Buenos Aires' carried out at CEDES during 1979–82. This chapter was prepared with the collaboration of Maria del Carmen Feijoo, Juan José Llovet and Silvina Ramos.
2. In this study attention is focused on consumption strategies. The analysis of the division of labour and patterns of participation in productive activities is further developed in Jelin and Feijoo (1980).
3. As is usual in this type of study, all names have been changed.
4. References are to nominal quantities of money, exactly has they were registered during the interviews. Due to the extremely high inflation rates during the period in which the families were followed (three years

of periodic visits), the reader should not pay any attention to the figures mentioned by the subjects.

5. An analysis of risk calculation in granting credit to popular sector consumers in the United States is presented by Caplowitz (1967).

6. The family histories gathered show several cases of families that have lost their lots owing to delay in paying instalments though they had already paid part of the total price.

7. Access to mass consumption has been an important element in the conformation of the Argentine working-class identity since massive incorporation to national life through *Peronismo*.

8. The extension of these consumer goods is related to the opening up of the economy during the years of dictatorship, when the relative prices of these goods were remarkably reduced. It was also influenced, earlier, by the extension of the consumption credit system. There are no studies on these processes within the country. The expansion of consumption of household appliances in Brazil is analysed by Wells (1976). For a comparative analysis, see Filgueira (1981).

9. There is also the realization that friendship among youngsters establishes the bonds for future marriages, and for this a 'respectable' appearance is important.

10. In the families interviewed, some husbands were against their wives working outside the home. On the other hand, women had a different outlook on the matter, not considering domestic and working roles as incompatible options. They accepted the idea and wished to work outside their homes, but they also accepted domestic work as their main responsibility (Jelin and Feijoo, 1980).

11. An extreme example of this situation is Rosa Medina, who complains about her husband's drunkenness not only because of the money he spends on drink but also because he is incapable of work the following day. The complaint was similar when her husband decided to go to his province of origin to visit a sick sister, diverting resources meant for the family's maintenance – both the expenses related to the trip and his lack of earnings because of his absence.

12. Other crucial areas of consumption, not included in this study, cover decisions on health and education. The is analysed by Llovet (1981), Little is known about the latter's micro-social dynamics.

8

FAMILY AND CLASS IN CONTEMPORARY AMERICA: NOTES TOWARDS AN UNDERSTANDING OF IDEOLOGY

Rayna Rapp

This chapter is grounded in two contexts, one political and one academic. The political context is that of the women's movement, in which a debate concerning the future of the family always seems to be raging. Many readers will be familiar with the meeting in which someone stands up and asserts that the nuclear family ought to be abolished because it is degrading and constraining to women. Usually, someone else (often representing a Third World position) follows on her heels, pointing out that the attack on the family represents a white middle-class position and that other women need their families for support and survival. Evidently both speakers are, in some senses, right. And just as evidently they are not talking about the same families. Those different notions of family need to be explored if an important split in the women's movement is to be healed. This means taking seriously the things women say about their experiences in their families, especially as they vary by class.

The second context out of which this chapter grows is the academic study of the contemporary American family. Over the last few years, in reading eclectically in sociology, demography, urban planning, and policy literature, the author has tried to sort out what is known (or not known) about women's experiences in their families. Here, too, a debate is raging over the future of the family – books have included titles such as *The Fractured Family*: journals on family co-ordination and counselling, and courses at every level from high school to graduate studies speak of the family in crisis. On the other hand, *Here To Stay* (to name but one title) and a spate of studies re-analysing the divorce rate provide reassurance that the American family is simply changing, not disappearing. This debate seems to mystify the subject it claims to clarify (Bane, 1976; O'Neil, 1977; Novak, 1976),; which is not surprising, since the family is a topic that is ideologically charged. In order to gain some under-standing of the importance of ideology in analysing the family, there are two fields which ought to be considered for perspective. One is recent work carried out on the history of the family (Pleck, 1976; Lasch, 1975–6; Tilly and Scott, 1978.) A great many innovative studies reveal similar issues in historical perspective; for as long as modern records concerning families, have been kept it seems that people have been speculating on the future of the institution. The last decade of social history should caution us to moderate our alarmism. At the very least, we have learned that all societies contain a multiplicity of family forms, the structural arrangements of which respond to complex conditions.

The second field that adds perspective to the issue is anthro-pology, which studies the family and kinship systems both at home and abroad. Anthropology reminds us that we are *all* participant observers when we study the American family. It has been pointed out that our understandings often get in the way and more often express the ideology and norms of our culture than an analysis. This word of warning leads to an examination not only of what differing groups of people *say* about their families but also of what they actually *do* in their families. It also leads to an examination of the ways in which the concept of family itself is ideological in social science.

The archetypical political debaters arguing over the meaning of the family are not talking about the same families. Neither are the social scientists. A distinction should be drawn between families and households, and their relation to one another examined. The entities in which people actually live are not families, but house-holds (as any census-taker, demographer or fieldworking anthropol-ogist will agree). Households are the empirically measurable units within which people pool resources and perform certain tasks. Goody analyses them as units of production, reproduction and consumption (Goody, 1972). They are residential units within which personnel and resources are distributed and connected. Households may vary in their membership composition and in their relation to resource allocation, especially in a system such as the American one. That is to say they vary systematically in their ability to hook into, accumulate and transmit wealth, wages or welfare. This seems a simple unit to define.

Families, on the other hand, are a bit more slippery. In English, 'family' tends to mean household. But analytically, the concept means something else. For all classes of Americans, the word has at least two levels of meaning (Goody, 1972; Schneider and Smith, 1973). One is normative: husbands, wives and children are a set of relatives who should live together (that is, the nuclear family). the other meaning includes a more extended network of kin relations that people may activate selectively – the American family includes relations by blood and marriage. The concept of family is presumed in America to carry a heavy load of affect. We say, 'Blood is thicker than water,' 'Till death do us part,' 'You can choose your friends, but not your relatives,' and so on. This chapter will argue that the concept of family also carries a heavy load of ideology.

The reason for this is that the family is the normative, correct way in which people are recruited into households. It is through families that people enter into productive, reproductive and consumption relations. The two genders enter them differently. Families organize households, and it is within families that people experience the absence or presence, the sharing or withholding, of basic poolable resources. 'Family' (as a normative concept in American culture) reflects those material relations; it also distorts them. As such, the concept of family is a socially necessary illusion which simultaneously expresses and masks recruitment to relations of production, reproduction and consumption – relations that condition different kinds of household resource bases in different class sectors. Our notions of family absorb the conflicts, contradictions and tensions actually generated by those material, class-structured relations that households hold to resources in advanced capitalism. 'Family', as we understand (and misunderstand) the term, is conditioned by the exigencies of household formation, and serves as a shock absorber to keep households functioning. People are recruited and kept in households by families in all classes, yet the families they have (or don't have) are not the same.

Having asserted that households and families vary by class, that third concept, class, should now be considered. If ever a concept carried a heavy weight of ideology, it is the concept of class in American social science. There is a vast and muddled literature which attempts to reconcile objective and subjective criteria, to sort people into lowers, uppers and middles, to argue about the relation of consciousness to material reality (Otto, 1975; Anderson, 1974a and 1974b; Szymanski, 1972; Braverman, 1974). 'Social class' is shorthand for a process, not a thing. It is the process by which different social relations to the means of production are inherited and reproduced under capitalism. As the concept is developed by Marx, the process of capital accumulation generates and constantly deepens relations between two categories of people: those who are both available and forced to work for wages because they own no means of production, and those who control those means of production. The concept of class expresses a historical process of expanding capital. In the process, categories of people are swept up at different times and places and deposited into different relations to the means of production and to one another. People are then labelled blue-collar or white-collar; they may experience their social existence as mediated by ethnicity or the overwhelming legacy of slavery and racism. Yet all these categories must be viewed in the light of the historical process of capitalist accumulation in the United States. To a large extent, it is the changing categories of proletarians which are actually being accumulated. Class formation and composition is always in flux; it is relationships that are accumulated. Under advanced capitalism, there are shifting frontiers which separate poverty, stable wage-earning, affluent salaries and inherited wealth. The frontiers may be crossed by individuals, and in either direction – both upward and downward mobility are real processes. 'Class' is not a static place that individuals inhabit. It is a process determined by the relationships set up in capital accumulation.

Returning to the initial distinction between family and household, the variations of the two among differing class sectors in contemporary America will now be explored, and a composite picture drawn of the households formed around material relations by class, and the families which organize those households. It will be argued that those families mean different things by class, and by gender as well, because classes and genders stand in differing material relations to one another. It will further be argued that their meanings are highly ideological.

To begin with a review and interpretation of the studies carried out on the working-class family, these span the postwar decades from the late 1940s to the present. They are regionally diverse, and cover both cities and suburbs. The data provided by researchers such as Berger, Gans, Komarovsky, Howell, Rubin and others reveal a composite portrait (Berger, 1968; Gans, 1962 and 1967; Kapp Howe, 1970; Howell, 1973; Komarovski, 1962; Rubin, 1976; Ryan, 1973; Seifer, 1973 and 1976; Shostak, 1969; Sennett and Cobb, 1972; Sexton and Sexton, 1971). The most salient characteristic of household organization in the working class is dependency on hourly wages. Stable working-class households participate in relations of production, reproduction and consumption by sending out their labour power in exchange for wages. 'Sending out' is important: there is a radical split between household and workplace, yet the resources on which the household depends come from participation in production outside itself. How much labour power a working-class household needs to send out is determined by many things: the cost of reproducing (or maintaining) the household, the work careers and earning trajectories of individual members, and the domestic cycle (that is, the relations between the genders and the generations, which specify when and if wives and adolescent children are available to work outside the home). Braverman (1974) estimates that the average working-class household now sends out 1·7 full-time equivalent workers. That figure tells us that a high percentage of married women and teenaged children are contributing their wages to the household. In many ways, the work patterns for nineteenth-century European capitalism described by Tilly and Scott (1975) still leave their mark on the contemporary American working-class household; survival does not depend only on male heads of household.

The working class sends out labour power in exchange for basic resources. Labour power is the only commodity without which there can be no capitalism. It is also the only commodity for which the working class controls its own means of production (Gernstein, 1973). Control over the production of labour power undoubtedly affected women's experiences historically, as it does today (Gordon, 1976). In the early stages of industrialization, it appears that working-class households literally produced a lot of babies (future labour-power) as their strategy for dealing with a market economy (Tilly, 1977). Now workers produce fewer children, but the work of servicing them (social reproduction) is still a major process carried on in the household. Households are the basic units in which labour power is reproduced and maintained, in a location radically removed from the workplace. Such relations therefore appear as autonomous from capital, but of course they are not; without wages, households are hard to form and maintain; without the production of a disciplined labour force, factories cannot produce and profit.

The work carried out in households (primarily by women) does not simply concern babies. Housework itself has recently been rediscovered as work, and its contribution to arenas beyond the household is clear.[1] Housework cuts the reproduction costs of wage-workers. Imagine if all those meals had to be bought at restaurants, those clothes cleaned at laundry rates, those beds made by hotel employees! Housework is also exchanged by women for access to resources bought by their husbands' wages. As such, it is a coin of exchange between men and women. As housework is wageless, it keeps its workers dependent on others for access to commodities bought with wages. It makes them extremely vulnerable to the work conditions of their men. When women work (as increasingly they do), their primary definition as houseworker contributes to the problems they encounter in entering the paid labour force. They are available for part-time (or full-time) work in the lowest-paid sectors of the labour market, in jobs which leave them less economically secure than men. Participation in the 'sexregated' labour market then reinforces dependency on the earnings of other household members and the continued importance of women's domestic labour.[2]

Of course, these rather abstract notions of 'household participation' in the labour market or in housework are experienced concretely by family members. Working-class families are normatively nuclear. They are formed via marriage, which links men and women 'for love' and not 'for money' (Schneider and Smith, 1973). This relation is of course both real and a socially necessary illusion. As such, it is central to the ideology of the family. The cultural distinction between love and money corresponds to the distinction between private family life in the home and work life outside the home. The two are experienced as opposite; in fact they are interpenetrating. The seeming autonomy to exchange love at home expresses something ideological about the relation between home and work: one must work for the sake of the family, and having a family is the 'pay-off' for leading a good life. Founding a family is what people do for personal gratification, for love, and for autonomy. The working-class family literature is full of life histories in which young women saw 'love' as a way to get out of their own, often difficult families. Rubin's interviews, for example, are full of teenaged girls who said, 'When I grow up, I'll marry for love, and it will be better

202

than my parents' marriage.' You may marry for love, but what you mainly get is babies. Forty to sixty per cent of teenaged pregnancies are conceived premaritally, and approximately 50 per cent of working-class women marry in their teens (Rubin, 1976, ch. 4). It is a common experience for a woman to go from being someone's child to having someone's child in under a year. This is not exactly a situation that leads to autonomy.

For men, the situation is complementary. As one of the young working-class men in Rubin's study puts it:

> I had to work from the time I was thirteen and turn over most of my pay to my mother to help pay the bills. By the time I was nineteen, I had been working for all those years and I didn't have anything – not a thing. I used to think a lot about how when I got married, I would finally get to keep my money for myself. I guess that sounds a little crazy when I think about it now because I have to support the wife and kids. I don't know *what* I was thinking about, but I never thought about that then. (Rubin, 1976: 56)

What you get from the romance of love and marriage is in fact not simply a family but a household, and that is quite another matter. Romance is implicated in gender identity and ideology. We are all aware of the cultural distinction between the sexual identity of a good girl and that of a bad girl; a good girl is one who accumulates her sexual resources for later investment. Autonomy means escaping your childhood family to become an adult with your own nuclear family. For young men, the identity process includes the cultural role of wild boy – one who 'sows some wild oats', hangs out on street corners, perhaps gets in trouble with the police, and drinks (Rubin, 1976; Shostak, 1969; Howell, 1973). Ideally, the good girl domesticates the wild boy; she gives him love, and he settles down and goes out to work. Autonomy means becoming an adult with your own nuclear family as an escape. But, of course, autonomy is illusive. The family is classically seen as an escape from production, but it is in fact what sends people into relations of production, for they need to work to support their families. The meaning of production is simultaneously denied and experienced through family relations; working-class wives say of a good husband that he works steadily, provides for the kids, and never harms anyone in the family. The complementary statement is uttered by working-class husbands, who define a good wife as one who keeps the kids under control when he comes home from a hard day's work, and who runs the household well (Rubin, 1976; Shostak, 1969; Sennett and Cobb, 1972; Terkel, 1972). To exchange love is also to underwrite both the necessity and the ability to keep on working. *This* is the heritage that working-class families pass on, in lieu of property, to their children.

The family also expresses ideology in another sense – the distinction between norms and realities. The norms concerning families are that people should be loving and sharing within them and that they should be protective. The reality is too often otherwise, as the rising consciousness of domestic violence indicates. Even without domestic violence, there are more commonplace stresses to which families are often subjected. Rubin found in her study that 40 per cent of the adults she interviewed had an alcoholic parent. Fifty per cent had experienced parental desertion or divorce in their childhood. National statistics confirm these figures (Rubin, 1976; US Bureau of the Census, 1974). About half the adults in her study had seriously destabilizing experiences within their families. The tension generated by relations to resource base can often tear households apart. Under these conditions, to label the working-class personality 'authoritarian' seems a cruel hoax. When the household is working, it expresses work discipline.

Ideology is expressed in gender role in families in another sense as well. Throughout the urban kinship literature, across classes and ethnic groups, the work of reproducing families is in part undertaken by larger kinship groups (the family in the broader sense of relatives). Family networks in this larger sense are women-centred and tend to be serviced by women. There is extensive literature on women-centred kinship networks in which it is usually assumed that women minister to kinship because they minister to families in general. Sylvia Yanagisako suggests that there is also a symbolic level to the kinship work which women carry out; ideologically, women are assigned to 'inside, home, private' domains, while men are seen to represent the outside world (Yanagisako, 1977.). Nuclear families are under cultural constraints to appear as autonomous and private. Yet they are never as private in reality as such value might indicate. The ideal autonomy of an independent nuclear family is constantly being contradicted by the realities of social need, in which resources must be pooled, borrowed, shared. It is women who bridge the gap between a household's real resources and a family's supposed position. Women exchange babysitting, share meals, lend small amounts of money. When a married child is out of work, his (or her) nuclear family turns to the mother, and often moves in for a while. The working-class family literature is full of examples of such pooling (Yanagisako, 1977; Wilmott and Young, 1957; Bott, 1971). To the extent that women 'represent' the family, they facilitate the pooling needed at various points in the domestic cycle. Men maintain, at least symbolically, the autonomy of their families. Pooling is a norm in family behaviour, but it is a hard norm to live with, either to meet or ignore. To comply with the demands of the extended family completely is to lose control over material and emotional resources; to refuse is very dangerous, as people know they will need one another. The tightrope act that ensues is well characterized in the classic mother-in-law story, which usually concerns a wife and her husband's mother. The two women must figure out a way of sharing the small services, the material benefits and the emotional satisfactions one man brings to them both in their separate roles of mother and wife. The autonomy of the younger woman is often compromised by the elder's needs; the authority of the mother is sometimes undermined by the demands of the wife. Women must constantly test, strain and repair the fibres of their kinship networks.

Such women-centred networks are implicated in a process that has not yet been discussed. Production and reproduction have been considered as they affect the working-class household and family. Consumption should briefly be mentioned as well. As a household function, consumption includes turning an amount of wages into commodities so that labour power may be reproduced. This is often women's work. And work it really is. Weinbaum and Bridges tell us that the centralization and rationalization of services and industry under advanced capitalism may be most efficient from the point of view of capital, but it leaves a lot of unrewarding, technical work to be carried out by women in supermarkets, paying bills, dealing with huge bureaucracies (Weinbaum and Bridges, 1976). Women experience the pay packet in terms of the use values it will buy. Yet their consumption work is carried out in the world of exchange value. They mediate the tension between use and exchange, as exemplified in the classic tales concerning domestic quarrels over money in which the man blames the woman for not making his pay cheque stretch far enough. In stable working-class neighbourhoods, the consumption work is carried out in part by women united by family ties who exchange services, recipes, sales information and general lifestyle skills. Kinship networks are part of 'community control' for women. As Seifer notes, working-class women become involved in political issues that threaten the stability of their neighbourhoods (Seifer, 1973 and 1976), perhaps because their neighbourhoods are the locus of extended families within which both work needs and emotional needs are so often met.

When everyone submits to the conditions described here 'for the sake of the family', the pattern that Howell labels 'settled living' emerges (Howell, 1973). Its opposite he calls 'hard living', a family lifestyle that includes a lot of domestic instability, alcohol and rootlessness. Here we are departing from a 'culture of poverty' approach. The value of a label like 'hard living' is that it stresses a continuum made up of many attributes. It is composed of many processes of which the working class has a lot of experience. Given national statistics on alcoholism, desertion, divorce, premarital pregnancy and the like, everyone's family has such experiences, either in its own domestic cycle or in the wider family network.[3] Everyone had a wild brother, or was a bad girl, or had an uncle who drank too much or cousins who get divorced. In each case, everyone experienced the pooling of resources (or the lack of pooling), as families attempted to cope with difficult, destabilizing situations. In a sense, the hard livers keep the settled livers more settled: the consequences of leaving the normative path are well known and are not appealing. This, too, is part of the working-class heritage. In studies by Seifer, Howell, and Rubin, young women express their hopes of leaving a difficult family situation by finding the right man to marry. They therefore marry young, with little formal education, possibly about to become parents, and the cycle begins again.

Of couse, hard living is most consistently associated with poverty in the urban family literature. For essentially political reasons, black poverty has more frequently been the subject of social science analysis than white poverty, but the pattern is found across races. Black Americans have survived under extremely difficult conditions; many of their household and family patterns have evolved to deal with their specific history, while others are shared with Americans of similar class and regional backgrounds. The problems of household formation under poverty conditions are not unique to any group of people; some of the specific, resilient solutions to those problems may be. Because we know far more about black families in poverty than we do about whites, the following composite picture of households and families uses studies that are primarily black.[4] Even when talking about very poor people, analysts such as Liebow, Hannerz, Valentine and Stack note that there are multiple household types, based on domestic cycles and the relative ability to draw on resources. Hannerz (1969), for example, divides his black sample into four categories. Mainstreamers live in stable households composed of husband, wife and children. The adults are employed, and either own their homes or aspire to do so. Their households do not look very different from the rest of the working class. Swingers (Hannerz' second type) are younger, single persons who may be on their way into mainstream life, or they may be tending towards street-families (type three), whose households are headed by women. This type is most important for this study. The fourth category is composed of street-men who are peer-oriented, and predominantly hard-core unemployed or underemployed. They are similar to the men of *Tally's Corner* (Liebow, 1967). While Hannerz and Liebow both give us a wealth of information about what men are doing, they do not analyse their domestic arrangements in detail. Carol Stack (1974a, 1979b), who did her fieldwork from the perspective of female-centred households, most clearly analyses household formation of the very poor. She presents us with domestic networks: extremely flexible and fluctuating groups of people committed to resource pooling, to sharing, to mutual aid, who move in and out of one another's houses.

Given the state of the job market, welfare legislation and segregated slum housing, households are unstable. These are people essentially living below socially necessary reproduction costs. They therefore reproduce themselves by spreading out the aid and the risks involved in daily life. For the disproportionally high numbers who are prevented from obtaining steady employment, being part of what Marx called the floating surplus population is a perilous endeavour. In human terms, this means not only that the poor pay more (Caplowitz, 1967) but that the poor share more as well. Stack's monograph contains richly textured descriptions of the way in which food, furniture, clothing, appliances, kids and money make the rounds between individuals and households. She subtitles one chapter, 'What Goes Round Comes Round', and describes the velocity with which pooling takes place. People try to give what they can and take what they need. Meeting consumption requirements is hard work under these conditions, and domestic networks get the task done. The pleasures and pressures of such survival networks are predominantly organized around the notion of family.

Meyer Fortes tells us that 'domestic groups are the workshops of social reproduction' (Fortes, 1972). Whatever else they do, the families that organize domestic networks are responsible for children. As Ladner and Stack remind us (Ladner, 1971; Stack 1974a, 1974b), poverty, low levels of formal education and early age for first pregnancy are highly correlated; a lot of young girls have children before they are fully adult. Under these circumstances, at least among black families, there is tremendous sharing of the children themselves. On the whole, these are not kids who grow up in 'isolated nuclear families'. Stack, for example, found that 20 per cent of the ACD (Aid to Dependent Children) children in her study were being raised in a household other than that of the biological mother. In the vast majority of cases, the household was related through the biological mother's family. Organizing kinship networks so that children are cared for is a primary function of families. Men, too, often contribute to child-rearing. Like women, they share out bits and pieces of whatever they have. While some men make no contribution, others may be simultaneously contributing to sisters, to a mother and to an aunt, as well as to wives or lovers. They may sleep in one household, but bring groceries, money and affection to several others. Both Stack and Ladner analyse the importance of a father's recognition of his children, by which act he links the baby to his own kinship network. It is family in the broader sense of the term that organizes social reproduction.

Family may be a conscious construction of its participants. Liebow, Stack, Ladner and others describe fictive kinship, by which friends are turned into family. Since family is supposed to be more reliable than friendship, 'going for brothers/for sisters/for cousins' increases the commitment of a relationship, and makes people ideally more responsible for one another. Fictive kinship is a serious relationship. Stack (who is white) describes her own experience with Ruby, a black woman with whom she 'went for sisters'. When Ruby's child was seriously ill, Stack became deeply involved in the crisis. When the baby was admitted to the hospital, she and Ruby rushed over for visiting hours. They were stopped by a nurse, who insisted that only the immediate family could enter. Ruby responded, 'Caroline here is my sister, and nothing's stopping her from visiting this baby.' And they entered, unchallenged. Ruby was correct; under the circumstances, white Caroline was her sister.

Liebow notes that fictive kinship increases the intensity of relationships to the point where they occasionally explode: the demands of brothers and sisters for constant emotional and material aid may lead to situations that shatter the bonds. Fictive kinship is a prime example of family-as-ideology. In this process, reality is inverted. 'Everyone' gets a continuous family, even though the strains and mobility associated with poverty may conspire to keep biological families apart. The idiom of kinship brings people together despite centrifugal circumstances.

It is important not to romanticize this pattern. It has enormous benefits, but its participants also pay high costs. One of the most obvious costs is levelling: resources must be available for all, and none may get ahead. Variations in the chance for suvival are smoothed out in domestic networks via sharing. Stack tells the story of a central couple, Calvin and Magnolia, who unexpectedly inherit a sum of money. While the money might have enabled them to ensure their own security, it is gone within a few months. It disappears into the network to pay off bills, buy clothing for children, allow people to eat better (Stack, 1974: 105–7). Similar stories are told by Hannerz, Liebow, and Howell. No one gets ahead because individual upward mobility can be bought only at the price of cutting off the very people who have contributed to one's survival. Upward mobility becomes a terribly scarring experience under these circumstances. To get out, a person must stop sharing, which is unfamilial, unfriendly, and quite dangerous. It also requires exceptional circumstances. Gans (1962) speaks of the pain that working-class children face if they attempt to use school as a means of achieving mobility, for they run into the danger of being cut off from their peer group. The chance for mobility may occur only once or twice in a lifetime – for example, at specific moments in a school career or in marriage. People rarely get the occasion, and when they do, to grasp it may simply be too costly. the pressures to stay in a supportive and constraining network, and to level out differences may be immense. They contribute to the instability of marriage and the normative nuclear family, for the old networks compete with the new unit for precious resources.

The family as an ideological construction is extremely important to poor people. Many studies show that the poor do not aspire to less 'stable families', if that term is understood as nuclear families. They are simply much more realistic about their life chances. Ties to family, including fictive family, are the lifelines that simultaneously hold together and sustain individuals. My guess is that among the poor, families do not exhibit the radical split between 'private, at home' and 'public, at work' found in families of the stable working class. Neither work relations nor household relations are as continuous or as distinct. What *is* continuous is the sharing of reproduction costs throughout a network whose resources are known to all. There can be no privatization when survival may depend on rapid circulation of limited resources. In this process, women do not 'represent' kinship to the outside world. They become the nodal points in family nets which span whatever control very poor people have over domestic and resource-getting arrangements. Families are what make the huge gap between norm and reality survivable.

It is particularly ironic that the ideology of family, so important to poor people, is used by ruling class ideologies to blame the poor for their own condition. In a society in which *all* Americans sub-scribe to some version of the normative nuclear family, it is cruelty to attack 'the black family' as pathological. Mainstream culture, seeing the family as 'what you work for' (and what works for you), uses 'family language' to stigmatize those who are structurally prevented from accumulating stable resources. The very poor have used their families to cement and patch tenuous relations to sur-vival; out of their belief in 'family' they have invented networks capable of making next-to-nothing go a long way (Haley, 1976; Gutman, 1976). In response, they are told that their notion of family is inadequate. It is not their notion of family that is deficient, but the relationship between household and productive resources.

Returning to the political debate that opened this chapter, we can now see that there are two different concepts of family at work. To achieve a normative family is something many categories of Americans are prevented from doing because of the ways in which their households plug into tenuous resource bases. And when nor-mative families are achieved, it is at substantial and differential costs to both men and women.

The meaning of family and household among class sectors with regular or unstable relations to wages has been considered; those sectors for whom resource bases are more affluent should now be looked at. Analysing the family and household life of the middle class is a tricky business. The term 'middle class' is ambiguous; a majority of Americans identify themselves as part of it whenever they answer questionnaires, and the category obviously carries positive connotations. Historically, we take the notion from the Marxian definition of the petty bourgeoisie: that category of people who own small amounts of productive resources and have control over their working conditions in ways that proletarians do not. The term signifies a stage in proletarianization in which small-scale entrepreneurs, tradesfolk, artisans and professionals essentially stand outside the wage-labour capital relation. That stage is virtually over: there are ever fewer small-scale proprietors or artisans working on their own account in post Second World War America. The term is now used to refer to a different sector – employees in corporate management, government and organizational bureaucrats of various kinds, and professionals, many of whom work directly or indirectly for big business, the State, and semi-public institutions. On the whole, this 'new middle class' is dependent on wages; as such, it bears the mark of proletarianization. Yet the group lives at a level that is quite different from the wage levels of workers (Braverman, 1974, ch. 18). Such a category is obviously hard to define; like all class sectors, it must be historically situated, for the middle class of early twentieth-century America differs markedly from that of the late twentieth century. To understand the meaning of middle class for the different groups, we need to know not only their present status but also the ethnic and regional variations in class structure within which their families entered America.

✓ In a sense, the middle class is a highly ideological construction that pervades American culture; it is, among other things, the perspective from which mainstream social scientists approach the experiences of all the other sectors they attempt to analyse. To analyse middle-class household formations and family patterns, it is necessary not only to examine the data available on all the people who claim to be middle class, but also to explore the biases inherent in much of social science. This is a task beyond the scope of this chapter. Instead, a few tentative ideas as notes towards future research are suggested.

Households among the middle class are obviously based on a stable resource base that allows for some amount of luxury and discretionary spending. When exceptional economic resources are called for, non-familial institutions are usually available in the form of better medical coverage, expense accounts, pension plans, credit at banks, and so on. Such households may maintain their economic stability at the cost of geographical instability; male career choices may move households around like pieces on a chessboard. When far from family support networks, such households may get transitional aid from professional moving specialists, or institutions like the Welcome Wagon (Packard, 1977). Middle-class households are probably able to rely on commodity forms rather than kinship processes to ease both economic and geographic transition.

The families that organize such households are commonly thought to be characterized by egalitarian marriages (Schneider and Smith, 1973, ch. 4). Rubin comments that 'egalitarian marriage' may be a biased gloss for a communication pattern in which the husband's career is in part reflected in the presentation of his wife (Rubin, 1974). To entertain intelligently, and instil the proper educational and social values in the children, women may need to know more about the male world. They represent the private credentials of family to the public world of their men at work. If this is the case, then 'instrumental communication' might be a more appropriate term.

At this level, kinship probably shifts from the lateral towards the linear. That is, resources (material and economic) are invested lineally, between parents, children and grandchildren, and not dispersed into larger networks, as is the case in working-class and poor families. This pattern would of course vary with geographical mobility, and possibly with ethnicity. There is usually greater investment across generations, and careful accumulation within them. This kind of pattern can be seen, for example, in the sums invested in children's education, setting up professional practices, wedding gifts (in which major development of property may occur), and so forth.

Perhaps friendship, rather than kinship, is the nexus within which the middle class invests its psychic and 'familial' energies. Friendship allows for a great deal of affective support and exchange but does not usually include major resource pooling. It is a relation consistent with resource accumulation rather than dispersal. If the poor convert friendship into kinship to equalize pooling, it would seem that the middle classes do the converse: they reduce kinship exchanges, and replace them with friendship, which protects them from pooling and levelling.

There is one last sector of the American class system, the household and family patterns of which would be interesting to examine – the upper class, sometimes identified as the ruling class or the very rich. As one sociologist (either naïve or sardonic) commented, 'We know so little about the very wealthy because they don't answer

.our questionnaires.' Indeed! They fund them rather than answer them! The few studies we do have (by authors such as Domhoff, Amory, Baltzell, Veblen) are highly suggestive. The upper class seems to hang together as a cultural phenomenon. They defend their own interests corporately, and have tremendous ideological importance.

We know very little about the household structure of the very rich. They are described as having multiple households that are recomposed seasonally (Hoffman, 1971; Baltzell, 1958) and filled with service workers rather than exclusively with kin and friends. While there is a general tendency towards 'conspicuous consumption', we have no basic information on the relation of their resource bases to domestic arrangements.

A look at the family structure of the very rich, however, produces some interesting bits and pieces (which may possibly be out of date). Families are described as extremely linear and concerned with who they are rather than what they do. People have access to one another through their control of neighbourhoods, schools, universities, clubs, churches and ritual events. They are ancestor-oriented and conscious of the boundaries that separate the 'best' families from all others. Families are obviously the units within which wealth is accumulated and transmitted. Yet the link between wealth and class is not so simple; some of the 'best' families lose fortunes but remain in the upper class. Mobility is also possible. According to Baltzell (1958), under certain circumstances it is possible for non-members to enter the class via educational and work-related contacts. A sketch of a group emerges from the literature: perhaps the only face-to-face subculture that America contains.

Women serve as gatekeepers of many of the institutions of the very rich (Domhoff, 1971). They launch children, serve as board members at private schools, run clubs and facilitate marriage pools through events like debuts and charity balls. Men also preside over exclusive clubs and schools, but different ones. The upper class appears to live in a world that is very sex-segregated. Domhoff mentions several other functions fulfilled by very rich women including setting social and cultural standards, and softening the rough edges of capitalism by carrying out charity and cultural work. While he trivializes the cultural standards that women set to things like dress and high art, he is alerting us to something more important. In the upper class, women 'represent' the family to the outside world. But here, it is an outside world that is in many senses created by their own class (in the form of high cultural institutions, education, social welfare and charity). Their public presence is an inversion of reality; they appear as wives and mothers, but it is not really their family roles but their class roles that dictate those appearances. To the extent that 'everyone else' either has a wife/-mother or is a wife/mother, upper-class women are available to be perceived as something both true and false. What they can do because of their families (and, ultimately, for their families) is utterly, radically different from what other women who 'represent' their families can do. Yet what everyone sees is their womanness as family members rather than class members. They influence our cultural notions of what feminine and familial behaviour should be. They simultaneously become symbols of domesticity and public service to which others may aspire. The very tiny percentage of very wealthy women who live in a sex-segregated world and have no need to work are thus perceived as benevolent and admirable by a much larger group of women whose relation to sex-role segregation and work is not nearly so benign. 'Everyone' can yearn for a family in which sex-role segregation is valued; no one else can have a family in which it is valued as highly as theirs. In upper-class families, at least as they present themselves to 'the public', we see a systematic confusion of cultural values with the values of family fortunes. We have here an excellent illustration of how the ideas of the ruling class become part of the ruling ideas of society.

At each level of American society, households vary systematically as to resource base and their ability to tap wealth, wages and welfare. Households are organized by families (which means relatives both distant and close, imaginary and real). Families both reflect and distort the material relations within which households are embedded. The working-class and middle-class households may *appear* isolated from the arenas in which production takes place. But, in fact, their families are fomed to generate and deepen relations to those work processes that underwrite their illusion of autonomy. Women's experience with 'the family' varies systematically by class, because class expresses the material and social relations on which their household bases rest. We need to explore their transformatory potential as well as the constraints that differential family patterns provide.

Women have structurally been put in the position of representing the contradictions between autonomy and dependence, between love and money, in the relations of families to capitalism. The ideological role women have played needs to be demystified as we struggle towards a future in which consumption and reproduction will not be determined by capitalist production, in which households will not have access to such uneven resource bases, and in which women will neither symbolically nor in their real relations be forced to bridge the gap between affective norms and contradictory realities in the name of love. To liberate the notion of voluntary relations which the normative family is supposed to represent, we have to stop paying workers off in a coin called love. ⟵

Notes

1. The economic value of housework has been the subject of vigorous debate in Marxist literature in recent years. The debate began with the publication of Mariarosa Dalla Costa (1972), and continued with Secombe (1974), Gardiner (1975), Vogel (1973), Gernstein (1973), and others. See also Hartmann (1974) and Vanek (1974) for American case historical materials, and Glazer-Malbin (1976) for a review of the field.
2. For historical, sociological, and political-economic analyses of women's economic position in the labour market, see the special issue of *Signs*, (Reagan and Blaxall, eds., 1976); also the US Bureau of the Census (1974), for statistical data on demography and workforce participation rates of women.
3. Throughout her work, Rubin (*Worlds of pain*) is especially sensitive to this issue and provides an excellent discussion of individual life cycles in relation to domestic cycles. She explains why the labelling issue is so critical (Rubin, 1976: 223, note 5).
4. Howell's study (*Hard living on Clay street*) provides important and sensitive insights into the domestic lives of poor and working white families, collected in the style of Oscar Lewis. Composite black family studies include Hannerz, 1969; Ladner, 1971; Liebow, 1967; Rainwater, 1970; Scanzoni, 1971; Stack, 1974a, 1974b.

BIBLIOGRAPHICAL
REFERENCES

Agricultura em Sao Paulo, 1952 al presente. San Pablo, Boletim da Divisao de Economia Rural, Secretaria de Agricultura,

Allen, Walter, 'The search for applicable theories of black family life', *Journal of Marriage and the Family*, 40(1), 1978: 117–22

Allub, Leopoldo and Marco A. Michel. 'Migración y estructura ocupacional en una ciudad petrolera: Villahermosa, Tabasco' in Allub, L. and M. A. Michel (eds.), *Impactos regionales de la politica petrolera en Mexico*. Mexico, Centro de Investigación para la Integración Social, 1982

Altimir, Oscar. 'La dimensión de la pobreza en América Latina' *Cuadernos de la CEPAL*. Santiago de Chile: CEPAL. 1979

Anderson, *Toward a new sociology*, (rev. edn.). Homewood, ll. 1974

Anderson, Charles H. *The political economy of social class*. Englewood Cliffs, Prentice Hall, 1974

Anderson, Michael. *Family structure in nineteenth century Lancashire*. Cambridge, Cambridge University Press, 1971

André, Jacques. 'Tuer sa femme, ou de l'ultime façon de devenir pere', *L'Homme*, 22(2), 1982: 69–86

Aries, Philippe. *Centuries of childhood: a social history of family life*. New York, Vintage, 1962

Arizpe, Lourdes. *Indigenas en la ciudad de Mexico. El caso de las 'Marias'*. México, SEP-setentas, 1975

'Women in the informal labour sector: the case of Mexico City,' *Signs*, 3(1) 1977

'Mujeres migrantes y economia campesina: análisis de una cohorte migratoria a la ciudad de México, 1940–1970,' *América Indigena*, 38(2), 1978

Migración, etnicismo v cambio económico (un estudio sobre migrantes campesinos a la ciudad de México). México, el Colegio de México, 1978a

'La migración por relevos y la reproducción social del campesinado' in Balan, Jorge (ed.), *Poblaciones en movimiento*, pp. 205–29. Paris, Unesco, 1982, 229.

'El éxodo rural en México y su relación con la migración a Estados Unidos', *Estudios Sociológicos*, 1, 1983

Aubey, Robert T. 'Capital mobilization and the patterns of business, ownership and control in Latin America: the case of Mexico'. Grenfield, Strickon and Aubey (eds.), University of New Mexico Press, 1977

Bacelar, J. A. *A familia da prostituta*. Sao Paulo, Atica, 1982

Balan, Jorge. 'Estructuras agrarias y migración en una perspectiva histórica: estudios de casos latinoamericanos', *Revista Mexciana de Sociologia*. 52(1), 1981

Baltzell, E. Digby. *Philadelphia gentlemen: the making of a national upper class*. New York, 1976

Bane, Mary Jo. *Here to stay: American families in the twentieth century*. New York.

Barret, Michele and Mary McIntosh. *The anti-social family*. London, Verso, 1982

Barroso, Carmen. 'Sozinhas ou mal acompanhadas – a situacao das mulheres chefes de familia', *Anais do Primeiro Encontro Nacional de Estudos Populacionais*, (ABEP), 1978

Bender, Donald R. 'A refinement of the concept of household: families, co-residence and domestic functions', *American Anthropologist*, 69(5), 1967: 493–504

Bendix, Reinhard. *National building and citizenship: studies of our changing social order*. New York, Doubleday, 1969

Berger, Bennett. *Working class suburb: a study of auto workers in suburbia*. Berkeley, 1968
'The use and misuse of census data for the historical analysis of family structure: a review of household and family in past time', *Journal of Interdisciplinary History*, 5(4), 1975

Berkner, Lutz K. 'The stem family and the developmental cycle of the peasant household: an eighteenth-century Austrian example', *American Historical Review*, 77(2), 1972

Berlanstein, Lenard R. 'Illegitimacy, concubinage and proletarianization in a French town, 1760–1940', *Journal of family history*, 5(4), 1980: 360–74

Bilac, Elisabete. *Familias de trabalhadores: estratégias de sobrevivencia*. Sao Paulo, Simbolo, 1978

Blumberg, Rae Lesser and Márcia P. Garcia. 'The political economy of the mother–child family: a cross societal view' in Lenero-Otero, Luis (ed.), *Beyond the nuclear family model*. Sage, 1977

Bohman, Kristina. 'Woman of the barrio: class and gender in a Columbian city', *Stockholm Studies in Social Anthropology*, 13, 1984

Bollettino Ufficiale della Camara Italiana di Commercio ed Arti in Sao Paulo,. February 1903

Bott, Elizabeth. *Family and social network: roles, norms and external relationships in ordinary urban families*. London, Tavistock Institute of Human Relations, 1957
Family and Social Network, New York, 1971

Bourdieu, Pierre. 'Marriage strategies as strategies of social reproduction', in Forster, Robert and Orest Ranum (eds.), *Family and society. Selections from the annals: economies, societies, civilisations*. Baltimore, Johns Hopkins University Press, 1976
Outline of a theory of practice. Cambridge, Cambridge University Press, 1977

Braverman, Harry. *Labor and monopoly capital: the degradation of work in the twentieth century*. New York,' 1974

Brown, Susan E. 'Love unites them and hunger separates them: poor

217

women in the Dominican Republic, in Reiter, Rayna (ed.), *Toward an anthropology of women*. Monthly Review Press, 1975

Browning, Harley H. 'Propositions about migration to large cities in developed countries', in Browning, H. (ed.), *Rapid population growth*, pp. 273–314. Baltimore, Johns Hopkins Press, 1971

Burch, Thomas, Luis F. Lira and Valdecir F. Lopes (eds.). *La familia como unidad de estudio demográfico*. San José, Celade,

Butterworth, Douglas. 'Study of the urbanization process of Mixtec migrants of Tilaltongo in Mexico City', *America Indigena*. 22, 1962: 25–74

Buvinic, Mayra and Nadia H. Youssef. *Women-headed households: the ignored facto in development planning*. Washington, International Center for Research on Women, 1978

Cabrera, Gustavo. 'Selectividad por edad y sexo de los migrantes en México, 1930–1960', *Demongrafia y Economia*. 3(2), 1970

Calderon, F. R. 'Los Ferrocarriles', in Cosio Villegas (ed.), *Historia Moderna de Mexico*. El Porfiriato. Vida Economica. Mexico: Hermes, 1965

Caldwell, John C. 'Towards a restatement of demographic transition theory', *Population and Development Review*, 2(6), 1976

Campbell 1976 cff. 179

Caplowitz, David. *The poor pay more* New York, 1967

Cardoso, Fernando H. and Enzo Faletto. *Desarrollo y dependencia en América Latina*. México, Siglo XXI, 1969

Carrillo V. Jorge. 'La migración femenina hacia la zona fronteriza México Estados Unidos'. Paper prepared for the XI congreso Internacional de la Asociación de Estudios Latinoamericanos en México, DF, *mimeo*, 1983

Carvalho de Moraes, J. P. *Relatorio apresentado ao Ministerio da Agricultura*. Rio de Janeiro, Ministerio da Agricultura, 1870

Castells, Manual. *La cuestión urbana*. México, Siglo XXI, 1976

Charbit, Yves. 'Caribbean family structure: past research and recent evidence from the World Fertility Survey on Matrifocality', *Scientific Reports* (WFS), 65, 1984

Clacso. *Migración y Desarrollo* 5. México, El Colegio de México, 1980

Migración y Desarrollo 6. Buenos Aires, Clacso, 1983

Cordero, H. Salvador. 'Concentración industrial y poder económico en México', *Cuadernos del Centro de Estudios Sociológicos* 18. México, El Colegio de México, 1977

Coulson, Margaret, Branka Magas and Hilary Wainwright. 'The housewife and her labour under capitalism – a critique', *New Left Review*, 89, 1975: 159–72

Dalla Costa, Mariarosa. 'Women and the subversion of the community', *Radical America*, 1972: 67–102

Davatz, Thomas. *Memoria de um colono no Brasil (1850)*. San Pablo, Livraria Martins, 1941

Davila, R. 'Apuntes analiticos sobre el desarrollo económico, cambios en la estructura agraria y migraciones femeninas diferenciales', *Investigación Demográfica en México – 1980*. México, Consejo Nacional de Ciencia y Tecnologia, 1982

Dean, Warren. *Rio Claro: a Brazilian plantation system, 1820–1920*. Stanford, Stanford University Press, 1976

Deere, Carmen D. and Magdelena Leon. 'Produccion campesina, proletari-
zacion y la division sexual del trabajo en la Zona Andina', in Magdalena
Leon (ed.), *Debate sobre la mujer en America Latin y el Caribe* vol. 2. Bogota,
ACEP, 1982

Deere, Carmen D. and Alain de Janvry. 'Demographic and social differentiation among northern Peruvian peasants', *Journal of Peasant Studies* 8,
1981: 335–66

Dias, Maria O. L. *Quotidiano e Poder em Sao Paulo no século XIX*. Sao Paulo,
Editora Brasiliense, 1984

Domhoff, G. William. *The higher circles*. New York, 1971

Donzelot, Jacques. *The policing of families*. New York, Pantheon Books, 1979

Durham, Eunice R. *A reconstituicao da realidade: um estudo sobre a obra etnografica
de Bronislaw Malinowski*. Sao Pablo, Atica, 1978

'A familia operaria: consciencia e ideologia', *Dados*, 23(2), 1980: 201–13

Edholm, Felicity, Olivia Harris and Kate Young. 'Conceptualising women',
Critique of Anthropology. 3(9/10), 1977

Elshtain, Jean B. 'Antigone's daughters', *Democracy*. 2(2), 1982

Elson, Diane and Ruth Pearson. 'La ultima fase de la internacionalización
del capital y sus implicaciones para la mujer del Tercer Mundo', in
*Estudios sobre la muier, 1. El empleo y la mujer. Bases teóricas, metodológicas y
evidencia empirica*. México, SPP, 1982

Escobar, Gabriel. 'Análisis preliminar del parentesco y la familia de clase
media de la ciudad del Cuzco', in Mayer, E. and R. Bolton (eds.),
Parentesco y matrimonio en los Andes, pp. 681–191. Pontificia Universidad
Católica del Perú, Fondo Editorial, 1980

Feijoo, Maria del C. *Buscando un techo: familia y vivienda popular*. Estudios
Cedes, 1983

Fernandez Kelly, Patricia. 'Mexican border industrialization, female labor
force participation and migration', in Nash, June and Patricia Fernández
Kelly (eds.), *Women, men and international division of labor*. New York, State
University of New York Press, 1983

Figueiredo, Marisa. 'Le role socio-économique des femmes chefs de famil-
les', *Tiers monde XXI*. (84), 1980: 871–91

Filgueira, Carlos. 'Acerca del consumo en los nuevos modelos latinoamericanos', *Revista de la Cepal*, 15(78), December 1981

Fonseca, Claudia. 'Familia e classe: questionando algunos conceitos sobre
a familia de baixa renda', *Revista do Instituto de Filosofia e Ciencias Humanas*
8. Porto Alegre, 1983

'La violence et la rumeur: le code d'honneur dans un bidonville bresilien',
Les temps modernes, 455, 1984: 2193–235

'Valeur marchande, amour maternal et survie: aspects de la circulation
des enfants dans un bidonville brésilien', *Annales ESC*, 40(5), October
1985: 991–1022

'Orphanages, foundlings and foster mothers: the system of child circulation in a Brazilian squatter settlement', *Anthropology Quarterly*, 59(1),
January 1986: 15–27

'Pais e filhos em camadas populares no inicio do século: um outro tipo
de amor', in D'Incao, Mariangela (ed.), *Amor e familia no Brasil*. Sao
Paulo, Achiamé, in prep.

Fortes, Meyer. 'Introducción', in Goody, J. (ed.), *Development cycles in domestic groups*. Cambridge, Cambridge University Press, 1958
Kinship and the social order. Chicago, Aldine, 1969
'Introduction', in Goody, Jack (ed.), *The development cycle in domestic groups*. Cambridge, Cambridge University Press, 1972

Fortune, R. F. *Sorcerers of Dobu*. London, Routledge and Kegan Paul, 1963

Foster, George M. *Tzintzuntzam*. México, Fondo de Cultura Económica, 1972

Fox, Rubin. *Kinship and marriage*. Harmondsworth, Penguin Books, 1967

Franchetto, Bruna *et al*. 'Antropologia e feminismo', *Perspectivas Antropologicas da Mulher*, vol. 1. Rio de Janeiro, Zahar, 1981

Frazier, E. Franklin. *The negro family in the United States*. Chicago, The University of Chicago Press, 1939

Freire, Jurandir Costa. *Ordem medica e norma familiar*. Rio de Janeiro, Graal, 1979

Frey, Michel. 'Du mariage et du concubinage dans les classes populaires à Paris (1846–7). *Annales ESC*, 33(4), 1978: 803–29

Furtado, Celso. *La economia Latinoamericana desde la Conquista Ibérica hasta la Revolución Cubana*. México, Siglo XXI, 1973

Galbraith, John K. *Economics and the public purpose*. Boston, Houghton Mifflin, 1973

Gans, Herbert J. *The urban villagers*. New York, 1962
The levittowners. New York, 1967

Garcia, Brigida. 'Dinámica del empleo rural y urbano en el sureste de México: 1970–1980'. México, Centro de Estudios Demográficos y de Desarrollo Urbano, El Colegio de México, *mimeo*, 1984
Migración y fuerza trabaio en la ciudad de México. Cuadernos del CES 26. México, El Colegio de México, Centro de Estudios Sociológicos, 1979

Gardiner, Jean. 'Women's domestic labour', *New Left Review*, 89, 1975: 47–761

Geertz, C. 'Religion as cultural system', in Geertz, C. *The interpretation of cultures*. New York, Basic Books, 1973

Geertz, Clifford. *The interpretation of cultures*. New York, Basic Books, 1973

Gernstein, Ira. 'Domestic work and capitalism', *Radical America* 7, 1973: 101–30

Glazer-Malbin, Nona. 'Review essay: housework', *Signs*, 1, 1976: 905–22

Gonzalez, Nancie L. Solien. *Black Carib household structure – a study of migration and modernization*. Seattle, University of Washington Press, 1969

Gonzalez Navarro, Moises. 'El Porfiriato de vida social', in Cosio Villegas, (ed.), *Historia moderna de México. El Porfiriato, la vida social*. México, Ed. Hermes, 1973

Goody, Jack. 'The evolution of the family', in Laslett, Peter (ed.), *Household and family in past time*. London, Cambridge University Press, 1972
Production and reproduction: a comparative study of the domestic domain. Cambridge, Cambridge University Press, 1976

Goody, Jack, Joan Thirsk and E. P. Thompson (eds.). *Family and inheritance: rural society in Western Europe, 1200–1800*. Cambridge, Cambridge University Press, 1978

Gordon, Linda. *Women's body, women's right: a social history of birth control in America*. New York, 1976

Gough, E. Katleen. 'Nayar: Central Kenala' in Schneider, D. M. and Gough, E. K. (orgs.), *Matrilineal kinship*. Berkeley, University of California Press, 1962

Greenfield, Sidney. *English rustic in black skin – a study of modern family forms in a pre-industrial society*. New Haven, College and University Press, 1966

Greenhalg, Susan. 'Chinese chia and the level of income equality in Taiwan: rethinking the recipient unit in income distribution studies'. Liege, IUSSP, *mimeo*, 1981

Gutman, Herbert. *The black family in slavery and freedom, 1750–1925*. New York, 1976

Habermas, J. 'A familia burguesa e a institucionalizacao de uma esfera privada referida a esfera pública', in *Dialética da familia*. San Pablo, Brasiliense, 1981

Hagerman Johnson, Ann. 'The impact of market agriculture on family and household structure in nineteenth-century Chile', *Hispanic American Historical Review*, 58, 1978: 625–48

Haguette, Tereza. *Os mitos da sobrevivencia*. Fortalez, Ed. de la Universidad de Ceará, 1982

Haley, Alex. *Roots*. New York, 1976

Hannerz, Ulf. *Soulside: inquiries into ghetto culture and community*. New York, Columbia University Press, 1969

Hansen, Roger D. *The politics of Mexican development*. Baltimore and London, Johns Hopkins University Press, 1974

Hareven, Tamara K. (ed). *Family and kin in urban communities, 1700–1930*. New York, New Viewpoints, 1977
Transitions: the family and the life course in historical perspective. New York, Academic Press, 1978

Harris, Olivia. 'Households as natural units', in Young, Kate, Carol Wolkowitz and Roslyn McCullagh (eds.), *Of marriage and the market: women's subordination in international perspective*. London, CSE Books, 1981

Hartmann, Heidi I. 'Capitalism and women's work in the home, 1900–2930'. Ph.D. dissertation, Yale University, 1974
'Capitalism, patriarchy and job segregation by sex', *Signs*, 1(3), 1976: 17–69
'The family as the locus of gender, class and political struggle: the example of housework', *Signs*, 6(3), 1981

Hartmann, Heidi I. and A. R. Markusen. 'Contemporary Marxist theory and practice: a feminist critique', *The Review of Radical Political Economics*, 12(2), 1980: 87–93

Heller, Agnes. *The theory of need in Marx*. London, 1976

Herskowitz, Melville. *The myth of the negro past*. New York, Harper and Brothers, 1941

Heusser, C. *Die Schweizer auf den Kolinien in St Paulo in Brasilien*. Zurich, Bericht des Herrn Dr. H., an die Direktion der Polizei des Kantons Zurich, 1857

Himmelweit, Susan and Simon Mohun. 'Domestic labour and capital', *Cambridge Journal of Economics*, I, 1977: 15–32

Hoffman, William. *David: Report on a Rockefeller.* NJ Secaucus, 1971

Holloway, Thomas H. *Immigrants on the land: coffee and society in Sao Paulo, 1886–1934.* Chapel Hill, Univeristy of North Carolina Press, 1980

Howell, Joseph. *Hard living on clay street.* New York, 1973

Humphries, Jane. 'Class struggles and the persistence of the working-class family', *Cambridge Journal of Economics*, I, 1977: 241–58

Ianni and Reuss-Ianni 1973 cff.179

Jaguaribe Filho, Domingos. *Algumas palavras sobre a emigracao.* Sao Pablo, 1877

Jelin, Elizabeth. 'Migración a las ciudades y participación en la fuerza de trabajo de las mujeres latinoamericanas: el caso del servicio doméstico', *Estudios Sociales* 5, Buenos Aires, Cedes, 1976

'Migration and labor force participation of Latin American women: the domestic servants in the cities', *Signs*, 3(1), 1977: 129–141

'Las relaciones sociales del consumo: el caso de las unidades domésticas de sectores populares', in Cepal, *La Mujer en el sector popular urbano: América Latina y el Caribe.* Santiago, Cepal, 1984

Familia y unidad doméstica: mundo público y vida privada. Buenos Aires, Estudios Cedes, 1984

Jelin, Elizabeth and Maria del C. Feijoo. 'Trabajo y familia en el ciclo de vida femenino: el caso de los sectores populares de Buenos Aires', *Estudios Cedes*, 3(8/9), 1980

Jelin, Elizabeth, Juan José Llovet and Silvina Ramos. 'Un estilo de trabajo: la investigación microsocial', in *Problemas metodológicos en la investigación sociodemográfica.* México, Pispal, El Colegio de México, 1986

Johnson, Ann Hagerman. 'The impact of market agriculture on family and household structure in nineteenth-century Chili', *Hispanic American Historical Review*, 58(4), 1978: 625–48

Kaerger, Karl. *Brasilianische Wirtschaftsbilder: Erlebnisse und Forschungen.* Berlin, 1982

Kageyama, Angela *et al.* 'Diferenciación campesina y cambio tecnológico: el caso de los productores de frijol en Sao Paulo'. Universidad Estadual de Campinas, *mimeo*, 1982

Kapp Howe, Louise (ed.). *The white majority: between poverty and affluence.* New York, 1970

Karrer, L. *Das schweizerische Auswanderungswesen und die Revision und Vollziehung de Bundesgesetz uber den Geschaftsbertrieb von Auswanderungsangenturen.* Bern, 1886

Kemper, Robert V. *Campesinos en la ciudad.* México, SepSetentas, 1976

Komarovsky, Mirra. *Blue collar marriage.* New York, 1962

Kowarick, Lucio. *Capitalismo e marginalidade na America Latina.* Rio de Janeiro, Paz e Terra, 1975

Kunstadter, P. 'A survey of the consanguine or matrifocal family', *American Anthropologist*, 65, 1963: 56–66

Kuznesof, Elizabeth A. 'Household composition and headship as related to changes in mode of production: Sao Paulo, 1765 to 1836', *Comparative studies in society and history*, 22, 1980: 78–108

Kuznets, Simon. 'Demographic aspects of the size distribution of income: an exploratory essay', *Economic development and cultural change*, 25(1), 1976

Ladner, Joyce. *Tomorrow's tomorrow: the black woman.* New York, 1971

Lamphere, Louise. 'Estratégias, cooperacao e conflito entre mulheres em grupos domésticos', in Rosaldo, M. Z and Lamphere, L. (orgs.), *A mulher, a cultura e a sociedade.* Rio de Janerio, Paz e Terra, 1979

Larguia, Isabel and John Dumoulin. 'Aspects of the conditions of wowmen's labor', *Nacla's Latin America and Empire Report,* IX, 1975

Lasch, Christopher. 'The family and history', *New York Review of Books 22,* 18, 19, 20, 1975–6
Haven in a heartless world: the family besieged. New York, Harper & Row, 1977
The cutlure of narcissism: American life in an age of diminishing expectations. New York. W. W. Norton, 1979

Laslett, Peter (ed.). *Household and family in past time.* London, Cambridge University Press, 1972

Leeds, Anthony and Elizabeth Leeds. 'Brasil and the myth of urban rurality experience work and values in squatments of Rio de Janeiro and Lima', in Field, Arthur V. (ed.), *City and country in the Third World,* pp. 229–85. Cambridge, Schenkman, 1970

Leff, Gloria. 'Algunas caracteristicas de las empleadas domésticas y su ubicación en el mercado de trabajo de la ciudad de México'. México, Facultad de Ciencias Politicas y Sociales, Unam, doctoral dissertation, 1974
'Las migraciones femeninas a la ciudad de México. Informe de investigación'. México, El Colegio de México, Centro de Estudios Sociológicos, *mimeo,* 1976

Leiss, William. *The limits of satisfaction: an essay on the problem of needs and commodities.* Toronto, Univeristy of Toronto Press, 1976

Levine, David. *Family formation in an age of nascent capitalism.* London, Academic Press, 1977

Levi-Strauss, C. 'L'analyse structurale en linguistique et en anthropologie', in Levi-Strauss, C., *Anthropologie structurale.* Paris, Plon, 1958

Levi-Strauss, Claude. *Les structures élémentaires de la parenté.* Paris, Mounton, 1968

Levy, M. J. and L. A. Fallers. 'The family: some comparative considerations', *American Anthropologist,* 61(4), 1959: 651–74

Liebow, Eliot. *Tally's corner: a study of negro street-corner men.* Boston, Little, Brown & Co, 1967

Llovet, Juan José. *Los lustrabotas de Buenos Aires.* Buenos Aires, Cedes, (Estudios Cedes, vol. 3, 4/5), 1981

Lobo, Susan. *A house of my own.* Tucson, University of Arizona Press, 1981
'The history of a Mexican urban family', *The Journal of Family History,* 3(4), 1978: 392–409
'Kinship structure and the role of women in the urban upper class of México', *Signs,* 5(1), 1979
'Family and Enterprise: The History of a Mexican Kinship Group.

Lomnitz, Larissa. *Cómo sobreviven los marginados?* México, Siglo XXI, 1975
Life in a Mexican shanty town. London, Academic Press, 1977

Luna, Francisco Vida and Iraci del Nero Costa. 'Devassa nas Minas

Gerais: observacoes sobre casos de concubinato', *Anais do Museu Paulista*, 31, 1982

Macedo, Carmen Cinira. *A reproducao da desigualdade: o projeto de vida familial de um grupo operario*. Sao Pablo, Hucitec, 1979

Machado Neto, Zahidé. 'Mulher: vida e trabalho – um estudo de casos com mulheres faveladas', *Ciencia e Cultura*, 31(3), 1979: 280–9

Maistrello, Guido. 'Fazendas de cafe – costumes (Sao Paulo)', in Ramos, Augusto (ed.), *O cafe no Brasil e no estrangeiro*. Rio de Janeiro, Santa Helena, 1923

Malinowski, B. *Argonauts of the Western Pacific*. London, Routledge and Kegan Paul Ltd, 1922

Malinowski, B. *A scientific theory of culture and other essays*. New York, Oxford University Press, 1960

  La vida sexual de los salvajes del noroeste de la Melanesia. 3. ed. Madrid, Morata. 1975

Malos, Ellen (ed.). *The politics of housework*. London, Allison & Busby, 1980

Manyoni, Joseph. 'Legitimacy and illegitimacy: misplaced polarities in Caribbean family studies', *Canadian Review of Sociology and Anthropology*, 14(4), 1977: 417–27

Marguilis, Mario and Rodolfo Tuiran. 'Crecimiento y migración en una ciudad de frontera: el caso de Reynosa, Tamaulipas'. México, Centro de Estudios Demográficos y de Desarrollo Urbano, El Colegio de México, *mimeo*, 1984

Marino, A. 'Family, fertility and sex rations in the British Caribbean,' *Population Studies*, 24(2), 1970: 159–72

Marshall, T. H. *Class, citizenship, and social development*. New York, Doubleday, 1964

Martin, Elmer P. and Joanne Mitchell Martin. *The black extended family*. Chicago, University of Chicago Press, 1978

Martinez, Marielle P. L. 'L'économie paysanne d'une communauté indienne au Mexique: San Pedro Jicayán, Oaxaca'. Doctoral dissertation presented in Parish 1980

Martinez, Marielle and Teresa Rendon. 'Las unidades domésticas campesinas y sus estrategias de reproducción', in Appendini, K. *et al. El campesinado en México: dos perspectivas de análisis*. México, El Colegio de México, 1983

Martinez-Alier, Verena and Armando Boito. 'The hoe and the vote: rural labourers and the national elections in Brazil in 1974', *Journal of Peasant Studies*, 4, 1977: 147–70

Mathis, Arthur. 'Contrasting approaches to the study of black families', *Journal of Marriage and the Family*, 40(4), 1978: 667–76

Meillassoux, Claude. *Muieres, graneros y capitales*. México, Siglo XXI, 1977

Modell, John, Frank F. Furstenberg, Jr. and Douglas Strong. 'The timing of marriage in the transition to adulthood: continuity and change, 1860–1975', in Demos, John and Sarane S. Boocok (eds.), *Turning points*. Chicago, American Journal of Sociology, 1978, suppl. to vol. 84

Morris, Lidia. 'Women in poverty: domestic organization among the poor of Mexico city', *Anthropological Quarterly*, 54(3), 1981: 117–23

Mott, Luiz R. B. 'Os pecados da familia na Bahia de Todos os Santos (1813)', *Cadernos do Ceru*, 18, 1983: 91–130

Munoz, Humberto and Orlandina de Oliveira. 'Migración, oportunidades de empleo diferencias de ingreso en la ciudad de México'. *Revista Mexicana de Sociologia*, 38(1), 1976

Murdock, George P. *Social structure*. New York, Macmillan, 1949

Murphy, R. F. *Headhunters' heritage*. Berkeley, University of California Press, 1960

Natsch, Rudolf Arnold. *Die Haltung eidgenossischer und kantonaler Behorden in der Auswanderungstrage, 1803–1874*. Zurich, Keller, 1966

Neves, Delma Pessanha. *Nesse terreiro, galo nao canta*. Presentado en la 'Reuniao Anual da Anpocs', Nova Friburgo, 1982

Novak, Michael. 'The family out of favor', *Harper's Magazine*, April, 1976

Nun, José. 'Sobrepoblación relativa, ejército industrial de reserva y masa marginal', *Revista Latinoamericana de Sociologia*, 5(2), 1969

Nutini, Hugo. *San Bernardino Contla*. Pittsburgh, University of Pittsburgh Press, 1968

Oliveira, Orlandina de. *Migración y absorción de mano de obra en la ciudad de México: 1930–1970*. Cuadernos del Des, 14. México, Centro de Estudios Sociológicos, El Colegio de México, 1976

Oliveria, Orlandina de and Brigida Garcia. 'Migración a grandes ciudades del Tercer Mundo: algunas implicaciones sociodemográficas', *Estudios Sociológicos*. El Colegio de México, 4, 1984: 71–103

O'Neil, Luis Decker. 'The changing family', *Wilson Quarterly*, winter, 1977

Oppong, Christine. 'Family structure and women's reproductive and productive roles: some conceptual and methodological issues', in Anker, Richard, Mayra Buvinic and Nadia H. Youssef (eds.), *Women's roles and population trends in the Third World*. London, Croom Helm, 1982

Otto, Luther B. 'Class and status in family research', *Journal of Marriage and the Family*, 37, 1975: 315–32

Ozorio de Almeida, Anna Luiza. 'Parceroa a tamanho da familia no Nordeste brasileiro', *Pesquisa a Planejamento Economico*, 7, 1977: 291–332

Packard, Vance. 'Mobility: restless America', *Mainliner Magazine*, May 1977

Palacios, Marco. *Coffee in Colombia, 1850–1970: an economic, social and political history*. Cambridge: Cambridge University Press, 1980

Papaterra Limongi, J. *O trabalhador nacional*. Boletim do Departamento do Trbalho, 5, Sao Pablo, 1916

Peattie, Lisa. 'La oganización de los "marginales" ', in Kaztman, Ruben and José L. Reyna (eds.), *Fuerza de trabaio y movimientos laborales en América Latina*. México, Colegio de México, 1979

Pinheiro, Paulo Sergio de M. and Michael M. Hall. *A classe operaria no Brasil: Documentos 1889 a 1930*. vol. I. Sao Pablo, Editora Alfa Omega, 1979

Pleck, Elizabeth H. 'Two worlds in one: work and family', *Journal of Social History*, December, 1976: 178–95

Poster, Mark. *Critical theory of the family*. Connecticut, Seabury Press, 1978

Potash, Betty. *Widows in African Societies: choices and constraints*. Stanford, Stanford University Press, 1986

Przeworski, Adam. 'Teoria sociológica y el estudio de la población:

reflexiones sobre el trabajo de la Comisión de población y desarrollo de Clacso', in *Reflexiones teórico-metodológicas sobre la investigación en población*. México, Pispal, El Colegio de México, 1982

Quijano, Anibal. 'Dependencia, cambio social y urbanización en América Latina', *Revista Mexicana de Sociologia*, 1968

Radcliffe-Brown, A. F. and D. Forde (orgs.). *African systems of kinship and marriage*. London, Oxford University Press, 1958

Rainwater, Lee. *Behind ghetto walls: black families in a federal slum*. Chicago, 1970

Ramos, Augusto, (ed.). *O cafe no Brasil e no estrangeiro*. Rio de Janeiro, Santa Helena, 1923

Ramos, Donald. 'City and country: the family in Minas Gerais, 1804–1838', *The Journal of Family History*, 3(4), 1978: 361–75

Ramos, Silvina E. *Las relaciones de parentesco y de avuda mutua en los sectores populares urbanos. Un estudio de caso*. Buenos Aires, Estudios Cedes, 1981

Rapp, Rayna. 'Family and class in contemporary America: notes toward an understanding of ideology', *Science and Society*, 42(3), 1978
'Anthropology', *Signs*, 4(3), 1979

Rapp, Rayna, *et al.* 'Examining family history'. *Feminist Studies*, 5(1), 1979

Roberts, Bryan. *Cities of peasants: the political economy of urbanization in the Third World*. London, Edward Arnold, 1978

Rodman, Hyman. *Lower-class families: the culture of poverty in Negro Trinidad*. London, Oxford University Press, 1971

Rodriguez, Miriángela. 'La proletarización del trabajo artesanal femenino', *Yucatán: historia y economia*, 4(23), 1981. Mérida, Yucatán. Centro de Investigaciones Regionales de la Universidad de Yucatán.

Roldan, Marta. 'Subordinación genérica y proletarización rural: Un estudio de caso en el Noroeste de Mexico', in Leon Magades (ed.), *Debate sobre la mujer en America Latina y el Caribe, vol. 2. Bogota, ACEP, 1982*

Romney, *Kimball and Romanine Romney. The Mixtecas of Juxtlahuaca, Mexico*. New York, John Wiley & Sons, 1966

Rosaldo, Michelle Z. 'A mulher, a cultura e a sociedade: uma resivao teórica' in Rosaldo, M. Z. and L. Lamphere (orgs.), *A mulher, a cultura e a sociedade*. Rio de Janeiro, Paz e Terra, 1979
'The use and abuse of anthropology: reflections on feminism and cross-cultural understanding', *Signs*, 5(3), 1980

Rubbo, Anna. 'The spread of capitalism in rural Columbia: effects on poor women' in Reiter, Ryana (ed.), *Toward an anthropology of women*. Monthly Review Press, 1975

Rubin, Lillian. *Worlds of pain*. New York, 1976

Ryan, Joseph A. *White ethnics: life in working class America*. Englewood Cliffs, 1973

Sacks, Karen. *Sister and wives: the past and future of sexual equality*. Westport, Greenwood Press, 1979

Salles, Vania. 'Una discusión sobre las condiciones de la reproducción campesina', *Estudios Sociologicos*, 4, 1984

Sallum, Brasilio, Jr. *Capitalismo e cafeicultura, oeste Paulista: 1888–1930*. Sao Pablo, Livraria Duas Cidades, 1982

'Casamento e papéis familiares em Sao Paulo no século XIX', *Cadernos de pesquisa*, 37, 1981: 17–25

A familia brasileira. Sao Pablo, Brasiliense, 1983

Scanzoni, John. *The black family in modern society*. Rockleigh, NJ, 1971

Schmukler, Beatriz. 'Mujer y familia en la reproducción de la pequexa burguesia' in Aguiar, Néuma (ed.), *Mulheres na forca de trabalho na America Latina*. Rio de Janeiro, Editora Vozes, 1981

Schneider, David M. and Raymond T. Smith. *Class differences and sex roles in American kinship and family structure*. Englewood Cliffs, 1973

Class differences in American kinship. Ann Arbor, University of Michigan Press, 1978

Secombe, Wally. 'The housewife and her labour under capitalism', *New Left Review*, 83, 1974: 3–24

Secretaria de Programación

'Domestic labour – a reply to critics,' New Left Review, 895 1975: 85–96

presupuesto. *Caracteristicas de los marginados en las áreas urbanas de México*. México, Coordinación del Sistema Nacional de Información, 1979

Seifer, Nancy. 'Absent from the majority: working class women in America'. Middle America Pamphlet Series, National Project on Ethnic America, American Jewish Committee, 1973

Nobody speaks for me: self-portraits of American working class women. New York, 1976

Sen, Gita. 'The sexual divison of labour and the working class family: toward the conceptual synthesis of class relations and the subordination of women', *Review of Radical Political Economy*, 12(2), 1980: 76–86

Sennett, Richard and Jonathan Cobb. *The hidden injuries of class*. New York, 1972

Sexton, Patricia Cayo and Brendan Sexton. *Blue collars and hard hats*. New York, 1971

Shostak, Arthur B. *Blue collar life*. New York, 1969

Singer, Paul. *Economia politica da urbanizacao*. Sao Pablo, Editora Brasiliense, 1975

Economia politica do trabalho. Sao Pablo, Editora Hucitec, 1977

Skolnick, Arlene. 'The family revisited: themes in recent social science research', *Journal of Interdisciplinary History*, 5(4), 1975

Smith, M. G. *West Indian family structure*. Seattle, University of Washington Press, 1962

Smith, R. T. *The Negro family in British Guiana*. London, Routledge and Kegan Paul, 1956

'The matrifocal family' in Goody, J. *The character of kinship*, Cambridge, Cambridge University Press, 1973

Stack, Carol B. *All our kin: strategies for survival in a black community*. New York, Harper & Row, 1974a

'Sex roles and survival strategies in an urban black community', in Rosaldo, Michelle Z. and Lousie Lamphere (eds.), *Women, culture and society*. Stanford, Stanford University Press, 1974b

1975 cff 184/221

Stinchcombe, Arthur. 'Formal organizations' in Smelser, Neil J. (ed.), *Sociology: an introduction*. New York, Wiley, 1967

Stolcke, Verena. 'Women's labours: the naturalisation of social inequality and women's subordination' in Young, Kate, Carol Wolkowitz and Roslyn McCullagh (eds.), *Of marriage and the market: women's subordination in international perspective*. London, CSE Books, 1981

Stolcke, Verena and Michael Hall. 'The introduction of free labour into Sao Paulo coffee plantations', *Journal of Peasant Studies*, 10, 1983: 170–200

Stone, Lawrence. 'The new eighteenth century', *The New York Review of Books*, 31(5), 1984: 43–8

Szymanski, Alfred. 'Trends in the American class structure', *Socialist Revolution*, 10, July–August, 1972

Terkel, Studs. *Working*. New York, 1972

Tilly, Louise. 'Reproduction, production and the family among textile workers in Roubaix, France.' Paper presented at the Conference on Social history, February 1977

Tilly, Louise and Joan Scott. 'Women's work in nineteenth century Europe', *Comparative Studies in Society and History*, 17, 1975: 36–64
Women, work and family. New York, 1978

Torrado, Susana. 'The "family life strategies" approach in Latin America: theoretical-methodological trends'. Paper presented at the IUSSP General Conference, Manila, *mimeo*, 1981

Turenne, P. de. 'L'immigration et la colonisation au Brésil', *Revue Britannique*, February 1879: 437–61

US Bureau of the Census. *Statistical abstract of the US*. 1974

Unesco. *Efectos de la migración rural urbana sobre la función y la condición de la mujer en América Latina. Informes y Documentos de Ciencias Sociales*, 41. Paris, Unesco, 1980

Valentine, Charles. 'Black studies and anthropology: scholarly and political interest in Afro-American culture', *McCaleb Module in Anthropology*, 15, n.d.
Culture and poverty: critique and counter-proposals. Chicago, 1968.

Van Gunsteren, Herman. 'Notes on a theory of citizenship', in Birnbaum, Pierre, Jack Liveley and Geraint Parry (eds.), *Democracy, consensus and social contract*. London, Sage, 1978

Vanek, Joann. 'Time spent in housework', *Scientific American*, November 1974: 116–20

Verduzco, Gustavo. *Campesinos itinerantes. Colonización, ganaderia y urbanización en el trópico petrolero de México*. Zamora, El Colegio de Michoacán, 1982

Visconde de Indaiatuba, (*c*.1878). 'Introducao do trabalho livre em Campinas' in *Monografia historica do municipio de Campinas*. Rio de Janeiro, 1952

Vogel, Lise. 'The earthly family', *Radical America*, 7, 1973: 9–50

Wallerstein, Immanuel and William Martin. 'Changes in household structure and labor-force formation', *Review*, 3(2), 1979

Webster, Steven S. 'Parentesco y afinidad en una comunidad indigena quechua' in Mayer E. and R. Bolton, *Parentesco y matrimonio en los Andes*. Lima, Pontificie Universidad Católica del Perú, 1980

Weinbaum, Batya and Amy Bridges. 'The other side of the paycheck: monopoly capital and the structure of consumption', *Monthly Review*, 28, 1976: 88–103

Wells, John. 'The diffusion of durables in Brazil and its implications for recent controversies concerning Brazilian development', *Cambridge Journal of Economics*, 1(3), 1977: 259–79

Whitehead, Ann. ' "I'm hungry, mum": the politics of domestic budgeting', in Young, Kate, Carol Wolkowitz and Roslyn McCullagh (eds.), *Of marriage and market: women's subordination in international perspective*. London, CSE Books, 1981

Whitehead, Tony L. 'Residence, kinship and mating as survival strategies: a West Indian example', *Journal of marriage and the family*, 40(4), 1978: 817–28

Willis, Robert J. 'The direction of intergenerational transfers and demographic transition: the Caldwell hypothesis revisited.' Paper presented to the IUSSP, Seminar on individuals and families and income distribution. Honolulu, *mimeo*, 1971

Wilmott, Peter and Michael Young. *Family and kinship in East London*. London, 1957

Woortman, Klaas. *A familia das Mulheres*. Rio de Janeiro, Tempo Brasileiro, 1987

Yanagisako, Sylvia J. 'Women-centred kin networks in urban, bilateral kinship', *American Ethnologist*, 4, 1977: 207–26

'Family and household: the analysis of domestic groups', *Annual Review of Anthropology*, 8, 1979

Young, Kate. 'Economia campesina, unidad doméstica y migración', *América Indigena*, 38(2), 1978

'Formas de apropiación y la división sexual del trabajo: un estudio de caso de Oaxaca, México' in Leon, Magdalena (ed.), *Debate sobre la mujer en America Latina y el Caribe*, vol. 2, Bogota, ACEP, 1982

Zemelman, Hugo. 'Problemas en la explicación del comportamiento reproductivo' in *Reflexiones teórico-metodológicas sobre investigaciones en poblaciones*. México, El Colegio de México y Pispal, 1981